SOCIAL CONFLICT IN PRE-FAMINE IRELAND

To Róisín

SOCIAL CONFLICT IN
PRE-FAMINE IRELAND

The case of County Roscommon

Michael Huggins

FOUR COURTS PRESS

This book was set in 11 on 13 Ehrhardt for
FOUR COURTS PRESS LTD
7 Malpas Street, Dublin 8, Ireland
email: info@four-courts-press.ie
http://www.four-courts-press.ie
and in North America by
FOUR COURTS PRESS
c/o ISBS, 920 N.E. 58th Avenue, Suite 300, Portland, OR 97213.

ISBN 978–1–85182–653–7

A catalogue record for this title
is available from the British Library.

Printed in Great Britain
by Cromwell Press Ltd., Trowbridge, Wiltshire.

Contents

Conclusions

Acknowledgments

The customary absolution of research supervisors from blame for what follows must be extended to two people in the case of this study. Professor John Belchem first suggested that I explore the work of E.P. Thompson and others in relation to my interest in Irish agrarian conflict. I thank him sincerely for that stimulus, plus the debates and good company that ensued. I thank Professor Elizabeth Malcolm, who also went far beyond what might reasonably be expected in her willingness to assist my work.

Professors Sean Connolly and Marianne Elliott have made a number of useful and challenging points. I thank them for the interest they have taken in this work.

A number of people gave me much practical help. Dr and Mrs P. Mooney and their son, Patrick, of Childwall, Liverpool, were unfailingly generous when I needed accommodation. Peter McConnell provided moral support when it was much needed. Juliet Doherty helped with a whole range of things, for which I am truly grateful. The staff at the Institute of Irish Studies, University of Liverpool, have given me much encouragement. Phil Potter and Dr Malcolm Rhodes of the University of Chester allowed me time and money to undertake the research.

I would also like to acknowledge the efforts of staff at the institutions where the research was undertaken, particularly the National Archives of Ireland. My sincere thanks to all at Four Courts Press for their help.

I thank (belatedly) my parents, Mary and James, for their enthusiasm for learning.

Finally, I would like to acknowledge publicly the ways in which my Auntie Kathleen, Uncle Alf and Mr Gerard Kavanagh encouraged my interest in history. I think it started during two weeks in Letterfrack, many years ago.

Abbreviations

CSORP	Chief Secretary's Office registered papers.
Devon Commission	Royal commission of inquiry into the state of the law and practice in respect to the occupation of land in Ireland: *Report, Minutes of evidence, Part I*, 1845 (605)(606) xix.1, 57; *Minutes of evidence, Parts II and III*, 1845 (616)(657) xx.1, xxi.1.
HL 1825	Select committee of House of Lords to inquire into state of Ireland with reference to disturbances: *Minutes of evidence*, 1825 (181) ix.1; *Minutes of evidence, appendix, index*, 1825 (521) ix.249; *Report* (1825), 1826 (40) v.659.
Keogh, *Statistical account*	A statistical account of the county of Roscommon by the Revd John Keogh drawn up for Sir William Petty superintendant [*sic*] of the Down Survey, Anno Domini 1683, John Rylands University Library of Manchester MS 498, a copy of the original manuscript, Trinity College, Dublin.
NLI	National Library of Ireland, Dublin.
OR	Outrage reports, National Archives of Ireland, Dublin.
OS extracts	Extracts ... relating to the topography and antiquities of County Roscommon collected by the Ordnance Survey, MS 14, vol. 6, Royal Irish Academy, Dublin.
OS letters	Letters containing information relative to the antiquities of the county of Roscommon, collected during the progress of the Ordnance Survey in 1837, by John O'Donovan. MS 14 F.8–9, Royal Irish Academy, Dublin.
OS memoirs	Ordnance Survey memoirs, Box 50, Co. Roscommon. Royal Irish Academy, Dublin.

RLG	*Roscommon and Leitrim Gazette.*
RJ	*Roscommon Journal and Western Impartial Reporter* (later *Roscommon Journal and Western Reporter*).
SC 1824	Select committee to inquire into disturbances in Ireland. *Report, appendix,* 1824 (372) viii.1; *Minutes of evidence, indices,* 1825 (20) vii.1.
SC 1825	Select committee of the House of Lords to inquire into state of Ireland with reference to disturbances: *Reports, minutes of evidence, index,* 1825 (129) viii.1.
SC 1831–2	Select committee on disturbed state of Ireland: *Report, minutes of evidence, appendix, index,* 1831–2 (677) xvi.1.
SC 1839	Select committee of House of Lords on state of Ireland: *Report, minutes of evidence, appendix, index,* 1839 (486) xi.1, xii.1.
SC 1852	Select committee on outrages (Ireland). *Report,* 1852 (438) xiv.1.
SOCP1	State of the Country Papers, first series, National Archives of Ireland, Dublin.
SOCP2	State of the Country Papers, second series, National Archives of Ireland, Dublin.
Whitworth, *Statement*	A statement of the nature and extent of the disturbances which have recently prevailed in Ireland, and the measures which have been adopted by the government of that country, in consequence thereof. From the lord lieutenant of Ireland, Lord Whitworth, to Lord Sidmouth, 5 June 1816. PP (479) ix.569.

Co. Roscommon was allotted number 25 for the registration of papers in the Chief Secretary's Office but, for the sake of clarity, this numerical prefix has been omitted when citing references from the CSORP and OR series.

A note on spellings and language

As far as possible, quotations from manuscript and other contemporary sources have been rendered exactly as written there. Where deemed necessary, a square-bracketed explanation has been added. Direct quotations from secondary sources are given as published. Words originally underlined are italicized.

Spellings of proper nouns have been rendered as in the manuscript sources. Some names may thus appear to have been spelled incorrectly. However, where many alternative spellings of parish and townland names were previously used, the modern spelling has been substituted. Unless specifically alluded to in the text, references to parishes are to civil parishes.

Some terms and phrases developed by historians and used regularly in this text, such as 'modernization', 'pre-modern', 'underground gentry' and 'moral economy', are presented without quotation marks or footnote references. However, no inference should be made that these are given, uncontested terms.

The champions of the rural world were able to defend themselves with much hardened political sense against feudal-capitalist exploitation, but they idealized the past. The expansion of the large estates, and the tiny size of properties insufficient to support a single family, were the paradoxical result of the agrarian laws passed in the nineteenth century, and in particular the Organic Regulations of 1831. The latter had broken with traditional law of custom and asserted private property in the modern sense. The ancient peasant communities had thus lost their control on the village, and the new agrarian contracts imposed on the rural masses had delivered them to the tender mercies of the landowners.

Iorga, writing just after the 1907 Revolution, and contesting the boyar claim to have possessed the land since time immemorial, conjured up the harmonious image of an ancient village community, in which at one time the boyar played his part on equal terms with the others. Even Mihail Sadoveanu, a democratic and revolutionary writer, depicts an archaic world in which the rural poor and masters are free men with ancient rights; however Panait Istrati, the rebel anarchist who extolled the bloody vendettas of the Haiduks against the feudal lords, the governors and the cruel, corrupt prelates, refers to a primitive era of collective harmony, when the boyars were not landowners but the chief men in the various communities, while the land belonged only to the community. Even Eminescu defends 'the ancient classes' against 'modern' capitalistic exploitation and Zamfirescu, in *Country Life* (1894), praises the healthy traditional orders of the nation, peasant and nobleman, as against the new, brutal class of *nouveau riche* farm bailiffs, who use their money to destroy the link with the land.

This romantic anti-capitalism over-idealizes the archaic peasant world, the warm cowshed atmosphere of the community, which was so often permeated with gloomy poverty and black violence ... But the intellectuals who transfigured the peasant world, as Iorga did, had no intentions of restoring the lost idyll. This idealization gave them the impetus not to return to the past, but to fight against the evils of the present. Nostalgia for times past made them look to the future.

Reflections on a visit to the Village Museum, Bucharest, in C. Magris, *Danube*, trans. P. Creagh (London, 2001 ed.), 376–7. Published by the Harvill Press. Reprinted by permission of the Random House Group Ltd.

Introduction

This book reconsiders whiteboyism in Ireland from the beginning of the nine-teenth century until the great famine. Nationalist histories have explained the 'recurring state of war between the authorities and the rebellious peasants in many parts of the country' from the mid-eighteenth century until the great famine in terms of national oppression, but more recently a number of histo-rians have re-examined the shibboleths established in the cause of nation- and state-building. Particularly since J.S. Donnelly's pioneering work in the 1970s, agrarian conflict has been subject to considerable re-evaluation.[1]

This study examines the legitimizing discourses and repertoires of collective action in terms of conceptual models used by historians to understand the behaviour of contentious crowds in England during the same period. This means that it is not restricted to specifically agrarian collective actions. As will become apparent, agrarian grievances formed part of a broader consciousness of the rights of the poor, a consciousness that had a political inflection. Broad-ly speaking, agrarian conflict became endemic, rather than episodic, from around the turn of the nineteenth century; for that reason the subsequent fifty years are the main focus of this work.

Revisionist historians have seen popular historiography as perpetuating myths that a socially homogeneous Gaelic nation was dispossessed by conquest and then oppressed by an alien Saxon élite. Irish agrarian conflict, which will be referred to generically in this study as 'whiteboyism' (named after the Whiteboy movement in Munster during the 1760s), was the response of a national com-munity suffering oppression, particularly in respect of land. The popular ver-sion of national history portrayed the post-Williamite inheritors of Ireland as absentees, enjoying an extravagant life in the clubs of Dublin and London, thanks to rents extorted from the defeated Gael. Estates were neglected or left in the hands of unscrupulous, rack-renting middlemen, who also profited great-ly from the misery of the peasantry. The nationalist rendition of Irish history was of considerable political use, both in justifying the struggle for indepen-dence and, after independence, in establishing the authority and legitimacy of the Free State.

---

1 When used generically, the lower case – whiteboy, whiteboyism, whiteboys – will be used. The Whiteboys of the 1760s take an initial capital; J.S. Donnelly, *Landlord and tenant* (1973), 27.

In recent years a number of historians have sought to refute perceptions of agrarian conflict as being embryonically nationalist. However, there have only been rare, and then usually tangential, attempts to use conceptual techniques developed in the historiography of other societies to illuminate further the nature of collective identities and actions in pre-famine Ireland. This book does not attempt to trace the story of particular movements and their immediate economic stimuli. Donnelly has undertaken such work with great success for the major eighteenth-century movements. Instead, it will consider the endemic agrarian conflicts of the first half of the nineteenth century from a variety of historiographic perspectives.[2]

In a now-famous 1971 essay Edward Thompson attempted to understand the ways in which custom, culture and reason affected the responses of the English poor to hunger in the late eighteenth century. Thompson chose to view collective actions by the poor as more than mere 'rebellions of the belly', in which the actions of the crowd (or, as it was often labelled, the 'mob') were simple reflexes of hunger. His investigation of crowd actions at a point of breakdown in social consensus was able to shed significant light on popular conceptions of how society ought to be ordered. The consideration of Co. Roscommon protest in similar terms offers valuable insights. Co. Roscommon protest was characterized by a consciousness that sought to assert the primacy of customary rights, but it was also mingled with a nascent political consciousness of French revolutionary and, later, English radical provenance.

This study does not try to provide a history of Co. Roscommon during the period, nor of rural social and economic relations in Ireland. Other regions experienced different economic circumstances, or had different social profiles that affected both the forms taken by, and the beliefs expressed in, popular collective actions. Roscommon has been selected as the focus for this study because it offers a reasonable median in terms of economic development and social relations. This book is, in effect, a case study that helps shed light on aspects of the collective consciousness and social identity of the rural poor in pre-famine Ireland.[3]

The historiography of popular discontents and protest in other societies offers conceptual tools that have not been used in a sustained study of Irish popular protest in the half century before the famine. Unfortunately, the recent development of Irish Studies as a distinct academic discipline, with a marked

2 See, for example, T. Bartlett, 'An end to moral economy' (1987), K. Whelan, 'An underground gentry?' (1996); J.S. Donnelly, 'The Rightboy movement, 1785–8' (1977–8); J.S. Donnelly, 'The Whiteboy movement, 1761–5' (1978).   3 E.P. Thompson, 'The moral economy of the English crowd in the eighteenth century' (1971). The same essay was republished without changes in idem, *Customs in common* (London, 1993), and subsequent references to it in this book will be to the 1993 edition.

emphasis on literary and postcolonial theory, has left some lacunae in the study of Irish social and cultural history. Furthermore, the 'linguistic turn' that has in recent years informed the historiography of English popular protest breathes new life into nationalist historical narrative, rejuvenating nationalist narratives of social identity.

Part 1 considers whiteboyism from a historiographic perspective. The first chapter reviews various accounts of whiteboyism, including the influential and important contemporary work of George Cornewall Lewis and the ways in which the historiography of whiteboyism was developed within the nationalist master-narrative; it considers how that narrative has been qualified or rejected by more recent research. This is followed by a more general survey of the fault lines in late eighteenth- and early nineteenth-century Irish society. This provides an important context for the consideration of the historiography of whiteboyism, particularly as these fault lines have been defined largely within popular nationalist narratives that have remained, for the most part, unchallenged. In Part 2 of the book, the focus shifts to Co. Roscommon and an examination of the rich body of evidence from the county. Part 3 considers social differentiation within rural populations and the ways in which it has been characterized by some historians and social theorists; this is an issue of particular relevance in considering the multi-layered social pyramid of pre-famine Ireland. Finally, the usefulness of Thompson's idea of a 'moral economy' as an approach to pre-famine social conflict in Co. Roscommon is considered, as well as some recent critiques of his approach.

Accounts of whiteboyism

Popular protest movements in Ireland became endemic following the 1798 rebellion, yet their roots were not in nationalism but in economic conflict. The movements frequently involved nocturnal assemblies of many people, swearing oaths of solidarity and airing economic grievances. These often resulted in the posting of notices that threatened violence unless their demands were complied with. The objects of these grievances might be landlords or, more often, people who had taken land from which someone else had been evicted. Historians often supposed that land was the main cause of whiteboy conflict, but it is clear that a range of complaints could form the basis of the protest movements that sprang up in Ireland from the mid–eighteenth century. The movements had some success in recruiting or intimidating people and spread to cover counties or even regions. They operated in circumstances of illegality and were given names like Threshers, Carders and Whitefeet.

Contemporary views

GEORGE CORNEWALL LEWIS

A useful starting point will be to consider the early analysis of whiteboyism undertaken by George Cornewall Lewis, and how the historiography of whiteboyism has developed, before placing popular nationalist perceptions of whiteboyism within the broader current of nationalist histories of social relations on the land.

Lewis was the first significant analyst of whiteboyism. His interest in the Irish poor had been aroused while serving as a Poor Law commissioner for England and Wales. He was also subsequently invited by the government to report on the established church in Ireland. This led to the publication of his *On local disturbances in Ireland and the Irish church question* in 1836. Lewis drew much of his evidence from the numerous parliamentary enquiries into the sources of conflict and poverty in rural Ireland conducted in the first half of the nineteenth century. It is apparent from his work that the nationalist understanding of Irish history in terms of ethnic and religious conflict was mirrored by some British opinion. He summarized that attitude adroitly:

some have attributed the turbulence of the inferior Irish to their inherent barbarism; some to their religion, some to their hatred of England;
some to their poverty, some to their want of education.

Lewis was something of a revisionist in his own day, however, claiming that
agrarian rebels were not disloyal, despite being characterized as such by local
magistrates and property owners. His assertion that the 'Whiteboy association
may be considered as a vast trades' union for the protection of the Irish peasantry' has been quoted widely.[1]

Lewis's main concern was to demonstrate that the disturbances were neither insurrectionary nor proto-nationalist, in response to the widespread view
among British parliamentarians that behind much whiteboy activity there was
a nationalist conspiracy. Despite the recent experiences of the 1798 rebellion,
the emancipation campaign and the tithe war, he was convinced that whiteboyism was not a nationalist rebellion. He quoted one witness to a parliamentary committee who said that an English gentleman travelling through Ireland,
either from motives of curiosity or commerce, would do so in perfect safety –
proof, according to Lewis, that national identity was not part of whiteboyism.[2]

Hindsight makes Lewis's prescription for the ills of the countryside seem
rather feeble (the conclusion of all his work on the question was a demand for
the extension of the new poor law to Ireland), but even so, his analysis was per-
suasive. It also pointed towards the complexity of rural social relations, beyond
the simple bipolarity of antagonistic confessional, ethnic or national blocs.

THE VIEW FROM ABOVE

The rural poor made themselves known directly only through threatening
notices and through their actions. There was no whiteboy press, although it
will become apparent later that towards the mid-century the Molly Maguires
approached that level of associational organization. The archival material available to the historian is quite rich, but it should be remembered that politicians'
perceptions of agrarian conflict were very much conditioned by the experience
and recollection of the 1798 rebellion. Their perceptions have been transmitted through parliamentary enquiries, newspapers, pamphlets and, in particular, the vast mine of manuscript sources in the National Archives of Ireland.

There were frequent parliamentary enquiries into agrarian disturbances in
Ireland during the first half of the nineteenth century, the evidence submitted
ranging from detailed examinations of local *causes célèbres* to the most general

1 G.C. Lewis, *On local disturbances* (1977 ed.), ix, 10, 80. For the significance of Lewis, see M.
Beames, *Peasants and power* (1983).   2 Lewis, *On local disturbances*, 200, quoting a Mr Griffith, engineer, evidence to SC 1824, 230–1, 233.

overviews of the state of Ireland provided by experts. An 1824 enquiry, for example, heard evidence from, among others, four barristers, two inspectors of constabulary, a yeoman, a civil engineer, two Catholic priests, two Church of Ireland ministers, a member of the committee who was a major landlord in Ireland, a magistrate, a Catholic middleman, and a landlord's agent. The following year another enquiry heard evidence from a similar range of witnesses, including Daniel O'Connell, bishops of both Catholic and Established churches and a political economist.[3]

However, the enquiries in the half century following the 1798 rebellion appear to have been motivated by a quest for political stability and a desire to identify any potential connection between agrarian conflict and nationalist rebellion. It has been pointed out that whereas in England popular protest was perceived as a form of negotiation between the poor and their social superiors, all similar disturbances in Ireland were seen as potentially subversive. Committee deliberations about agricultural production, judicial reorganization and police reform should be seen in this context: insofar as they examined social and economic matters, these were intended to discover remedies for perceived problems of economic and social organization which would create a basis for political stability. This is not to say that perceptions of popular protest were uniform. An examination of the evidence illustrates the diversity of élite opinion.[4]

An 1839 Lords committee on the state of Ireland was addressed by a range of local officials, professionals and gentry, including Hill Wilson Rowan, a resident magistrate with nine years' experience. Rowan warned the committee that 'Ribandism' was centrally directed, had the objective of overthrowing the lawful government in Ireland, and sought to establish a Roman Catholic monarchy in the country. Although he acknowledged that local ribbon societies operated as agrarian combinations, he told the committee of legal funds, printed forms and regulations, books of proceedings and membership tickets. It seems likely that this witness was less rigorous in distinguishing between agrarian combination and urban conspiracy than historians have been more recently. He saw all collective mobilization that was not élite-sponsored as potentially subversive and nationalist.[5]

What is revealing about Rowan's evidence is not only the anti-Catholic hysteria that characterizes it, but also the seriousness with which it was considered. Some members of this committee displayed similar instincts, explaining Orange anti-Catholic notices found in Mullingar as black propaganda produced by papists. Similarly, a Catholic priest had told the 1824 committee that a Pastori-

3 See list of witnesses, SC 1824; SC 1825.   4 J. Bohstedt, *Riots and community politics*
(1983), 5.   5 SC 1839, 546, evidence of William Kemmis.

ni notice posted on his chapel door was the work of Orangemen; the Pastorini prophecies, which enjoyed a brief but widespread vogue in the 1820s, were millenarian accounts of the final days, involving the end of Protestantism. It is apparent that the attitudes of the committee members assumed rebellion to have a nationalist and confessional character. Even when agrarian conflict was seen in terms of the revolt of a particular social group, it was not usually distinguished from nationalism. Astute observers like Lewis may have made such distinctions, but not all politicians took the same discerning approach. Such was the alarm caused by Rowan's evidence that the committee recalled him for further questioning, and later still asked William Kemmis, crown solicitor on the Leinster circuit, for his opinion of Rowan's views; Kemmis said he could not remember any political rebellion since 1803. Ribbonism and whiteboyism were, of course, sometimes impossible to distinguish in an agrarian context. This does not mean that the politics of agrarian combinations and of the urban proto-nationalist conspiracies usually identified as ribbonism were the same.[6]

John Lewis O'Ferrall, commissioner of police in Dublin city, offered a rather different view when he was questioned in 1839 whether agrarian protesters had central leadership or national objectives. He suggested that there was no such leadership, nor broader aims, because no more was known about the secret societies than had been known in 1822. In all that time of meeting and levying, there had never been more than local outrages. O'Ferrall believed that agrarian outrages and Dublin trade combinations had analogous aims, pursuing local economic objectives such as (in Dublin) stopping the employment of persons who had not served a regular seven-year apprenticeship. People who had violated some regulation of the combination were assaulted, much as agrarian rebels sought to regulate their specific economic circumstances and ensure future security. Historians have tended to view anti-stranger motifs in the language of combinations as evidence of parochial loyalties. However, they might be reinterpreted as protectionist measures similar to those that modern associations might demand. O'Ferrall's observations matched Lewis's view of whiteboyism as a vast trades union of the rural poor, and they help clarify the distinction between whiteboyism and ribbonism. It seems highly likely that the economic associations of the rural poor were less formally constituted as secret societies than the proto-nationalist Ribbonmen, who printed membership cards, catechisms and rule books. Indeed, identifying the loose whiteboy associations as secret societies may be misleading.[7]

Parliamentary committees were also anxious about the manufacture, sale and theft of weapons. This means that arms raids assumed a special significance.

6 SC 1839, 602, evidence of Thomas Uniacke; SC 1824, 379, evidence of Revd Michael Collins; SC 1839, 546, evidence of William Kemmis.   7 SC 1839, 399-400, evidence of John

Arms raids (an infrequent whiteboy undertaking), usually involved a nocturnal visit to someone known to possess weapons. The 1839 Lords committee, for example, asked Westmeath magistrate Robert Kelly about the sale of gunpowder to the lower orders. The correspondents whose reports are contained in the manuscript sources also saw arms raids as especially significant, and for similar reasons. The lord lieutenant, Whitworth, reported to the home secretary, Viscount Sidmouth, in June 1816 that the collection of arms was a 'principal object' of agrarian rebels. There were many instances of arms raids being reported with no attribution of motive. This illustrates presumptions about the nature of arms raids that the correspondents, and the parliamentarians, did not think they needed to state explicitly. Louis Cullen has claimed that 'firearms had a political message, not the usual agrarian one attributed to the issue'. The distinction is an important one, but many politicians were unable to make it in the first half of the nineteenth century.[8]

Another aspect of whiteboyism that suggested general objectives to the committees of enquiry was any sectarian basis attributed to the agrarian organizations. Those local disturbances that were considered in detail by the committees frequently concerned questions of sectarian antagonism, alleged or actual. However, many witnesses believed that the almost completely Catholic make-up of agrarian combinations was due less to exclusivism than to the general social and economic status of the Catholic and Protestant populations. Francis Blackburne, a barrister in Limerick, told the 1824 select committee that because landlords were all Protestants 'religion happened to become enlisted in the cause' and the disturbances assumed a religious character 'at least in appearance'. Matthew Barrington, crown solicitor for Munster, told the 1839 Lords enquiry that, in his experience, outrages 'have been quite indiscriminate; they have had no particular Selection of Protestant or Roman Catholic', while another crown solicitor said that Catholics were assaulted, as well as Protestants. Piers Geale, a crown prosecutor on the home circuit (Dublin and adjacent counties), said that Ribbonmen assaulted their fellow Catholics as well as Protestants, and that outrages connected with religion were not common; Geale knew only one political case – a notice encouraging rebellion that referred to the example set recently by the Canadian colony. The 1824 enquiry was preoccupied by the question of tithes – an indication of how Westminster perceived issues associated with religion as being connected with nationalism and rebellion. In this way contemporary parliamentary enquiries, as well as later historiography, conspired to force the investigation of agrarian conflict into a confessional, and by extension national, mould.[9]

O'Ferrall.   8 SC 1839, 501, evidence of Robert Kelly; Whitworth, *Statement*, 4; L.M. Cullen, 'Catholics under the penal laws' (1986), 25.   9 SC 1824, 22, evidence of Francis

The question of the recovery of estates forfeited by ancestors was also seen as a potential indicator of latent political rebellion. George Bennett, a crown prosecutor in King's County and Co. Kildare, told the 1824 select committee that the memory of the seventeenth-century confiscations remained alive:

> I have heard that in many instances they kept an idea in their minds that they would, at one time or other, recover their property.

Agrarian conflict increasingly accompanied the breakdown of any residual loyalties to the descendants of Irish nobles dispossessed after the Cromwellian and Williamite wars, a process described in Kevin Whelan's work on the underground gentry, which will be discussed in the next chapter. In 1825 Colonel John Irwin, a Sligo magistrate, told the committee of enquiry about a map on the wall in McDermott's pub near Boyle, Co. Roscommon, which showed all the forfeited estates in Connacht. Hill Wilson Rowan alleged to the 1839 Lords enquiry that Catholic priests kept lists of forfeited estates in order to restore them to their rightful owners when the occasion might arise. Captain Samuel Vignoles, a stipendiary magistrate who had served all over Ireland, told the same committee that the intention of all the variously named secret societies was to recover the estates their ancestors had been dispossessed of, but that there was no desire to destroy the monarchy. Like Rowan, Vignoles believed the Catholic clergy to be implicated. This contrasted with the earlier evidence of Meath chief constable John Hatton, who told the committee that the Catholic clergy opposed 'ribandism'. Meath stipendiary magistrate George Despard told the committee of efforts by Catholic priests to subdue ribbonism. The same committee heard of oaths of both loyalty and disloyalty to the monarch.[10]

There were many other witnesses who demurred from the views of Vignoles and Rowan, claiming that the objects of agrarian secret societies were local, economic and, generally, non-sectarian. There was no evidence of gentry or clerical leadership among them, they said (most witnesses did not imagine that the rural poor might produce their own leaders), and the combinations were as likely to punish Catholics as Protestants for breaking their laws. Viscount Whitworth reported in 1816 that he could not ascertain that the various combinations proposed to themselves any definite object of a political nature. The redress of local grievances was their object. George Bennett told the 1825 hearings:

Blackburne; SC 1839, 584, evidence of Matthew Barrington; SC 1839, 673, 676, evidence of Piers Geale. 10 SC 1824, 94, evidence of George Bennett; SC 1825, 698, evidence of Col. John Irwin; SC 1839, 171, evidence of Hill Wilson Rowan; SC 1839, 301–2, evidence of Captain Samuel Vignoles; SC 1839, 244, evidence of John Hatton; SC 1839, 269, evidence of George Despard; SC 1839, 198–9, evidence of William Fausset, magistrate, Sligo. Fausset read a paper to the committee that purported to be 'obligations of the Fraternal Society'

I do not think the lower class of the peasantry of Ireland care two-pence about emancipation.

He added that the better class of farmers and professional men were the only ones who mentioned the state of the law regarding Catholics. Indeed, the 1824 committee had been told that

> the Catholic having acquired property, and having been admitted into professions, became ambitious and anxious to participate in all the privileges of the constitution.

Religious distinctions were indeed more marked among the upper orders, although Catholics of the lower orders might be persuaded that they had a common interest with their Catholic betters. John Irwin agreed that the Catholic peasantry cared little about emancipation.[11]

Oliver Kelly, archbishop of Tuam, attempted to sell the idea of Catholic emancipation to the 1825 select committee on the basis that, while the members might think that poorer Catholics would not gain anything immediately from emancipation, 'it would tend most materially towards tranquillizing their minds ... It would have the most soothing effect.' Kelly's words demonstrate a belief that the removal of confessional disabilities held a symbolic significance for all Catholics and would thus be welcomed, as well as contribute towards the maintenance of social order. Kelly may not have intended to commend the duping of lower-class Catholics, but he was clearly acknowledging that the impact of emancipation would be merely symbolic as far as they were concerned.[12]

George Warburton, the inspector of constabulary who played a major part in attempting to control popular protest in Co. Roscommon, was one of those who made a distinction between two different kinds of secret society, co-existing and occasionally overlapping. One was local, agrarian and economic; the other national, sectarian and political. In terms of the former, he testified to the 1824 select committee that the oaths he had seen did not discriminate between Catholics and Protestants; similarly, Roman Catholic gentlemen worked as hard as Protestant gentlemen to put down disturbances. Michael Collins, a Catholic parish priest from Skibbereen, Co. Cork, told the same hearings that Catholic peasants viewed Catholic and Protestant gentlemen similarly; in nearby Dunmanway, a Catholic magistrate was particularly unpopular because he was a considerable dealer in tithes.[13]

and proclaimed loyalty to William IV. At HL 1839, 328, however, Despard told of similar obligations that included a disavowal of allegiance to the king.   11 Whitworth, *Statement*, 4; SC 1824, 101, evidence of Richard Willcocks; SC 1824, 204, evidence of Sergeant Lloyd; SC 1825, 695, evidence of Col. John Irwin.   12 SC 1825, 245, evidence of Oliver Kelly, archbishop of Tuam.   13 SC 1824, 345; SC 1824, 389, evidence of John O'Drischol, barrister.

The views of those, like Lewis, who comforted parliament by saying that the conflicts were not national, have provided material for those who have sought to explain agrarian conflict as part of a process of modernization. Tomkins Brew, a stipendiary magistrate, former Orangeman, Irish language speaker and landlord, made this connection quite clear. He told the 1824 committee that 'outrages' occurred due to a 'want of land' when tillage was turned into pasture to raise cattle for markets in Dublin and Liverpool. The views of such witnesses have become another historiographic orthodoxy. The Limerick barrister Francis Blackburne, for example, told the 1824 parliamentary enquiry that agrarian conflict was the outcome of demography, subdivision of holdings and the resulting high rents, and that it was more intense where landlords were absent. Matthew Barrington told the 1839 Lords committee that agrarian conflict invariably concerned land. These appraisals tell only part of the story, at best.[14]

Cormac Ó Gráda has suggested that absenteeism, while providing potent images of profligacy for nationalist propagandists, was not of critical significance in the management of estates. However, the witnesses who offered reassurance to parliament that there was little prospect of agrarian combination becoming nationalist rebellion also habitually failed to identify the alternative social and political content frequently expressed in such collective mobilization. This was partly due to their assumptions about what form political mobilization in Ireland would take, but also because of the lack of leadership by members of a higher social order and because of the evident conflicts between lower-order Catholics and their wealthier co-religionists. Those witnesses were right to claim that there was little evidence to connect agrarian upheaval with nationalist political revolt, but their complacency about the lack of leadership by élite Catholics obscures the significance of agrarian combination. There was a tone of relief, for example, in Lord Whitworth's 1816 report to the home secretary that there appeared to be no general political object in the disturbances. In seeing the potential for rebellion in national or religious terms, and as something requiring élite leadership, people like Whitworth overlooked other senses of identity among the rural poor. The line of questioning pursued by the 1839 committee, for example, assumed that if agrarian disturbance was not national, it could not have any other political character. In such ways was the zero-sum relationship between nationalism and unionism constructed.[15]

Similarly, the historiography of modernization also assumes that the agrarian rebels could see no further than their plot of land, would not generate political impulses independently of élite leadership, and would not readily draw

14 SC 1839, 1038, evidence of Tomkins Brew; SC 1824, 6, 14, evidence of Francis Blackburne; SC 1839, 577, evidence of Matthew Barrington.   15 C. Ó Gráda, *Ireland: a new economic history* (1994), 125; See, for example, SC 1839, 400, evidence of John O'Ferrall.

general political conclusions about the world and their place in it. The two paradigms of nationality and modernization seem to be derived from the parliamentary enquiries into pre-famine agrarian conflict. It is an aim of this study to disengage from those assumptions that have informed historians' views of agrarian conflict ever since Lewis's analysis. Parliamentary enquiries also frequently reduced the rebelliousness of the rural poor to racial stereotypes of a quasi-mystical attachment to land. Such stereotypes may have helped parliamentarians explain the ferocity of the rebellions, but the Irish rural poor were concerned with economic security as much as any metaphysical identification with the land.

Recent historians of Irish agrarian unrest have mined the parliamentary archives to interrogate the nationalist story of agrarian conflict. They have also used the manuscript material extensively, but have nevertheless often failed to move significantly beyond the paradigms constructed by the early parliamentary enquiries. The parliamentary papers do provide material that challenges the nationalist narrative, but as sources they are limited significantly by Westminster's preoccupations with the prospects for political stability. If some witnesses before committees were able to provide comfort in this respect, it was mainly because of their assumptions about the nature of any political challenge Westminster might face in Ireland. The more thoughtful contemporary commentators provided an analysis that has formed the basis for more recent modernization explanations of pre-famine agrarian conflict.

The views of landlords and magistrates are important insofar as they were a step closer to the agrarian rebels themselves. The local newspapers of the time could offer much more detailed views of disturbance – and were free to make observations outside the discipline of set-piece committee hearings of parliamentarians in London, with their carefully selected witnesses and stage-managed lines of questioning. However, they reflected the same concerns with national rebellion. The case of the two most significant newspapers published in Co. Roscommon illustrates this. The *Roscommon and Leitrim Gazette* was published each Saturday in Boyle from April 1822 until beyond the period that concerns this study. The *Roscommon Journal and Western Impartial Reporter* (in November 1832 it became the *Roscommon Journal and Western Reporter* and it is referred to hereafter as the *Roscommon Journal*) appeared weekly in the county town from July 1828. Boyle was a town noted for demonstrations of sectarianism by its significant Protestant population, and the political stance taken by the *Gazzette*'s proprietor, John Bromell, reflected this hostility to Catholicism: his unreconstructed loyalism meant that the *Gazette* was aligned wholeheartedly behind the parliamentary opposition to emancipation, supporting the 'free and independent principles of the British constitution'. The local landlord, Viscount Lorton, was eulogized almost weekly. He was complimented for reducing the size of his tenantry, for residing at nearby Rockingham and for the fact that rent arrears on his lands were very low. There would be no need for an Insurrection Act, Bromell asserted, if other areas had landlords like Lorton. Another landlord was Godfrey Hogg of Gillstown. A member of the local Brunswick Club (the militantly Protestant society founded to oppose the extension of constitutional rights to Catholics after the suppression of the Orange Order), he was nevertheless 'an indulgent landlord', according to the *Gazette*. It will become apparent that the newspaper had a very different view to that of less partisan observers, including the local chief constable.[16]

A nationalist, Charles Tully, published the *Roscommon Journal*. In sharp contrast to Bromell, he wrote disparagingly of Lorton and the activities of the Boyle Brunswick Club, describing the Brunswickers as 'blood hounds' and Lorton's home as the 'Rockingham kennel', a headquarters for the 'old beagles, which were discarded as unfit for hunting, and their young cubs'. The imagery reveals an interesting perception of the Ascendancy and its profligate sons held by a member of the vigorous, economically virile Catholic middle class. In November 1829 Lorton summoned a meeting at Elphin to call for the introduction of the Insurrection Act. Tully sarcastically reported that the meeting was held at Elphin to 'save wear and tear on our Courthouse' (Elphin was nearer Lorton's estate in the north of the county than Roscommon town). Lorton had taken the chair 'spontaneously'. Almost everyone at the meeting was related to Lorton by blood, marriage or employment as agents, and they called for the '*benign influence* of the Insurrection Act', which would give them 'the power of *transporting* every poor idiot who (after hours) may wish to gaze at his *prototype* the *man in the moon*'. Tully was challenging the patronage-led politics of the Ascendancy, which was being replaced by an increasingly professional police and judiciary. Lorton's holding of an unofficial meeting at Elphin, rather than appearing in the county's administrative centre, was evidence of this. Electoral rivalry lay behind the conflict between these two groups. One group was represented in parliament by Lorton's son, and the other by the O'Conor Don. This appears also to confirm that confessional differences (particularly the frustration of Catholic aspirations before 1829) were felt more keenly among these groups than among the poor.[17]

If the editorial approach of the *Roscommon and Leitrim Gazette* represented a local rearguard action of Protestant ascendancy, then the *Roscommon Journal* was the voice of members of an emergent élite that was increasingly to find a voice in Westminster, through O'Connell. Bromell's opposition to emancipation and repeal reflected the anxiety of a once-dominant group that believed itself threatened by the emergence of a new local economic élite, typified by people

16 RLG, 27 Apr. 1822, 31 Jan. 1824, 7 Mar. 1829.   17 RJ, 11 Oct. 1828, 21 Nov. 1829.

like Tully. Indeed, Tully's nationalism did not deter him from writing to the lord lieutenant in the same sycophantic terms habitually used by local Protestant magistrates and landowners when he perceived himself under threat from his rebellious co-religionists. In May 1839 he claimed that the M'Donell family had made a number of attempts on his life, following the publication in his newspaper of an unsympathetic report of the trial of a member of the family.[18]

The perceptions of these two local newspaper proprietors therefore reflected different attitudes to whiteboyism on the bases of religion and nationality. For Bromell (rather like Rowan and Vignoles), popular protest was a sign of latent nationalist rebellion. For the moderate nationalist Tully, it was a sign of national oppression, and the necessary panaceas were emancipation and repeal.

The fear of nationalist revolt conditioned not only the views taken by parliamentarians and some local newspaper proprietors, but also those taken by local élites such as landowners, military personnel and law enforcers. Like parliamentarians, men of authority in Co. Roscommon presumed 'political' to mean sectarian or nationalist and, if there was no evidence of such politics, dismissed agrarian conflicts as mere economic reflexes. They tended to scrutinize each incident for evidence of nationalist taint, neglecting other possible explanations for whiteboyism. For example, Matthew Wyatt of Loughglynn House, near Castlerea, reported a case of conflict between a man called O'Hara and O'Hara's father-in-law. That conflict had led to two outrages. Wyatt added:

> I am happy to say that – savage and inhuman as these outrages are ... they are fortunately unassociated by any party or political spirit whatsoever.

Such relief, unfortunately, does not make the cause of the conflict any more apparent.[19]

Likewise, Stephen Mahon (MP and heir to the Strokestown estate) replied to Peel's enquiries about incidents in Co. Roscommon that had come to his attention in July 1816: 'It however appears to me that the burnings and outrages have arisen from private resentment, and not from a General Inclination to Disturbance.' The specific event he was talking about was the burning down of a house that belonged to a wealthy farmer named Charles Tinsillant in Dysart parish. Tinsillant was the manager of an estate and when he took a 180-acre farm and built a new house, it was burned down. Mahon's comment presumed Peel's concern to be with insurrectionary disturbances, but his assurance that these matters were not broader in scope leaves the student of whiteboyism unclear about the nature of the events.[20]

---

18 OR 1839/3453, Charles Tully to Viscount Ebrington, lord lieutenant, undated, [May 1839].   19 SOCP1 1767/52, Matthew Wyatt to Peel, 21 Oct. 1816.   20 SOCP1 1767/46,

Just as it is apparent that politicians and parliamentary witnesses like Rowan believed that nationalist politics was immanent in whiteboyism, important men in Co. Roscommon like the Protestant bishop of Elphin discerned nationalist or sectarian conspiracies in the actions of agrarian protesters. In a series of near-hysterical letters to the under-secretary, William Gregory, during the Thresher conflicts in 1813, the bishop said he had been told that all Protestants were to be murdered the following week and that the magistrates were all either 'timid and incapable old women' or 'corrupt and disaffected'. The bishop did not trust the militia, two thirds of which he believed to be disloyal. He added that all the men in the county were Threshers. Similarly, Lorton wrote frequently to Peel in 1816 to request the implementation of the Insurrection Act. However, it appears Peel was unimpressed by Lorton's belief that 'the activity of the Gentry has had a great effect towards intimidating the disaffected'. It was reform instigated by Peel that began the end of the dominance of policing by people like Lorton. Such accounts as Lorton's reveal as much about the consciousness of the writers as about the nature of agrarian collective action.[21]

In a similar vein, Dublin Castle frequently received letters warning of massacres of Protestants that were to take place at appointed times. In August 1817 a memorial was sent to the lord lieutenant suggesting that all the Protestants of Strokestown were to be put to death 'on the 8th of next month'. A man wrote from Castlerea to warn that 'a general massacre of Protestants is to take place'. Such forecasts were never fulfilled, but the fact that they were treated at all seriously is revealing. They expose a sense of embattlement among magistrates, yeomen, landowners, Protestant clergy and the military. A letter from the Co. Roscommon magistrate John Wills to Gregory, complaining of a number of arms raids in which 'all the persons from whom arms were taken were Protestants', reveals acutely the problems with the perceptions of local élites. It was something of a self-fulfilling prophecy that, if most legally held arms were in the hands of Protestant members of the local élite and their employees, then Protestant houses were likely to be the targets of such raids. A short time later, a Dublin civil servant demonstrated élite assumptions about the confessional nature of agrarian polarization and conflict when recommending that a Co. Roscommon landlord gather about him only 'Protestants and unquestionably loyal Catholics'.[22]

Stephen Mahon to Robert Peel, chief secretary, 28 July 1816; SOCP1 1767/43, William Bowles to Peel, 17 July 1816.   21 SOCP1 1538/19, 20, 21, 22, 23, Power Le Poer Trench, Church of Ireland bishop of Elphin, to William Gregory, under-secretary, 4 Aug., 5 Aug., 7 Aug., 8 Aug., 12 Aug., 1813; SOCP1 1767/64, 65, 66, Viscount Lorton to Robert Peel, 19 Dec., 23 Dec., 31 Dec. 1816.   22 SOCP1 1833/32, anonymous memorial to Viscount Whit-

Numerous letters from resident magistrates in 1845 warned of seasonal migrants returning from England with weapons. The writers always presumed that this made agrarian conflict a close relative of nationalist rebellion. George Warburton, who became inspector of constabulary for Connacht in the emerging professional policing system, had the same tendency. For example, he attributed the swearing of a man to give up his holding in 1830 to the man's employer being a Protestant. It seems much more likely that the man was sworn because he was a herdsman, as agrarian combinations tended to presume in favour of tillage, which could yield subsistence for the rural poor. Just as the parliamentary sources reveal much about the preoccupations of the governing class nationally, the manuscript sources reveal the concerns of local magistrates, landowners and clergymen.[23]

This overriding concern, which could lead to a significant misreading of the situation, was shared by the lord lieutenant. A draft letter on the state of Ireland from the lord lieutenant, Viscount Whitworth, to the home secretary, Viscount Sidmouth (which formed the basis of a parliamentary statement on 5 June 1816) attributed disturbances to conflict between Catholics and Protestants of the lower orders. Whitworth understood conflict in such terms alone. As with parliamentary enquiries, questions of political revolt and confessional conflict were never far from the minds of the local élites in their correspondence with Dublin Castle.[24]

Thus it can be seen that there were two broad strands of contemporary élite opinion, both locally and nationally, in respect of the nature of whiteboyism. Both have their origin in the concern of political élites to achieve stability. One found political rebellion in each popular action, while the other saw whiteboyism as the action of economic rabbles. These two broad approaches have been reflected to some extent in later treatments of whiteboyism.

Later accounts

THE NATIONALIST PERSPECTIVE
Popular nationalist historians of Ireland wrote somewhat different accounts of whiteboyism to those of local and national élites. The Home Rule MP and

worth, lord lieutenant, Aug. 1817; SOCP1 2176/6, H. Caldwell to General P. O'Loghlin, 28 Jan. 1820; SOCP1 2176/3, John Wills, magistrate, Strokestown, to Gregory, 14 Jan. 1820; SOCP1 2176/12, Hewitt (no first name given), Custom House, Dublin, to Charles Grant, under-secretary, 10 Feb. 1820.   23 See for example OR 1845/14253, Edmond Blake, resident magistrate, to Edward Lucas, under-secretary, undated, summer 1845; CSORP 1830/W18, police inspector of police George Warburton, Roscommon, to Gregory, Dublin Castle, 2 Feb. 1830.   24 SOCP1 1567/1, Whitworth to Viscount Sidmouth, 5 Jan. 1814.

publisher of *The Nation*, A.M. Sullivan, described it as 'ribbonism' and believed it had continued almost until the year he published *New Ireland* (1877). However, he appeared to make no distinction between agrarian combination and urban proto-nationalist conspiracy, alluding to a Dublin leader named Jones, whose letters were full of talk about liberating Ireland. Sullivan believed that such combinations were the product of a 'vicious land system'.[25]

Subsequent historians have sought to distinguish more carefully than did O'Sullivan between agrarian combinations and the urban nationalist conspirators, more commonly called Ribbonmen. These distinctions have usually been drawn on the basis of social composition and objectives. In Sullivan's defence, it ought to be acknowledged that many contemporaneous accounts of whiteboyism used the moniker 'ribbonism' freely when reporting agrarian collective action. More recently, McCartney has asserted that 'ribbonism was mainly an urban movement', that it was 'opposed to mere agrarianism' and that it had a more significant political content than agrarian combinations.[26]

This view could be justified by an examination of parliamentary accounts of whiteboyism. Some witnesses were careful to distinguish between whiteboyism and ribbonism. The Meath chief constable, John Hatton, told the 1839 parliamentary enquiry that 'they are very different … The one is connected with the taking of Land, and that kind of System; the other is a revolutionary System.' He conceded that people who were whiteboys could also be 'ribandmen', but suggested a general social division between agrarian rebels and the nationalist conspirators: 'they will not allow any Person to become a Ribandman who is not a Man of Character for Industry and sober Habits'.[27]

It is, however, impossible to make absolute distinctions between agrarian and ribbon activity. The Co. Roscommon evidence suggests that not only were agrarian protesters more politically conscious than previously supposed, but also that their politics was not proto-nationalist, a politics usually associated with ribbonism. The name 'Ribbonmen' first appeared in the State of the Country Papers relating to Co. Roscommon in April 1815, although in connection with exactly the same kind of agrarian activity that had recently been attributed to Threshers. Conversely, some correspondents continued to call Roscommon agrarian rebels 'Threshers' for some time after the first appearance of the name 'Ribbonmen'. The confusion among contemporary observers reflects the ebb and flow of political tides.[28]

25 A.M. Sullivan, *New Ireland* (1877), 77, 69.   26 See, for example, D. McCartney, *The dawning of democracy* (1987), 63–109, especially 82–3; idem 82, 84.   27 SC 1839, 240, evidence of John Hatton.   28 SOCP1 1713/21, John Wills, magistrate, Strokestown, Wills to Gregory, 13 Apr. 1815. SOCP1 1956/18, on 8 Jan. 1818 Arthur Mahon of Cavetown, Co. Roscommon, wrote to Peel of 'those insurgents usually called Thrashers'. SOCP1 1956/23, informations of Denis and Peter Rush. The two men swore on 6 Feb. 1818 that they had

In another nationalist narrative of rural social relations, the journalist R. Barry O'Brien, wrote:

> the unfortunate Irish peasant, in addition to supporting the religion in which he believed, was obliged to pay rents to 'absentee' landlords, and tithes to the ministers of an 'alien' church.

The critical word is 'alien'. Such a linguistic usage is characteristic of a historiography that insisted on the primacy of the national struggle between natives and foreigners. John Redmond's introduction to the book described the land system more generally as the 'curse of the country', and O'Brien concluded that even where the landlord was Irish-born, 'the bayonets of England ... were behind the landlords'. Sullivan had suggested that these rural conflicts pitted Irishman against Irishman and were thus wretched aberrations. However, both Sullivan and O'Brien were Home Rule MPs who, while sharing the nationalist consensus about the source of the problems faced by the rural Irish, had no enthusiasm for the violence used by agrarian rebels. Indeed, they had a contemporary anti-Fenian agenda. Insofar as these wrongs were the result of British rule, they fitted the nationalist view of the agrarian problem, but the solution was not violent direct action by the rural poor. This may at least partially explain the relative lack of attention paid by some Irish nationalist writers to agrarian conflicts. If rural conflict could not wholly be explained by English oppression, or if too close an examination revealed conflicts within the community of oppressed Gaels, it might be disregarded, or dismissed with a general comment about English oppression. O'Brien's sophistry concerning landlords and bayonets is an example of this approach. The historiography of the eighteenth-century 'penal era' was particularly prone to such approaches. Where difficulties arose, they were subsumed into a grand narrative of national and confessional unity. For example, more recently Brady and Corish acknowledged the conflicts between Whiteboys and clergy in the 1760s over dues for the performance of Catholic rites, but offered no explanation of this in the midst of a discourse on the heroic unity of priests and poor during the eighteenth century.[29]

---

stopped at an inn near Boyle where around 30 men, 'who all stiled themselves Captain Thresher's men', were meeting. The State of the Country Papers are among the principal manuscript sources for this work. They consist of many thousands of unsystematic and miscellaneous reports from magistrates, clergymen, landowners and soldiers, collected in the National Archives of Ireland, Dublin. Agrarian conflict was one of the main foci of two series of State of the Country Papers (the second much smaller than the first) between 1798 and 1831. The papers reflect the amateur nature of law enforcement before the beginnings of the bureaucratization of the state apparatus under Peel. From 1835 to 1852 such conflict was

However, constitutional nationalism's dismay at the tactics of agrarian rebels was supplanted as nationalist orthodoxy by a view that treated whiteboyism more sympathetically. This perspective was derived from John Mitchel, who set the tone in his *Jail Journal*. Writing of eighteenth-century social relations on the land, Mitchel said that:

> the condition of the peasantry is embittered by subjection to an alien and hostile class of landlords, who hold by lineage and affection to another country, and whose sole interest in their tenantry is to draw from them the very uttermost farthing, that they may spend it in that other country.

P.S. O'Hegarty criticized Sullivan directly:

> He had condemned Ribbonism, but neither he nor anybody else, until Parnell, had any alternative to it, or realized that it was essential to the continued existence of the Irish rural population, as being their only defence against the Government which misgoverned them and the landlords who oppressed them ... They were forced to do hard and cruel things, but harder and more cruel things were done against them.

In a pithy statement of the popular nationalist understanding of whiteboyism, O'Hegarty concluded that 'if their objects were sectarian and agrarian in fact, they were national in spirit'. The difference between O'Hegarty's approach and that taken by O'Brien and Sullivan reflected the distinction between the republican view that violence may indeed have been both necessary and justified in the cause of national liberation, and the home rulers' rejection of such tactics.[30]

O'Hegarty's approach to whiteboyism can be located in the broader current of popular nationalist historiography concerning rural social relations. While it took a sympathetic approach to the problems of the rural poor, it was nevertheless situated on the same analytical continuum that allowed no source of conflict other than the struggle between native Gael and foreign oppressor. In passing, it is also worth noting O'Hegarty's suggestion of genocidal intent on the part of the government, a view often reflected in nationalist propaganda

reported in a series of Outrage Reports, arranged by county. The Chief Secretary's Office Registered Papers also contain many 'outrage reports'. An evaluation of the sources available for the study of whiteboyism follows later.   **29** R.B. O'Brien, *A hundred years of Irish history* (1911), 98, 28, 75; J. Brady and P.J. Corish, *A history of Irish Catholicism* (1971).   **30** J. Mitchel, *Jail journal* (1983 ed.), xxiii; P.S. O'Hegarty, *A history of Ireland under the Union* (1952 ed.), 419.

about the great famine and originating in Mitchel's celebrated assertion that
the famine was a deliberately genocidal act by the British government. In
Mitchel's opinion, landlords and government had colluded in 'a deliberate
scheme for the pauperization of a nation', culminating in the 'rage for exter-
mination' that became policy during the great famine.[31]

It is worth digressing briefly to consider what this popular nationalist historiography signified. Such versions of Irish history were popularized through the
history curriculum taught in the influential Christian Brothers' schools. B.M.
Coldrey has demonstrated how the educational ethos developed by the Brothers was of critical importance in the development of a popular nationalist
conception of Irish history. That history, defining the Irish nation as homo-
geneously Roman Catholic, Gaelic and oppressed, displaying a significant con-
gruity with the nationalist historiography of whiteboyism. Coldrey suggested:

> The principal theme of Irish history, as they [the Christian Brothers]
> expounded it, was that of Irish resistance to English invasion; of Irish
> suffering resulting from English persecution; of Irish struggle against
> English oppression.

Coldrey went on to analyze the Christian Brothers' texts. An example will give
an idea of the Brothers' approach to teaching history. The periodical *Our Boys*
was aimed at the Christian Brothers' pupils. In ten instalments one 1914 serial
included five examples of British cowardice, eleven of British cruelty towards
Irish people, six of Irish chivalry faced with British crudity, ten of the Irish
defeating the English in battle, three situations where Ireland was economically exploited by Britain and no examples where Englishmen dealt fairly or gen-
erously with Ireland or its people.[32]

The Brothers were a dynamic order, producing their own textbooks and
making a significant impact on the consciousness of generations of young Irish
men. The Brothers' version of Irish history informed popular apprehensions
of agrarian social relations (in the more general context of Irish history) before
and after independence, and arguably until the present.

Popular historical novels such as Walter Macken's trilogy based on the
Cromwellian Wars, the great famine and the 'war of independence' sustained
this version of history in independent Ireland. Macken's novel *The Silent People* dealt in some detail with whiteboyism. The hero mused on pre-conquest
vertical social ties in Irish society, 'when men were free and had access to the
boards of their lords to argue and declare their freedom and their rights'. The

---

31 J. Mitchel, *The last conquest of Ireland (perhaps)* (1861), 120.   32 B.M. Coldrey, *Faith and
fatherland* (1988), 113, 128.

violence of whiteboyism was contrasted with the orderliness of O'Connell's election supporters, and his death was described as 'the end of hope'. Although this approach reflected Sullivan's, Macken did suggest additional complexities, such as O'Connell's eviction of his tenants and the problem that a particularly unpleasant agent was a Catholic.[33]

However, perhaps the most significant statement of the approach which sought to unite all native Gaels, humble or exalted, in a homogeneous Irish nation, was made by the Cork author and critic, Daniel Corkery. His book *The hidden Ireland* (1924), ostensibly about eighteenth-century Irish-language poetry in Munster, was premised on the social, cultural and political unity of Ireland before the seventeenth-century confiscations. The Gael in the hovel and the Gael in the 'Big House' had shared an ancient and noble culture and society, based on communal ideals derived from race, language and religion. These ideals were fundamentally at odds with the alien, acquisitive, culture of the conquerors. Corkery asserted:

> The Gaels in the big houses were one with the cottiers in race, language, religion and, to some extent, culture.

The political consequences of such a view were a belief that the fundamental cleavage in Ireland was between the alien oppressors and the oppressed, conquered Irish. The limitations of Corkery's approach were first outlined by L.M. Cullen more than thirty years ago. For Corkery, as for the Christian Brothers or home rule MPs, the main problem of Irish society was the relationship with Britain, and only national independence would resolve it. The colonial relationship to Britain oppressed the peasant in the hovel, the dispossessed Gaelic aristocrat and the Catholic professional. Of course, this suggested these groups shared political interests. The confiscations of the Gaelic aristocracy's estates had underpinned Ireland's subjection to the British crown. National independence was required for Irish society to develop, unimpeded by colonial handicaps. It is indeed questionable whether some of the advocates of an 'Irish Ireland' sought economic 'development' at all, for they seemed to imply that social ills which are incompatible with a pious, Catholic people would accompany such development. De Valera's well-known image of comely maidens dancing at the crossroads was self-consciously articulated in opposition to the perceived vulgar materialism of industrial society, Britain being paradigmatic. This perception of Irish society continues to surface in the modern historiography of pre-famine Ireland, even where it is otherwise good history. For example, Kevin O'Neill's useful investigation of pre-famine social

33 W. Macken, *The silent people* (1965 ed.), 43, 201–2, 344, 327.

relations on the land asserts that, 'isolated from their rulers by language, customs, and religion, the peasantry were able to preserve much of their traditional Gaelic culture'. While Kevin O'Neill acknowledges that Ireland's proximity to the first industrial revolution made it significant for the study of 'the expansion of capitalism into isolated rural areas', he unfortunately suggests that this signified a clash of social and economic systems that amounted to a confrontation between native and planter. These represented a clash between different 'social and moral values', much as Corkery and nationalist politicians had narrated them.[34]

For nationalist writers like O'Brien, Sullivan and O'Hegarty, the conflicts that racked the country over land from the 1760s until the great famine were proto-national, in so far as they pitted the colonists against the native Irish. The tenants, oppressed by the exactions of middlemen, an alien church and a hostile legal system combined to oppose their oppressors. The popular images of landlord and tenant relations in eighteenth- and nineteenth-century Ireland are those of rapacious middlemen enforcing distress warrants or evictions, aided by a partisan police and magistracy. Furthermore, popular fiction and education confirmed the nationalist master-narrative, thus rendering whiteboyism as the unfortunate but understandable outcome of national oppression.

RECENT ANALYSES

Professional historians of Ireland were largely concerned with other issues until relatively recently. This was so much the case that the chapters on the eighteenth and nineteenth centuries in a survey of history scholarship published by the Irish Committee of Historical Sciences in 1971, reprinted from *Irish Historical Studies*, failed to mention the conflicts that afflicted the countryside in the century before the famine. It was only with the publication of *Secret Societies in Ireland* in 1973 that agrarian conflicts really became a focus of studies (although the earlier warning about the relatively informal organization of agrarian rebels ought to be borne in mind). Two essays in the book are particularly relevant, in that they imply new approaches to pre-famine agrarian conflicts. Maureen Wall asserted that both Catholics and Protestants had been involved in whiteboy agitations, and that both Catholic and Protestant clergy had been targets. Less surprising, in view of the dislike of secret societies expressed by mainstream nationalist figures like Sullivan, was her suggestion that the Catholic church had frequently been in conflict with its congregation over rural rebellions. However, her essay was a significant revision of the popular conception of a peasantry

---

34 D. Corkery, *The hidden Ireland* (1967 ed.), 64; L.M. Cullen, 'The hidden Ireland: reassessment of a concept' (1969). For a more recent discussion of Corkery, see S.J. Connolly, 'Eighteenth century Ireland' (1996); K. O'Neill, *Family and farm* (1996), 4, 14, 15.

oppressed by an alien church and landlords. Joseph Lee's contribution to the book asserted bluntly that such agrarian movements were not nationalist. However, Lee repeated Sullivan's dubious nomenclature of a century earlier, using the term 'Ribbonmen' to describe clandestine agrarian organizations.[35]

In the 1970s and 1980s James Donnelly's contribution to the study of Irish agrarian movements was critical in developing professional approaches to the subject. In a succession of detailed papers he profoundly revised the nationalist orthodoxy. Donnelly explicitly described his efforts as revisionist, and drew on sources which had previously been relatively unexplored. His findings were revelatory. His examination of the Whiteboys of the 1760s demonstrated conflict among the Catholic population, as well as a distaste among contemporary Catholic commentators for their rebellious lower-order co-religionists, rather similar to the distaste that home rulers like Sullivan were to feel a century later.[36]

The nationalist orthodoxy was challenged most directly in Donnelly's work on the Rightboy movement. Not only did he discover conflict among Catholics, but also he found Protestant gentry in positions of leadership in the movement, albeit in particular local circumstances. Such findings led Donnelly to conclude that the social composition of agrarian movements varied according to the economic stimulus that provoked collective action. He also attempted to impose some sort of conceptual order on the mass of evidence he had considered. This included a consideration of theories of collective action and modernization.[37]

Historians have also found evidence of divisions in Irish society which were not based on nationality, race or religion in the activities of early nineteenth-century factions, such as the Caravats and Shanavests of east Munster. These factions were gangs that met almost ritually, particularly on fair days, to engage in combat for the sake of family or community pride. They were particularly associated with leading families (often the descendants of local pre-confiscation landowners and possibly associated with the 'underground gentry', although gentlemen were less willing to be associated with factions after the turn of the nineteenth century) or certain neighbourhoods. For example, Boyle fair days in the early nineteenth century were accompanied by confrontations between the mountain men and the plains men, factions from distinct areas near the town (there is also the fascinating but unverifiable possibility that the Boyle fair factions reflected political distinctions like those between the radical Mountain and

35 T.W. Moody (ed.), *Irish historiography, 1936-70* (1971); M. Wall, 'The Whiteboys' (1973); J. Lee, 'The Ribbonmen' (1973).   36 J.S. Donnelly, 'The social composition' (1983). Donnelly's major articles on eighteenth century agrarian movements in Munster often used contemporary newspaper accounts as sources. This was, in itself, a significant change in approach; Donnelly, 'Whiteboy movement', 21, 37-8.   37 Donnelly, 'Rightboy movement', 127; Donnelly, 'Social composition', 154; S. Clark and J.S. Donnelly, 'General Introduction' (1983).

the conciliatory Plain factions in the French national convention during 1792 and 1793). A convention which excluded firearms from such conflicts was breaking down in the early nineteenth century, and the conflicts were no longer restricted to market-place confrontations. Paul Roberts's examination of the Shanavests suggests that the faction was a vigilante gang formed by middle-class nationalist farmers connected with the 1798 rebels:

> The Shanavests were an unprecedented middle-class anti-Whiteboy movement formed specifically to combat the Caravats. They seem to have combined vigilantism and informing with the propagation of an ideological alternative to Whiteboyism, namely, nationalism.

Roberts's analysis of 28 members of the Shanavests reveals that 21 were tenant farmers, although four were labourers, possibly because they had family ties with members or because, while the social status of a family had changed, their gang loyalty remained. The significance of family loyalties will be examined shortly. The faction was based on local groups who were bound by family ties that expressed hereditary family conflicts, not through the arms raid or the threatening letter but through fighting and prosecuting the Caravats, who more closely resembled a whiteboy association. Roberts considers that rather than being kin-based factions, the Caravats and Shanavests represented opposing class interests among the rural population.[38]

However, David Fitzpatrick has suggested that hereditary kin rivalries were the likely precipitant of conflicts over land and, indeed, that conflicts between or within families and communities were much more significant than any between either native Gaels and oppressive Saxon landlords, or indeed between social classes. His study of the Outrage Reports for one Co. Leitrim parish, Cloone, between 1835 and 1852, identified a range of motives behind agrarian conflicts which left him in little doubt that neither nationality nor class divisions in non-élite rural society were the main causes of conflict in rural Irish society before the mid-nineteenth century: community or family loyalty (or disloyalty) was more likely to be the source of outrage:

> Many of the outrage cases ... discussed in a class context may be reinterpreted more profitably as intra-family disputes.

Thus the apparently 'individual' crime might be the enforcement of a particular family solidarity against another member of the same family. Rather than any

38 J.S. Donnelly, 'Factions in prefamine Ireland' (1988). The term 'underground gentry' was deployed in Whelan, 'An underground gentry?'; RLG, 10 Oct. 1823; Donnelly, 'Factions in prefamine Ireland', 115; P.E.W. Roberts, 'Caravats and Shanavests' (1983), 67, 89-90.

more general sense of class solidarity, the need for subsistence security and to ensure the viability of family farm units created particular solidarities and conflicts within families and communities. This finding is somewhat at odds with Lewis's study. Lewis was convinced that the phenomenon under consideration was 'social' crime in a wider sense than the enforcement of an individual family member's desires against another's. It was not 'ordinary' thieving:

> The persons who commit these crimes do not, like the bandits of Italy or the London thieves, follow crime as a profession: they are merely called out by their brethren for the occasion.

Nor was it merely 'the banding together of a few outcasts ... but the deliberate association of the peasantry, seeking by cruel outrage to insure themselves against the risk of utter destitution and abandonment'.[39]

The question was clearly of some significance to Lewis, who appeared particularly concerned to show that rural disturbances were the pursuit of individual ends through a collective discipline. This is a point he emphasized repeatedly. He noted the lack of petty theft associated with whiteboy raids on houses (they took money only to help cover legal costs and not for personal gain), where they removed arms and little else:

> Conduct of this kind clearly evinces the feeling of the Whiteboys, that they are the administrators of a general system, meant for the benefit of a *body*, and by which *individuals* are not to be allowed to profit;

and again:

> The Whiteboys do not seek plunder in the individual case but to enforce a law for the general advantage of the poor.

For Lewis, the system was a generalized one, demanding the loyalty of a wide range of people, rather than expressing the desires of a particular family or community against another, so that 'homicides are considered, not as casual acts of individual malice or vengeance, but as exemplary infliction, intended to deter all others'. The people had a general sympathy with the cause of whiteboys and saw their own interests as bound up with the success of such combinations. Lewis distinguished between public and private grievances, noting that it was much easier to find witnesses in cases where the nature of the offence was pri-

---

39 D. Fitzpatrick, 'Class, family and rural unrest' (1982); Lewis, *On local disturbances*, 183, 247.

vate (he cited the example of the case of a murder of a husband by his wife and her lover). Alexis de Tocqueville was shocked when he was told of the murder of an agent who evicted a sick woman and then destroyed her home before the woman's eyes. The agent was killed by a man 'who was not personally interested in any way in the act ... but who acted out of vengeance for that deed'.[40]

Lewis did allow that 'although the Whiteboys' union was for the protection of a class, occasionally there were hatreds among the factions contained in that class'. Fitzpatrick, however, suggests that where there were family rivalries over claims to coveted farms, houses or jobs, the claimants were strongly tempted to reinforce their claims through intimidation, factional combination and outrage. Indeed,

> Conflicts apparently between classes may often be reinterpreted as struggles within families; conflicts within classes may be construed as struggles between family factions.

For Fitzpatrick, these conflicts between and within social strata mean that concepts like class or community 'carry little conviction'. Avowed egalitarianism merely legitimized factional exclusivism.[41]

Fitzpatrick's work not only rejects the perceptions conveyed in popular nationalist historiography, but also any determining significance being placed upon class relations in the pre-famine countryside. In doing so, Fitzpatrick's work can be located in a broader historiography of modernization which identifies solidarities in 'pre-modern' societies as based largely around the parochial, familiar world of the peasant's family and vertical ties to local community élites. This was a period in which class solidarities in the 'modern' urban and industrial sense did not yet exist. Fitzpatrick states his modernization approach explicitly when he quotes Cullen approvingly:

> The changing character of manifestations of unrest in the nineteenth century ... are a subtle indication of the progress of modernization.

Donnelly and Clark considered the impact of modernization when discussing conceptual approaches to Irish agrarian conflict, and placed such conflicts in a framework developed by Charles Tilly, in which conflicts were transformed over many years from local to national, reactive to active and communal to associational.[42]

40 Lewis, *On local disturbances*, 223, 172, 192, 82, 164, 207; E. Larkin (trans. and ed.), *Alexis de Tocqueville's Journey* (1990), 42.   41 Lewis, *On local disturbances*, 228; Fitzpatrick, 'Class, family and rural unrest', 45, 68, 43, 47.   42 Fitzpatrick, 'Class, family and rural unrest', 38; Clark and Donnelly, 'General introduction', 5; C. Tilly, *From mobilization to revolution* (1978).

Tilly identified three types of collective violence – the primitive, the reactionary and the modern. The primitive stage was characterized by struggles between communal groups, the reactionary by small-scale conflict between communal groups or loosely organized members of the population, and the modern was undertaken by the complex, durable organizations of a significant section of the population against local authorities or representatives of a central power. Tilly has since rejected this analysis, and has attempted to understand how changes in patterns of collective struggle (which he now calls 'popular contention') occur without the need to build them into a narrative of modernization in which reactionary social forces like the peasantry were swept aside by the development of commerce, capitalism and the consolidation of a centralized state apparatus. What may be significant in terms of the historiography of Irish popular protest is that Clark and Donnelly add the important qualification that both reactionary and modern forms could co-exist for a time. It will be necessary to return to the notion of modernization when discussing conceptual models, but it is clear that Fitzpatrick's approach does mark a significant break from the popular nationalist historiographic consensus and also from other revisions of that consensus.[43]

The suggestion by Fitzpatrick that agrarian collective actions were characterized by group identities springing from pre-modern sources of social identity, especially kin groups, echoes the work of George Rudé and Eric Hobsbawm, which reflect the widespread view that collective agrarian conflict was descended formally from individual brigandage and banditry. In this analysis, the Italian *bandito*, the Balkan *haidouk* and the Irish Tory or Rapparee all shared similar status as defenders of the community's values, resisting incursions of the modern state into the community's life. For example, at the time of the revolutions of 1848 the Kingdom of the two Sicilies was beset by widespread social disorder. This was attributed to land hunger after small proprietors had taken possession of the commons and let them on onerous terms. The view from above was, as in Ireland, that the disturbances did not have a political character. Hobsbawm's study of brigandage in southern Europe suggests that the social brigand appeared only until such time as the poor achieved more effective means of social agitation, 'when the jaws of the dynamic modern world seize the static communities'. Hobsbawm's discussion of the secrecy and symbols of the brigands may appear familiar to the student of Irish agrarian movements, and he locates movements characterized by such 'primitive' symbols as ones where 'bonds of kinship or tribal solidarity which ... are the key to what are thought of as primitive societies, persist'.[44]

43 C. Tilly, 'Collective violence in European perspective' (1968); C. Tilly, *Popular contention in Great Britain* (1995), 37; Clark and Donnelly, 'General introduction', 10.   44 A. Sciroc-

Rudé suggested that the result of the process was that 'the machine wrecker, rick burner and "Church and King" rioter have given way to the trade unionist, labour militant and organized consumer of the new industrial society'. Pre-modern peasant bands were 'fired as much by memories of customary rights or a nostalgia for past utopias as by present grievances or hopes of material improvement, and they dispense a rough-and-ready kind of "natural justice" '.[45]

This attempt to preserve customarily held rights was noted in an Irish context by Lewis. He quoted evidence given to a Commons select committee in 1831 which related the story of a peasant insisting on occupancy rights because his forefathers had been in possession of the small plot of land he was under pressure to relinquish. One of the objects of the Whiteboys in 1761 had been to level enclosure fences – reversing a 'modern' encroachment on customary rights. As people became increasingly desperate, appeals to custom were often expressed in a quasi-legal language, based on an alternative sense of legal authority. Lewis, discussing threatening notices, observed, 'These mandates are often written in a style resembling a legal notice.'[46]

In his study of the downwardly mobile Catholic gentry after the Williamite wars, Kevin Whelan detected a sense of obligation between landlords and tenants. Whelan noted the sense of mutuality between the 'shadow gentry ... perhaps facilitating access to jobs, subleases, conacre or cottier holdings', and the rural poor, but also that, under the impact of economic change the 'underground gentry' abandoned their patrician role and immersion in popular culture:

> By the late eighteenth century, these common ties in the informal intimacy of collective engagement in popular culture had snapped, to be replaced by a more formal, distant relationship.

(More generally, Peter Burke has described how during the early modern period in Europe the 'clergy, nobility and bourgeoisie alike were coming to internalise the ethos of self-control and order'.) As a consequence, said Whelan,

> The great redresser movements, the Whiteboys and Rightboys, sought a return to the days when the moral economy blunted the impact of the real one.

Whelan, then, offers an explanation of the causes of whiteboy conflict in terms of a modernization process. Like Hobsbawm and Rudé, he sees whiteboyism as

co, 'Fenomeni di persistenza' (1981), 262, 261, 250; E. Hobsbawm, *Primitive rebels* (1969 ed.), 24, 3.   **45** G. Rudé, *The crowd in history* (1964), 268, 5.   **46** Lewis, *On local disturbances*, 61, 2, 178.

a reactionary phenomenon. Furthermore, Whelan uses Edward Thompson's term moral economy in a modernization framework. It will become clear later that Thompson did not impose such a rigid teleology on the concept. Appeals to the legitimizing power of the past and of memory were significant, and not limited to the restoration of Rudé's 'past utopias'. Indeed, social and economic relationships and structures that conferred order on the world could, at the same time, be the source of conflicts within that world. Further, the ways in which such relationships and structures were re-ordered were contingent upon the outcomes of such conflicts, and the outcomes were not predetermined by a modernizing teleology.[47]

It was the 'underground gentry' that was to re-emerge as the Catholic middle class and 'strong farmer' interest in the nineteenth century and as the backbone of O'Connell's movement, adopting policies of 'improvement' on the land, emancipation from religious penalties in public life and nationalism in politics. As part of this adoption of improvement they came increasingly into conflict with their Catholic tenants and sub-tenants. Near Tuam in the summer of 1835, a Catholic priest acknowledged to de Tocqueville that Catholic and Protestant landlords 'oppress the people in about the same way'. It may be just such farming interests that were identified by Lewis when he quoted evidence to a Commons committee which suggested that factions were led by farmers or sons of farmers. Membership of a particular faction may, indeed, have been an echo of eighteenth-century vertical loyalties between descendants of the dispossessed Catholic gentry and the poor. Donnelly notes that factions were often known by family names, which signified particularly powerful or authoritative families. The historiographic trend that identifies whiteboyism as an expression of pre-modern kin loyalties thus originates in the assumption, shared by some of the more perceptive contemporaneous observers of whiteboy conflict, that because it did not enjoy élite patronage or leadership, whiteboyism had no political inflection. It expressed only parochial or pre-modern collective identities, such as to the family. It is apparent that whiteboyism must be located within a broader matrix of social relations in the pre-famine Irish countryside. It is now necessary to consider these relationships, in relation particularly to Catholicism (most commonly associated with nationalism) and in relation to the vertical social relations between the landlord and tenant.[48]

47 Whelan, 'An underground gentry?', 16, 24, 26; P. Burke, *Popular culture* (1994 ed.), 272.
48 Whelan, 'An underground gentry?', 18; Larkin, *De Tocqueville's journey*, 118; Lewis, *On local disturbances*, 231; Donnelly, 'Factions in prefamine Ireland', 116, S.R. Gibbons, *Captain Rock, night errant* (2004), 12.

Pre-famine rural social relations

Priests and people

Nationalist historians considered the image of the mass rock, of people and priests suffering together under penal statute, to be paradigmatic of relations between the Catholic church and its congregation, but revisionist accounts have suggested otherwise. They have drawn attention to conflict between co-religionists as well as numerous instances of discord between the Catholic rural poor and their own clergy – over the dues levied by the clergy for the performance of various rites, the exclusion of priests from chapels so that oaths could be administered, or threats that were made to persuade priests not to interfere in the business of secret combinations. Donnelly's study of the Rightboys even suggested that one tactic of protest could be to go so far as to join a Protestant church. In early 1786 several entire Co. Cork parishes seceded to the Church of Ireland and clergy of both denominations were attacked and assaulted. Clearly, it was not only tithes payable to the established church that were a source of conflict between churches and the rural population.[1]

Michael Beames saw the pre-famine conflicts between Catholic clergy and congregations as reflecting a concerted effort by the Catholic church to consolidate its ideological control over the populace. This process – and the contrast between earlier 'folk' versions of Catholicism and Paul Cullen's ultramontane church – has been dissected by Emmet Larkin and Sean Connolly. Larkin suggests that before the 1840s mass attendance was as low as 40 per cent and that the ratio of priests to people was so low as to severely limit 'any effective service on the part of the clergy'. Also significant for the purposes of this study are Larkin's examples of the 'performance' of the pre-Cullenite clergy – and their conflicts with Catholic congregations. He observes that the clergy were guilty of drunkenness, womanizing and avarice. In one 1840 case, parishioners from Co. Mayo petitioned the pope about alleged abuses by the clergy; there were fifteen different complaints registered in a petition which, according to Larkin, 'was the product of a fierce local struggle for power, with the contending parties prepared to say and write the worst about their opponents'. Connolly has noted the work of George Thomas Plunket, Catholic bishop of Elphin between 1814 and 1827, to reform 'drunken, immoral and disorderly clergy'.[2]

---

1 Donnelly, 'The Rightboy movement', 170; Beames, *Peasants and power*, 29. 2 Beames,

Larkin's 'devotional revolution' began rather earlier than he suggested. Connolly has pointed out the efforts of the Catholic church to impose a stricter discipline on its adherents before the great famine. It is often supposed that the reform process began with Cullen's accession to the see of Dublin in 1850, but the synod held that year at Thurles was the consolidation of a half-century of reform and reorganization. Connolly suggests that conflicts between priests and congregation 'contrast sharply with the pious picture ... of a clergy and laity united by common social origins and shared grievances'. He has also, interestingly, compared the attempts of the Irish Catholic clergy to impose order and discipline on their congregations with the efforts of moral reformers in England.[3]

There were also economic reasons for conflict between Catholic priests and people. Michael Beames has described how, during the Whiteboy movement of the 1760s, 'Catholic clergy were equally liable to the attentions of Whiteboys when their charges were deemed excessive.' Priests' dues continued to be an issue well into the nineteenth century. Indeed, in 1831 the Dublin archdiocese set statutory tariffs for the performance of clerical tasks such as baptisms, weddings and funerals. These dues and their impact expose the inadequacy of the nationalist image of priest and people suffering oppression together, enduring oppression steadfastly for the faith. In 1807 a magistrate in Swinford, Co. Mayo, identified dues payable to Catholic clergy as a reason for disturbances by Threshers – alongside tithes payable to ministers of the established church. Later that year Lord Hartland of Strokestown Park, Co. Roscommon, wrote to a fellow landlord after disturbances on his own estate:

> This business is a quarrell between the priests and their flocks about clerical dutys viz. Christenings, marriages and for which they have lately considerably raised their fees.

On 6 January 1814, magistrate John Wills read the riot act to an assembly of several hundred people at the Catholic church of Ballagh, also in Co. Roscommon, after the parish priest refused to say Mass because of their conduct. As late as 1839 George Warburton told the Lords committee investigating disturbances in Ireland that violence was used against Catholic priests to discourage them from interfering in the activities of the oath-bound secret societies. George Cornewall Lewis noted antipathy between the rural poor and Catholic clergy. He confirmed that Catholic priests' dues, as well as tithes, had been the cause of the Thresher disturbances in Connacht in late 1806 and 1807. Lewis also cited a

Peasants and power, 28; E. Larkin, 'The devotional revolution in Ireland' (1972), 627, 633; S.J. Connolly, *Priests and people* (1982), 71.   3 Connolly, *Priests and people*, 72, 252, 172.

case from 1775 in Co. Kildare, when a priest was buried to his neck in thorns. The Catholic clergy, nobility and gentry had, in his view, been 'most active' in the suppression of disturbance, and he recounted the case of a murder in Co. Kilkenny of a landjobber who was the brother of the Catholic bishop of Ossory. A parliamentary witness was quoted as lamenting that the 'Whitefeet pay little respect to their clergymen'. The Whiteboy and Rightboy movements were not to be interpreted as nationalist or religious rebellion: 'the Munster disturbances, although they were carried on by Catholics ... were not intended to serve the cause of Catholicism'.[4]

Landlords and tenants

The popular nationalist views of the social relations that form a general context for whiteboyism have also been revised on a number of grounds, including landownership and agrarian class composition and structure. It is useful to consider some of these revisions, relating in particular to the period prior to the uninterrupted whiteboyism of the first half of the nineteenth century. Sean Connolly has summarized these revisions thus: 'Ireland in this period can no longer be conceived in terms of the simple duality of anglicized landlord and Gaelic peasant.'[5]

Kevin Whelan and others have suggested that the significance of the post-confiscation Catholic landlord bloc has previously been underestimated. Legal devices such as holding land in trust were adopted widely to ensure the continuity of the Catholic landed interest, in such a way that as much as 20 per cent of the land may have remained in the hands of the descendants of its former owners, the most conspicuous in Co. Roscommon being the O'Conor Don of Clonalis House, near Castlerea.[6]

Whelan argues that even where, as on the majority of estates, eighteenth-century landlords were disposed to hire Protestants as middlemen, in practice it was not possible to do this. The former owners of the land became middlemen in a significant number of cases and retained an honoured status within the 'indigenous' population. Arthur Young noted in north Co. Cork:

4 Beames, *Peasants and power*, 114; SOCP1 1121/53, Major General Robert Taylor, Athlone, to unnamed, Dublin Castle, 1 Oct.1807, relating statement of William Brabazon, Swinford, Co. Mayo; SOCP1 1192/9, Lord Hartland, Strokestown, to Mahon, 7 Dec. 1808; SOCP1 1558/24, Wills to Gregory, 10 Apr. 1814; SC 1839, 70, evidence of George Warburton; Lewis, *On local disturbances*, 33, 24-5, 94, 117 (quoting W.W. Despard's evidence to SC 1831-2), 26.   5 S.J. Connolly, ' "Ag déanamh *commanding*" ' (1998), 2.   6 Whelan, 'An underground gentry?', 6.

> All the poor people are Roman Catholics, and among them are the
> descendants of the old families who once possessed the country, of
> which they preserve the full memory, insomuch, that a gentleman's
> labourer will regularly leave to his son, by will, his master's estate.

David Dickson has also noted the presence of Catholic former proprietors
among the middlemen, suggesting that they may have enjoyed some 'residual
authority' among the poor. It will be necessary to return to this 'underground
gentry', but for now it should be observed that the continued existence of
Catholic land-owners, and the role of former owners as middlemen (a rôle
reserved by nationalist histories for the worst Saxon parasites) are a challenge
to nationalist orthodoxy.[7]

In an investigation of the many layers that existed in land relations in rural
Ireland, Samuel Clark has proposed further grounds for qualifying any suggestion that all Gaels were united in suffering at the hands of the alien oppressor. It is necessary, he argued, to distinguish not only the cottier and labouring
poor from the more substantial tenant farmers, but also an intermediate layer
of smaller tenant farmers. In circumstances of relative impoverishment, these
men might side with one or other of the distinct classes that Clark was able to
distinguish among the rural population, beneath the landowning group that
occupied the apex of the social pyramid. Clark correctly saw conflict in the
nineteenth-century Irish countryside as primarily between the tenant farmer
and cottier/labourer class. He made plain his disagreement with the popular
perception of a united peasantry fighting the landed colonial élite:

> Popular accounts hold that in the eighteenth end nineteenth centuries
> the rural Catholic population fought continuously to resist the oppres-
> sion from which it suffered at the hands of heartless and mostly absen-
> tee landlords ... If one examines this unrest carefully, one finds that it
> did not consist of one continuous struggle but of a number of different
> collective efforts by members of distinguishable social groups within the
> rural population, whose interests were not identical and sometimes dia-
> metrically opposed.

Clark proceeded to construct an elaborate table that divided the rural population into five different classes: non-farming élites, large independent landholders, small independent landholders, labourer-landholders and landless
labourers. He attributed struggles over various issues to conflicts between dif-

7 A.W. Hutton (ed.), *Arthur Young's tour in Ireland* (1892), 300; D. Dickson, 'Middlemen'
(1979).

ferent permutations of these groups. Clark's studies demonstrated hetero-geneity among the non-élite rural population in Ireland in the eighteenth and nineteenth centuries. Further evidence of this has been provided by Joseph Lee, who has examined 'outrages' in Co. Roscommon. Of 163 incidents in the first five months of 1846, 103 were attributable to 'disputes between labour-ers and either landlords or, far more frequently, farmers'.[8]

David Fitzpatrick took up and disagreed with Clark's finely stratified model of the rural population, asserting that small and large farmers should not be separated into classes and accorded the potential for hostile mobilization. Indeed,

> The subtle stratification of agrarian society was a ladder which one could climb up or slip down, not a pyramid on which each man felt he had been assigned (perhaps unfairly) his proper station.

The slippery ladder image may be more appropriate for farming families (who were relatively upwardly mobile) than for the desperately poor cottiers and labourers, for whom social mobility could scarcely be considered 'vigorous'.[9]

Donnelly noted Fitzpatrick's enthusiasm for a kin and community model of agrarian conflict, and conceded that there is evidence that class, kin or com-munity identities could be at the root of conflict – particularly when consider-ing factions, which may have been led by a local family that retained vestigial authority or power. However, Donnelly argued that Roberts, Beames and Fitz-patrick all underestimated the impact of economic fluctuation on the social composition of whiteboy movements. In making this point, Donnelly in effect accepted Clark's model of conflict between various non-élite social strata as being of primary importance in agrarian unrest. His work has frequently been underpinned by examinations of how prevailing economic conditions influ-enced the social profile of those who became involved in whiteboy activity and the groups who actually come into conflict. Donnelly showed how, for exam-ple, during the Rightboy movement, relatively benign economic conditions led to increased concern across a broader social range with issues like priests' dues, tithes and rates (issues like conacre rents were unknown as sources of conflict during the Rightboy movement). However, while Donnelly delineated the unique features, economic stimuli and social compositions of various move-ments, he did not examine the frequently similar legitimizing notions used by agrarian rebels to justify their actions, despite acknowledging that similar griev-

8 S. Clark, 'The importance of agrarian classes' (1982), 13; J. Lee, 'Patterns of rural unrest in nineteenth century Ireland' (1980), 224.   9 Fitzpatrick, 'Class, family and rural unrest', 55, 53, 69.

ances were aired throughout the whiteboy period. Appeals to custom, whether ancient or created contemporaneously to legitimize some new demand, were highly significant.[10]

Clearly, then, the nationalist notion of social homogeneity (conferred by Corkery's touchstones of race, language and religion) among the rural population beneath the landowning élite has faced a profound challenge, with Whelan going so far as to suggest that the landowners were nowhere nearly so uniformly English, Protestant and absentee as previously claimed.

Toby Barnard has criticized Whelan's model, but for the purposes of this work there is a significant area of agreement between them concerning the pervasive culture of landlordism in the eighteenth century. Whelan has suggested that hospitality, gaming and leisure were the principal pursuits of the 'underground gentry', and Barnard has added that the new Protestant landlord and middleman élite adopted a similar ethos (although he disagrees with Whelan about some details of lifestyle). Barnard, like Whelan, rejected the popular image of the absentee landlord who enjoyed huge profits from a suffering peasantry. Rather, landlords and middlemen had vertical ties and a sense of mutuality with their tenants, irrespective of their confessional affiliation. The corollary of this is that where conflict did arise, it was not necessarily legitimized in terms of ethnic or religious difference, but more commonly in terms of the customary duties of the rich to the poor.[11]

Maria Edgeworth's novel, *Castle Rackrent*, illustrates Whelan's and Barnard's findings. The novel is narrated by a faithful Gael, Thady Quirk, whose family has lived rent-free on the Rackrent estate since 'time out of mind'. The novel also shows how old families could retain possession of their estates by means of legal sophistry. The Rackrents had earlier been called O'Shaughlin. In the figure of the narrator's son, who becomes a lawyer and eventually owner of the estate, Edgeworth anticipates the trajectory that Whelan suggests Catholic professionals and farmers were to take. O'Connell reported to a House of Lords select committee in 1825 that property in Catholic hands had 'increased enormously' over the previous thirty years (since the relaxation of restrictions on Catholic landowning) and that Catholics were very heavily involved in the mortgage business. As William Kinsella, bishop of Ossory, observed to de Tocqueville:

> Everyday we see the rich Catholics of the towns lend money to Protestants ... many estates pass gradually into the hands of Catholics.

10 Donnelly, 'Factions in prefamine Ireland', 116; Donnelly, 'Social composition', 154; Donnelly gives detailed accounts of the economic context for whiteboyism in, for example, 'Whiteboy movement', at 30–1 and 'Rightboy movement', at 139; Donnelly, 'Rightboy movement', 124.   11 T.C. Barnard, 'The gentrification of eighteenth century Ireland' (1997).

The Rackrent dynasty's patriarch 'lived and died a monument of old Irish hospitality', allowing his tenants to fall into arrears of rent (this was customary on
many estates). The Rackrents are ruined by their spendthrift lifestyle. The tone
of the novel – at least when focused on the landlord class – is decidedly iron-
ic, but there is an epiphanic moment when the people who live on the estate
cheer their hard-pressed landlord, for fear of his being replaced by the hard-
headed Catholic lawyer. The novel is pervaded by a sense of affection between
the landowning class and the poor who live on the estate, even when the landlord is frequently absent in Bath. The landowner's apparent benevolence is
illustrated when he throws the narrator a guinea from his waistcoat pocket.
The poor gather to welcome the last Rackrent and his wife back from honey-
moon and are 'much more alert in doffing their caps to these new men, than to
those of what they call *good old families*'. The novel is also characterized by
imagery of decay. By the end, it is only possible to enter the house by walking
to the rear entrance. The front is too narrow for a carriage 'and the great piers
have tumbled down across the front approach, so there's no driving the right
way by reason of the ruins'. Eventually the house lies empty, with the wind
blowing through it. It is a striking image of the end of land relations characterized by mutual obligation and vertical ties.[12]

Thomas Bartlett has suggested that these relations came conclusively to an
end at the time of the anti-militia riots of 1793, following the disappointment
of lower-class Catholic hopes by the Catholic Relief Act, which had been a vic-
tory for the Catholic middle classes, clerical and lay. In his view, relative harmony had characterized social relations in the eighteenth-century countryside,
dependent on easygoing practices – long leases, low rents and the tolerance of
arrears. This picture is consistent with the accounts given by Barnard and
Whelan, and rendered fictionally by Edgeworth. One judge quoted by Lewis
suggested that the cause of agrarian conflict is the 'relations disseevered, which
between the higher and lower classes are the offspring of reciprocal protection
and dependence.' Similarly, de Tocqueville noted at around the same time as
Lewis, and more than forty years after the militia riots: 'The natural link that
should unite the upper and lower classes is destroyed.'[13]

Lewis commented that the rural poor in Ireland received no 'interested protection and relief which a master would afford to his bondman'. However, it is
not clear that this mutuality was abandoned by those seeking to legitimize
agrarian protest quite as suddenly as Bartlett suggests. Rudé has argued that

12 M. Edgeworth, *Castle Rackrent* (1995 ed.), 7; SC 1825, 64, evidence of D. O'Connell;
Larkin, *De Tocqueville's journey*, 64; Edgeworth, *Castle Rackrent*, 37, 79, 19, 21, 47, 61.   13
Bartlett, 'An end to moral economy', 216; Lewis, *On local disturbances*, 240-1; Larkin, *De Toc-
queville journey*, 40.

there is a time lag between the existence of new economic situations, social forms and forces on the one hand and the languages they are expressed in on the other. However, it will become apparent that appeals to custom did not merely look backward: many of the demands legitimized by such language were relatively new formulations based on new circumstances. This study will demonstrate the continued legitimization of agrarian protest through appeals to mutuality, custom and tradition during the first half of the nineteenth century and, in addition, that Irish agrarian rebels appropriated freely from other languages and repertoires of dissent to legitimize their collective actions. The use of such repertoires was already evident in the daylight marches of the Rightboys in the 1780s, disturbing the strictly linear evolution of the development of popular protest suggested by terms like 'pre-modern' and 'modern' and implied in Rudé's approach. In a strict modernization scheme, protest in the 1780s should still have been confined to the anonymity conferred by darkness.[14]

It is clear, then, that historians have progressed from nationalist narratives of popular protest to a more complex reading of whiteboyism. The next part of this book will move from the broad picture of conflict and social relations in the pre-famine Irish countryside to examine the evidence in the case of Co. Roscommon.

14 Lewis, *On local disturbances*, 44; Rudé, *Crowd in history*, 197.

3

'The sensational and the routine'

Co. Roscommon was among neither the most disturbed nor the most peaceful counties of Ireland during the period under consideration. Some studies have focused upon especially turbulent counties like Tipperary, or on particular categories of crime. Fitzpatrick's study of agrarian unrest examined evidence from Cloone, a Leitrim parish that was notoriously disturbed. In 1845 a correspondent from near Carrick-on-Shannon reported to Dublin Castle that he feared 'another Cloon in one of the heretofore most quiet parts of Roscommon'. It has not been established that studies of such places as Cloone or Tipperary provide the best evidence to sustain generalizations about the nature of agrarian conflict. Further, counties that were relatively undisturbed (or were disturbed in particular untypical ways) may also not reveal the general character of agrarian conflict in the half century before the great famine. Donnelly's accounts of eighteenth-century Munster remain much the most comprehensive and detailed studies of specific whiteboy movements.[1]

Only in the mid-1840s could Co. Roscommon be said to be among the most disturbed counties in Ireland. Acknowledging that the conacre crisis was 'particularly acute in Roscommon' at that time, it may nevertheless be suggested that the conacre issue clarifies the essence of land problems, rather than demonstrating that Co. Roscommon was exceptional. The county had been one of the more disturbed counties during the Thresher disturbances in the second decade of the century and in the 1830s, but was relatively peaceful during periods when, for example, Munster was much disturbed. Beames also suggested that 'Roscommon ... exhibited a continuous propensity for outrage throughout the pre-famine period.' What is most important is to establish here that Roscommon did not exhibit any characteristics that made it so exceptional as to negate the value of making it a case study. The intention of this chapter is not to show that the findings from Roscommon may be transferred without qualification to Ireland as a whole during the period, but that it occu-

---

1 For example, Beames, 'Rural conflict in pre-famine Ireland' (1978), considers Co. Tipperary over a ten year period. The range of the investigation is limited further by focusing exclusively on murders. See also Fitzpatrick, 'Class, family and rural unrest'. Fitzpatrick criticizes the narrowness of Beames's approach but does not appear to consider whether the exclusive reliance on data from one notorious place may distort his own findings; OR 1845/8705, C. MacArthur, chief constable, Carrick on Shannon, to unnamed, Dublin Castle, 13 Apr. 1845.

pies a reasonable median for the conduct of a case study. Furthermore, it should be recalled that this study aims not to explain immediate causes of particular agrarian agitations, but to investigate the workings of a collective customary consciousness among the rural poor. While the economic stimuli for agrarian discontent may have varied between a county of many agricultural labourers like Roscommon and another where tenant farmers predominated, for example, actions could still have been legitimized in similar ways. This subject, however, would require further comparative study.[2]

The manuscript evidence for this on-going (if frequently unspectacular) conflict over a significant period is critical to the purpose of this study. However, it will also be useful to provide a brief account of the social and economic contexts of the county in the first half of the nineteenth century. Coleman has claimed that factors which could influence the incidence of and reasons for disturbance included soil capacity, types of agriculture, population and emigration levels, and the relative numbers of landless and agricultural labourers. An examination of Roscommon in terms of the factors suggested by Coleman shows the relatively unremarkable economic and social conditions that the county experienced in the period in question and the suitability of using the evidence from the county to draw more general conclusions about collective consciousness in pre-famine Ireland.[3]

Additionally, the traditional and cultural background of the county reveals that Roscommon complies with general accounts of social relations in the first half of the nineteenth century. Some of those typical features that will be explored here included the decline of middlemen, the end of rundale tenure arrangements, increased grazing and consolidation of holdings. Culturally, the traditions and customs associated with the county were also typical. They reflected the beginning of the end of the interchange between the great tradition and the little tradition. The great tradition was the culture of educated élites, learned at school and consolidated in political, social and economic networks. The little tradition was the customary culture worked out 'in the lives of the unlettered in the village communities'. The two were not mutually exclusive, and the little tradition, in particular, absorbed from the great. While this may be an oversimplified and unsatisfactorily bipolar model, it does have some value as a shorthand when considering the difficult relationship between paternalism and deference. The case of Lord Lorton demonstrates how paternalism

2 A. Coleman, *Riotous Roscommon* (1999), 14, suggests that Roscommon was statistically the most disturbed county in Ireland only in 1845; C. Mattimoe, *North Roscommon* (1992), 148, suggests that Co. Roscommon earned the reputation of being the fourth most disturbed county in Ireland; Beames, *Peasants and power*, 123; Lee, 'The Ribbonmen', 28; Beames, *Peasants and power*, 45.   3 Coleman, *Riotous Roscommon*, 56.

and deference persisted, although neither Lorton's paternalism nor the deference of the rural poor were uncomplicated.[4]

Skeffington Gibbon's witty 1829 account of the Roscommon gentry suggests that the county fell within a familiar discourse of Anglo-Saxon oppression and Irish poverty:

> The whole of the aristocracy of this fine county are absentees, and the soil is generally let to middlemen or opulent graziers, who expel the small farmers and oppress the working slaves.

It has already been suggested that such narratives of land arrangements in nineteenth-century Ireland must be treated with care, and it will become apparent that Gibbon's hyperbolic assessment of the county was inaccurate. There were significant numbers of resident landlords (although it has also been noted that the advantage of this is debatable); the middlemen were by this time declining in number; and small, directly-rented farms were proliferating. Grazing was on the increase, and the poor were increasingly reclaiming marginal land, which they rented directly from their landlord. This development accompanied their removal from farms that were being consolidated. However, Gibbon's comment demonstrates that his perceptions of Co. Roscommon were that it was not untypical, even if they were erroneous in detail. Emigration from the county before the famine was 'not unusually significant' and the county 'enjoyed neither the relative prosperity of the eastern maritime economy, nor the grinding poverty of the counties of the western seaboard'. Additionally, Roscommon occupied a median position in respect of farm sizes, proportions of tenants to labourers and commercial development.[5]

The county's physical geography is characterized by a mix of the celebrated limestone grazing lands and marginal carboniferous uplands. John Keogh had surveyed the county for Petty in 1683, although O'Donovan, working for the Ordnance Survey in the 1830s, said that Keogh's 'acquaintance with the places he describes was very imperfect and limited'. However, Keogh did note the geophysical diversity of the county:

> The soil is such wherein nature approximating extremes together here ... more sensibly than Elsewhere hath made some parts thereof extraordinary good both for pasture and corn and others again both extraordinary bad.

---

4 Burke, *Popular culture*, 24, discusses this model, first suggested in R. Redfield, *Peasant society and culture* (Chicago, 1956). 5 S. Gibbon, *The recollections of Skeffington Gibbon* (1829), 165; I. Weld, *Statistical survey* (1832), 297; Coleman, *Riotous Roscommon*, 7, 53.

The county was thus already known, long before Weld's 1832 survey, for the grazing plains extending from Roscommon town to Boyle, 'harbouring few other inhabitants but sheep'. The plains were dominated by large grazier ranches. On his travels around Ireland the English agronomist Arthur Young noted that 'a great part of Roscommon, particularly from Athlone to Boyle, 30 miles long and 10 broad, is sheep walk'. Keogh's and Young's findings (corroborated by Weld in his 1832 survey) provide the foundation for Donnelly's suggestion that the co-existence of rich pasture with adjacent tillage explains the severity of the conacre struggles in the county during the 1840s.[6]

Until the 1830s the marginal lands were dominated by the nucleated rundale settlements called clachans. During his 1776 tour, Young had been told that farms around Strokestown were generally let in rundale, with holdings ranging in size from two to 300 acres, farmed by from ten to fifteen families. Cawley has found that, from the 1830s onwards, there was a marked decline in clachan settlement in upland areas like Slieve Bawn. Weld also reported the end of rundale, noting that Lord Mount Sandford, a major absentee landlord with estates in the Castlerea district, had brought to an end the system of co-tenancies which still prevailed in many parts of the county. It will be seen that the end of rundale partnership arrangements was frequently accompanied by conflict, not least between the former partners. Such findings are consistent with the supposition that such agro-economic and tenurial arrangements were giving way to dispersed settlement patterns as Co. Roscommon experienced a process of economic change during the first half of the nineteenth century. Culturally, changes in inheritance patterns among stronger farmers in favour of impartible arrangements accompanied the growth of single-family, livestock-orientated farms.[7]

Tillage increasingly gave way to pasture in the 1820s. However, this change was also frequently accompanied by the direct renting from head landlords of ever-smaller plots on which to grow family subsistence crops. According to the 1828 Tithe Applotment book, on the Clonbrock estate at Eskerbaun in the south of the county there were sixty-two families consisting of 370 people, with an average holding of 4.72 acres. Before 1824 there had been four 72-acre leases on the same land. The drive to 'improve' estates meant that rundale partnerships and sub-lessees were increasingly removed and farms let to individuals, particularly from the mid-1830s onwards. The Revd John Finn, Catholic curate at Ballymote, told the Devon Commission during its sitting at Boyle in July 1844 that the extent of consolidation had been enormous for twelve years previous.[8]

6 M. Cawley, 'Aspects of continuity and change' (1982–3), 113; OS letters, 269; Keogh, *Statistical account*, 97–8, 99; Weld, *Statistical survey*, 182; Hutton, *Arthur Young's tour*, 215; Donnelly, *Landlord and tenant*, 33.   7 Hutton, *Arthur Young's tour*, 216; Cawley, 'Aspects of continuity', 115, 120; Weld, *Statistical survey*, 474.   8 Coleman, *Riotous Roscommon*, 18; W.

The realignment towards direct lettings accompanied the efforts on some estates to improve agricultural output and efficiency. For example, during the early 1820s the earl of Clancarty's tenants in Moycarn half-barony, in the south of the county, were encouraged to participate in a competition. Prizes were offered to the tenants with the 'neatest habitations'. To enter the competition, the tenants had to have a chimney and well, and a paved or gravelled space in front of the door. They had to whitewash the dwelling annually and keep their livestock in an outhouse, and the dung heap had to be at least six feet from the rear of the house. Quite apart from the issue of 'improvement', this may be viewed as an attempt to encourage cultural adjustment at the same time as impose economic change. The tendency of the Irish rural poor to share the same dwelling as their livestock and maintain adjacent dung heaps was widely commented upon. It is not so apparent, however, that the poor themselves saw such changes as the imposition of a foreign national culture upon their comfortable 'Gaelic' squalor. The Clancarty competition was accompanied in September 1822 by a 'plan for the encouragement of industry' which involved loans for flax production. Similarly, in 1824 Lorton gave land free for flax production. A Devon Commission witness attested that Lorton gave preferential terms to tenants who undertook improvements. Indeed, much of the focus of the Devon Commission was on the prospects for improvement.[9]

The county was much further integrated into wider United Kingdom markets than may have been supposed. Work on the historical archaeology of the county has shown that the ethos of improvement extended to everyday vessels. Charles Orser has found extensive evidence of the use of ceramic pottery, which was associated with 'modernity, progress and a bright future'. The 'redwares' of Irish country life were increasingly considered old-fashioned and as having no place at the modern table. Many styles of fine earthenware were imported into the county, intended to promote 'an entirely new way of eating'. Table settings were sold, promoting good manners and cultural change.[10]

As in many Irish counties, conacre and cottier land holders paid vastly more per acre than did more substantial farmers. The stipendiary magistrate John Wills wrote to the under-secretary in Dublin, Charles Grant:

Gacquin, *Roscommon before the famine* (1996), 39; Devon Commission, Part II, 234, evidence of Revd John Finn.   9 Clancarty manuscript, NLI, MS 31761; RLG, 23 Oct. 1824; Devon Commission, II, 249, evidence of Robert Lynch; Devon Commission, I, 51, reported that 'a large portion [of Co. Roscommon] is capable of improvement'. It was estimated that there were 130,000 acres of bog and unimproved land in the county, of which 40,000 acres might be reclaimed for cultivation, 80,000 drained for pasture and 10,000 that were unsuitable for improvement.   10 C.E. Orser, 'Archaeology and nineteenth century rural life' (1997), 17; Orser, 'In praise of early nineteenth-century coarse earthenware' (2000), 11.

Lands are set in this county from twenty to forty shillings an acre which is not considered high – average is thirty shillings – such as do not hold ground and take what is termed con acre in this country pay from five to seven guineas per acre.

Weld observed:

The rent of one of these cabins, with one quarter of an acre of land immediately behind it, payable to the middle-man, amounted, as I was informed on the spot by the tenants, to six guineas; but when out of lease the head landlord charges only £2 9s. 4d.

Similarly, it was reported to the Devon Commission that a tenant who held land from Lorton at 25s. to 27s. an acre, was letting conacre at £13 an acre. Scott, in his study of peasants in south-east Asia, noted that 'the overriding importance of family subsistence leads to paying more for land than "capitalist" investment criteria would indicate'; the poorest people in pre-famine Ireland evidently endured similar conditions.[11]

Rent payments were delayed, as elsewhere, so that most were paid at least six months in arrears. Indeed, Denis Kelly told the Devon Commission that it was the custom on his estate for the rent to be paid a year in arrears. The ratios of land holders to labourers and of farms to families occupied in agriculture also demonstrate Co. Roscommon's unexceptional position. The ratio of land holders to labourers was 1:0.66, against a national average of 1:0.86, and the ratio of farms to families was 1:1.2, placing the county ninth in a table that ranged from 1:1.96 to 1:0.8 (excluding Co. Dublin).[12]

The development of Roscommon's social profile may be traced through an examination of estate records dating from the mid-eighteenth century. From the 1750s to 1780s leases on the King estate around Boyle (more frequently known in the nineteenth century as Rockingham after Lorton built his new house on the shores of Lough Key) were typically granted for three lives in parcels of between 100 and 150 acres to people with names that were to recur among the social élite of the county in the early nineteenth century. By that time, leases on the same estate were more typically for 31 years, or a number of lives, whichever was shorter. In the third decade of the nineteenth century, leases on the estate were generally for 21 years, thus demonstrating the disengagement by landowners from commitments to long leases at low rents.[13]

11 SOCP1 2176/49, Wills to Grant, 8 June 1820; Weld, *Statistical survey*, 323; Devon Commission, I, 231, evidence of James M'Gan, agent for the O'Connor Don (*sic*); Scott, *Moral economy of the peasant* (1976), 13.   12 Weld, *Statistical survey*, 333; Devon Commission, Part II, 341, evidence of Denis Kelly, landlord and magistrate; Beames, *Peasants and power*, 18–19. 13 King papers, NLI, MS 4120; Lorton papers, NLI, MS 3104; Lorton papers, NLI, MS

Rents payable by tenants also rose dramatically in the early years of the nineteenth century. On the Mahon estate, for example, Christina Wynne was paying £15 10s. 8d. for Tansyfield in 1795, but her lease expired in November 1798 and the land was let to James Hughes the following May at £64. The rent on Luke Taaffe's land at Farnbeg was raised from £6 14s. 8d. to £25 15s. 0d. in 1804. Such significant increases very probably reflected the war-time boom, which led to the French family leasing back land for 2 guineas an acre 'during the height of the war prices' that they had let at 15s. At the same time the French family was letting land for conacre at 6 guineas an acre. Young had been told in 1776 that rents in the county were typically around 20s. an acre. Weld's survey described how the author had met an old man who held five acres on a 30–year lease at 25s. an acre, but expected that the rent would be raised significantly when the lease was renewed. In such circumstances it is perhaps not surprising that cottier rents and prices for conacre also rose steeply. However, while rents on the Mahon estate in the first decade of the century were more than £2 an acre, by 1846 smaller parcels of land were being let at a typical £1 10s. an acre, although rents had increased again to £2 an acre by 1848. These fluctuations are consistent with the general economic trends associated with the post-war slump.[14]

On the Lorton estate some cottier rents in the first decade of the century were in excess of £3 an acre. On 1 November 1802, for example, three men took leases of 2 acres and 3 roods at £7 2s. 6d. a year at Abbeytown. There were eight such tenancies at Abbeytown, plus one of an even smaller plot. Twenty-six years earlier, however, a 92–acre farm at Ardgower townland had been let at little more than £1 an acre. Even when the same land was let in 1851, the rent had increased only modestly, to £1 7s. an acre, again indicating that the significant rent increases of the early nineteenth century were not sustained.[15]

Ardkina in Estersnow parish was the scene of protests in 1838 when Lorton took action to clear at least part of the townland. The townland may be seen as a microcosm of developments on the Lorton estate and indeed more widely. Ninety-three acres at Ardkina had been let for named lives in March 1780 to Samuel Owens at 11s. an acre. The changes between then and 1850, when tenants held scraps of land of one acre, two roods and two perches at £1 5s. 0d. an acre directly from Lorton's agent, reflect the increased pressure on the land and the efforts of some landlords to improve their estates. It is notable that Lorton's lease book describes a lessee as having surrendered her tenancy at Ardkina in 1850. For the lessee, economic pressures that rendered continuing customary

3105.   14 Pakenham-Mahon papers, NLI, MS 2597, rent ledger 1795–1804, folios 25, 27; Weld, *Statistical survey*, 296, 297; Hutton, *Arthur Young's tour*, 217; Weld, *Statistical survey*, 255; Pakenham-Mahon papers, rentals and accounts, 1846–1854.   15 Lorton papers, NLI, MS 3104, lease book, folios 2/1, 2/2, 2/3, 10/1.

arrangements unviable were more probably perceived as compulsive. The collective action taken by the Ardkina tenants in 1838 will be considered later.[16]

The middlemen were on the decline, although they still attracted the wrath of Denis Browne, the splenetic MP from neighbouring Co. Mayo. Browne claimed that the poor of Co. Roscommon lived on mountains and were harshly dealt with by their immediate landlords. When they had reclaimed a few acres of mountain, the landlord planted grass seed and sent them off to reclaim another patch of upland. The land in Roscommon was 'much held by land jobbers, middlemen who have made by this trade great fortunes ... the laws entrusted to these men as mags are administer'd partially', according to Browne.[17]

Browne's assessment is striking, particularly as it was made by a man who was a leader of gentry opinion in Co. Mayo. He might have been speaking directly of such personalities as Godfrey Hogg (who was a witness before the Devon Commission when it took evidence in Roscommon town on 27 July 1844) and others whose names recur frequently in the manuscript sources. It is evident that Co. Roscommon had a number of middlemen who were involved intimately with the county administration, and whose rôles were reformed in the first half of the nineteenth century. Many were Protestants, but a substantial number were Catholics.[18]

By the 1840s 'the immediate landlord of most Roscommon tenants ... was likely to be a co-religionist' and it has been suggested that Catholicism was much weakened as a social bond between farmer and labourer, particularly when issues of property arose. For example, Protestants like Hogg were colleagues of Oliver Grace, a Catholic and chairman of the county's magistrates, who 'shared their attitudes on the rights of property and on law and order'. It was suggested in an earlier chapter that Catholic attitudes to the rights of property were increasingly aligned with economic imperatives, rather than customary usages. In this, Catholic landlords in Co. Roscommon were not untypical.[19]

The county was also typical of the southern counties in the proportions of Catholics to Protestants. Boyle was known to have a significant Protestant presence, but elsewhere Catholics predominated. The 1749 religious census enumerated 2,363 Catholics and 585 Protestants in Boyle, a ratio slightly exceeding four to one. More typical were the three parishes of Kilkeevin, Baslick and Ballintober, in the Castlerea area. There the figure was 4,483 Catholics and 338 Protestants, a ratio of 13.26 to one. Unfortunately, the censuses of 1821 to 1851 did not survey religious affiliation, but they do reveal the remarkable demographic explosion that reflected the national trend. Between 1749 and 1841 the

16 Idem, folio 14/1.   17 SOCP1 2175/9, Revd Denis Browne, Castlebar, to unnamed, Dublin Castle, 23 Jan. 1820.   18 D. Jordan, *Land and popular politics* (1994), 78; Devon Commission, II, 348–51.   19 Coleman, *Riotous Roscommon*, 2.

combined population of the three parishes grew from 4,821 to 17,141, an increase of 356 per cent. Cormac Ó Gráda has suggested a slightly higher national growth between 1741 and 1841 of around 425 per cent.[20]

The county also occupied a median position in terms of commercial development, lagging behind Leinster counties but ahead of those further west.

Table 1: Population statistics for selected parishes in Co. Roscommon

	1821	1831	1841	1851
Baslick	3,227	3,574	3,603	2,140
Ballintober	2,152	2,480	2,616	2,226
Kilkeevin (including Castlerea)	9,094	10,867	10,922	9,780

Source: Census of population of Ireland

Markets were established in the towns by the beginning of the nineteenth century, with new ones continuing to open, such as a linen market in Ballaghadereen in 1823. The markets held at numerous centres in the county sold corn, butter, home-produced linen and cloth. Weld observed:

> The roads which have been ... made through the country, and the numerous markets which have been opened, have increased tillage in a very remarkable degree.

Commerce was conducted through the Sligo and Athlone branches of the Provincial Bank, and its notes were circulating along with Bank of Ireland tender. Corn and butter were exported from the county by canal, and large numbers of carmen transported grain, flour and oatmeal to Dublin.[21]

Like other counties, faction fights troubled fairs and markets around the county. As already noted, battles between the plains men and the mountains men were regular features at Boyle fair in the 1820s. As late as 1846, Elphin fair was disturbed by clashes between 'two dreaded and rival factions', the Carneys

---

20 Religious census of the diocese of Elphin, 1749, NA, MS 2466; Ó Gráda, *Ireland: A new economic history*, 6.   21 RLG, 2 Aug. 1823; T.W. Freeman, *Pre-famine Ireland* (1957), 258; Weld, *Statistical survey*, 182, 206; Coleman, *Riotous Roscommon*, 7; Gacquin, *Roscommon before the famine*, 20; Freeman, *Pre-famine Ireland*, 258.

and Flanagans. Indeed, there is evidence to suggest that factions did not disappear in the years before the famine, upsetting historians' linear projections that such pre-modern practices ought to have disappeared. Faction fights were still being recorded in Co. Roscommon, for example, in December 1850 (although the quasi-recreational nature of such confrontations appears to have persisted, this particular fight being pre-arranged for a Christmas-time race meeting).[22]

The county had been subject to much the same kind of confiscations during the seventeenth century as others. Cromwell awarded Strokestown to the Mahons, and the Kings received Boyle as a reward for services rendered during the Williamite wars. Keogh recorded that 'the first breach that was made in Connaught upon the Irish party' had been in a battle in 1641 against a force led by the O'Conor Don.[23]

The O'Conor Don, however, had kept possession of his estates and was paid the greatest respect by his tenants, who sent him presents of cattle. This was the county's most significant landed family to remain Catholic from the seventeenth century to the nineteenth. Other landed Catholic families may have descended into the underground gentry. The middleman stratum had originally been seen as a bulwark against any landed Catholic resurgence but may well have shared a common repertoire of customary attitudes with the fallen Catholic gentry – and a certain level of cultural symbiosis with the rural poor. According to Young, one underground gentry figure, Macdermot, styled himself as the Prince of Coolavin, doubtless stimulating anxieties that forfeited estates were still coveted.[24]

The suggestion that there was a widespread underground gentry may be borne out by the common fascination with genealogy. This interest extended not only to the descendants of former land-owners displaced by such as the Mahons and Kings, but also to professional surveyors employed in the Ordnance Survey. O'Donovan filled many pages with accounts of the 'pedigrees of some respectable ancient families'. The Ordnance Survey memoirs for the county also contain a number of genealogies. A local study of Kiltoom and Cam parishes suggests that there were indeed several farmers who were descendants of the dispossessed Gaelic aristocracy. It has been established that 33 of 36 freeholders in a 1795–6 list from the two parishes were Catholics. Bryan Fallon of Coolagarry, a direct descendant of Redmond O'Fallon, the last elected head of Clann Uadach, rented 680 acres from

22 For example, see RLG, 4 Oct. 1823, 5 June 1824, 1 Jan. 1825; RLG, 13 Dec. 1845, 3 Jan. 1846; OR 1851/1, J.A. Kirwan, resident magistrate, Boyle, to unnamed, 31 Dec. 1850, outlined how two Catholic priests had attempted to persuade factions to disperse after a race meeting. 23 Gibbon, *The recollections*, 7; Keogh, *Statistical account*, 109. 24 Hutton, *Arthur Young's tour*, 219.

Henry Kenny in the mid-eighteenth century for 31 years. His family became Protestants in 1767.[25]

A stratum of Catholic farmers (and agents) was emerging, abetted by the relaxation of the anti-popery laws and the casuistry with which their eighteenth-century ancestors had conducted their legal arrangements in respect of property. These men came into conflict with the lower strata among the poor as they adopted the ethos of improvement. Unsurprisingly, the names of middlemen, agents and substantial farmers recur more frequently in the manuscript sources as objects of agrarian combination than do those of the head landlords, although this began to change to reflect the increasing number of the rural poor who rented tiny plots directly from landowners, as the mid-nineteenth century approached.

A picture thus emerges of a county that bears many of the features associated with general social and economic relations in rural Ireland in the half-century before the famine. Commercially, the wartime boom was accompanied by increased economic integration into the UK. The land was owned by a small number of men, some of whom were absentees. Their estates were let to middlemen, who were themselves under pressure and being replaced by agents and direct leases.

However, the landowning élite retained a certain cultural hegemony, remaining as leaders of opinion, despite the gradual replacement of the county oligarchy by a professional, centrally-directed judicial and fiscal apparatus. In 1817 Lorton acknowledged that he frequently went out at night to ascertain whether his tenants were at home. Yet within a few years Lorton and his colleagues had been replaced by a professional police force. Lorton's 1816 letter to Peel requesting help to suppress agrarian unrest revealed the gentry's anxiety about the processes Peel had begun. Lorton believed the 'resident gentlemen' to be as effective as a professional Peace Preservation Force in maintaining order. He thus resisted political and administrative change, holding decidedly conservative views, at the same time as he vigorously pursued economic improvement.[26]

The example of Lord Lorton and his complex relations with his tenants illustrates the persistence of a culture of paternalism and customary expectation, and its explosive potential in a context of economic and social change. Indeed, Lorton's complexity as a character arises directly from his espousal of change, which was nevertheless combined with a paternal expectation of continued deference and compliance by his tenants with the re-ordering of their economic relations. Holding 29,242 acres in the county, he was the single

25 OS Letters, vol. 2, 234; OS Extracts, 360–1, 370–405; Gacquin, *Roscommon before the famine*, 20.   26 SOCP1, 1833/29, Lorton to unnamed, Dublin Castle, 11 Jan. 1817; SOCP1, 1767/65, Lorton to Peel, 23 Dec. 1816.

largest landowner and was 'widely considered to be an improving landlord'. John Duckworth told the Devon Commission that Lorton demanded 25s. an acre for prime land, and the O'Conor Don's agent, James M'Gan, asserted that Lorton was 'not a high landlord'.[27]

Born Robert King in London in 1773, Lorton attended Eton College and inherited his father's Co. Roscommon estate in 1797, which was encumbered by debts of around £119,000 (the annual rental income of the estate was around £10,400 at this time). He has been described as a 'man of strong principle, dedicated to developing an efficient and economically viable estate. He strove to maintain a good tenant relationship and also to maintain law and order.' Another assessment suggests that 'to this day he survives in folk memory as an awesome figure'. What can certainly be said is that he was a staunch Protestant and believer in Ascendancy. Yet he combined this, not with the profligate lifestyle associated with that class in the eighteenth century (evidently including his forbears), but with an improving ethos and a close involvement in the management of the estate.[28]

Boyle was his family's town, and as well as owning it, Lorton (who was ennobled in 1806) was involved in providing its cultural identity. He was a president, patron and trustee of the Boyle Savings Bank (founded 1822), and patron of the Boyle Charitable Loan. Lorton wrote to the *Roscommon and Leitrim Gazette* in 1824 to declare that he was not an Orangeman. Skeffington Gibbon acknowledged that Lorton had ended 'Orange excesses' in the town, which had previously been notorious for its sectarian displays. However, Lorton was a vigorous champion of Protestantism. He spoke against emancipation in the Lords on 23 February 1827, describing the Protestants of Ireland as 'a proscribed and persecuted people'. In April the same year he published an address to his tenants, warning them against wicked men who claimed he was a bad landlord because of his opposition to emancipation. In 1845, 'ever faithful to the cause of Protestantism and truth', he voted against Peel's Maynooth grant bill in the Lords.[29]

Lorton saw no contradiction between his stances on emancipation and the relentless improvement of his estates on the one hand and a paternal care for the poor on the other. He chaired the first meeting of a Society for Improving the Condition and Increasing the Comforts of the Irish Peasantry in 1823, in which he attributed poverty to the absence of much of the county's gentry (his proselytizing did not end there, for he also chaired a Society for Promoting

---

27 Coleman, *Riotous Roscommon*, 8; Devon Commission, II, 237, evidence of John Duckworth, magistrate, Boyle; idem 231, evidence of James M'Gan.   28 A.L. King-Harman, *The Kings of King House* (1996), 43, 45, 48; Mattimoe, *North Roscommon*, 73.   29 OS Memoirs, ii, ii, 3; RLG, 25 Sept. 1824; Gibbon, *The recollections of Skeffington Gibbon*, 141; RLG, 3 Mar. 1827, 7 Apr. 1827, 14 June 1845.

Christianity among the Jews). He was behind a committee for the relief of the poor that was formed to deal with famine in 1822, employing 279 men and 60 boys, making daily soup and subsidizing meal prices. Of 4,000 people in Cloonygormican, Killukin and Kilcooley parishes, 2,400 were 'unable to procure for themselves the necessaries of life' at that time. It is notable that there was apparently no congruence between agrarian unrest and the famines that afflicted the county in 1817 and 1822. Indeed, it has been suggested that the 1822 famine ended an outbreak of agrarian conflict that had begun in 1820.[30]

Following emancipation, Lorton addressed his tenants in paternal terms, aiming 'to renew those precious relations between landlord and tenant and to resuscitate that reciprocity of good feeling'. When Michael McGlinn, a tenant holding fourteen acres, reached the age of 100 in 1822, Lorton gave him an annual allowance of 35s. for the remainder of his life. This was a fine example of a (possibly unselfconscious) theatrical paternalism, which could engage with popular sentiment at little cost to Lorton.[31]

In February 1837 ten of Lorton's tenants were fined £2 each or one month's imprisonment for cutting down timber belonging to Lorton at Tawnytaskin. Chief Constable Robert Curtis reported that wood was scarce and Lorton's steward marked more than 100 trees for cutting to give to tenants but 'a number of the tenants got into the wood with hatchets of their own and commenced cutting for themselves and did not confine themselves to the timber which was marked'. Before they could be stopped, they had cut more than 100 trees in excess of those marked for Lorton's gift. Lorton's paternal largesse required that his tenants receive it deferentially and passively. Self-help was punished severely.[32]

Lorton evidently believed in a combination of incentive and threat to cure his tenants of their customary notions of the correct economic relations between landlord and tenant, despite his own expectation of continued deference. His wife ran a free school in order to instil Protestant virtue and good habits in Catholic children, but Lorton was prepared to evict large numbers of tenants in order to put into effect his improvement and rationalization schemes. In addition to the clearance of Ardkina townland in May 1838, Mattimoe has recorded the clearing of 128 tenants in the early 1840s from other townlands around Boyle in order to rid Lorton's estate of perceived troublemakers. In May 1843 a memorial to the Boyle Board of Guardians claimed that 171 families had been evicted from land that had long been occupied by them

30 RLG, 7 June 1823, 21 Sept. 1823, 22 June 1822; G. Broeker, *Rural disorder and police reform in Ireland* (1970), 138.   31 King-Harman, *The Kings of King House*, 46; Lorton papers, MS 3105, Deerpark folio.   32 OR 1837/17, Robert Curtis, chief constable, Boyle, to Warburton, 15 Feb. 1837.

and their ancestors because 'his Lordship wanted to enlarge his holdings'. Others who had sheltered the evicted families were themselves served with notice to quit the estate, 'where so few have leases'.[33]

However, the *Roscommon and Leitrim Gazette* continued to perpetuate Lorton's paternal vision of landlord and tenant relations in May 1839, after a public meeting in Boyle expressed approval of Lorton. The newspaper suggested that the circulation of 'slanderous calumnies' against Lorton would make the country more wretched 'by severing the tie that should exist between Landlord and Tenant'. The meeting had followed the notorious murder of four Protestant tenants on Lorton's Co. Longford estate. The previous month Lorton had advertised in the *Gazette* that he would evict Roscommon tenants if similar events occurred there. Lorton explained to the 1839 Lords committee on the state of Ireland that the victims had been among nine Protestant farmers given land after he cleared (with compensation) many sub-lessees from the land at Ballinamuck. Lorton said the murderers had been protected by the community. He 'came to a Determination to level the Town; it was put into execution' with plenty of warning, so 'it was therefore at their own Option'. Forty 'miserable huts' were levelled. He knew the 'relative duties' of landlord and tenant and he had, indeed, recently received an address from his Co. Roscommon tenants complimenting him on his conduct towards them. A Co. Longford stipendiary magistrate also told the same committee, 'In the County of Roscommon he is a most kind and excellent Landlord'.[34]

There is a discernible iciness in Lorton's tone, as reported by the parliamentary committee, which would admit of no alternative. This was also reflected in an address, published in the *Gazette* in October 1846, warning people once more against the 'machinations of wicked and designing men' who on this occasion wanted 'to turn the awful infliction, which it has pleased the Almighty in his infinite wisdom, to visit upon this unhappy land, to their own account' by suggesting the hungry should resist paying rent or should take food from the fields for themselves. This attitude seems to have persisted for the duration of the famine, for in March 1851 Lorton evicted a number of tenants from Annagh townland in Kilronan parish, for non-payment of rent.[35]

The *Roscommon Journal* made a rather different assessment of Lorton. When the £10 freeholders were registered as electors following emancipation, a number of 'creatures in the pay of his Lordship' (the diction suggesting the

33 RLG, 30 Sept. 1837; Mattimoe, *North Roscommon*, 150; Memorial presented to the Boyle Board of Guardians on 26 May 1843, returns relative to the Boyle Union, Parliamentary Papers 1843 (443) L.403.   34 RLG, 4 May 1839, 20 Apr. 1839; SC 1839, 1,048, 1,052, 1,054, evidence of Viscount Lorton; SC 1839, 985, evidence of John Barnes;   35 RLG, 24 Oct. 1846; OR 1851/254, J. M'Mullen, sub-inspector, to unnamed, Dublin Castle, 19 Nov. 1851.

continued importance of patronage in electoral politics) objected to all Mr French's freeholders (French was a potential electoral rival to Lorton's son in the county). The following month the *Journal* published the sarcastic report of the meeting alluded to earlier that was chaired 'spontaneously' by Lorton at Elphin.[36]

It is appropriate to comment here upon the evident variance between the ideas of improvement and paternalism. The ethos of improvement, increasingly adopted by estate owners and substantial lessees, was at odds with the culture of paternalism and deference that had characterized much eighteenth-century estate management. Land was increasingly exploited more thoroughly for profit, and the conservative attachment of the rural poor to customary dealing in land and other economic necessities was an obstacle to such improvement. Terms requiring maintenance and improvement were increasingly inserted into leases. The Clancarty competition is just one example of the efforts of landlords to encourage change. While this may be considered a combination of 'carrot and stick', other change might well have been experienced as the use of the stick alone. Yet landlords (and their tribunes in the pages of newspapers like the *Roscommon and Leitrim Gazette*) continued to talk in terms of paternal care, while imposing unwelcome change on lessees. One historian, writing of Co. Mayo in this period, has suggested that these reforming efforts 'had closer affinities with industrial philanthropy than with the spirit of accord hypothesized by landlord and tenant during the eighteenth century'. However, the language of improvement is potentially misleading, suggesting a concern for the occupiers of land, when more often it led to insecurity and dispossession. Another historian, writing of the Bellew estate in east Co. Galway, has suggested that 'well-meaning, compassionate proprietors adopted the new philosophy of "improvement" ' but noted that by the 1820s 'the way forward no longer lay in improvement, but in coercion'. The critical point is that for the rural poor, improvement was not experienced as philanthropy or compassion but as coercion, even when it was accompanied by a sincere belief on the part of the landlord that it was being undertaken for the long-term welfare of tenants. Improvement should not be presented as evidence of paternalism on the part of the land-owner, but as a shift towards reifying land as a capital resource, rather than a life-support system for the gentry. It was a shift analogous to the effects of enclosure in the English countryside. While, in the long term, such changes may indeed have made the land more productive in strict terms of agricultural output, as apologists like Arthur Young claimed, the immediate effect was to polarize the relationship between owners (or substantial lessees) of land and the occupiers thereof. At these points of polarization and conflict it becomes possi-

36 RJ, 24 Oct. 1829.

ble to discern the significance of customary views of proper social and economic relations held by the rural poor.[37]

It is evident from the example of Lorton that people who belonged formally to the 'great tradition' could demonstrate a paradoxical consciousness, making it difficult to portray them simply as modernizers or patricians. What of
the 'little tradition'? Burke suggests that much that is transmitted orally may
originate in élite literary output and reflect a symbiosis between élite and popular cultures across Europe. Sean Connolly has recently noted an interaction
between élite and popular culture. O'Donovan claimed that many old tales he
heard were in fact passed on by people who had heard someone literate rendering an account of a story told by Keating. It seems that not only were the
collective actions of the poor not limited by a pre-modern position in a linear
historic process, but also that culturally they adapted freely both from the great
tradition and from other spatial and economic or social contexts, as it suited
their purpose. O'Donovan's note on oral tradition shows precisely how a story
often viewed as part of the little tradition might in fact have been an adaptation
from a source such as Keating's *Foras Feasa ar Éirinn*. Just as oral tradition did
not reflect a linear development, it will become apparent in the ensuing chapters that a traditional consciousness did not restrict the Roscommon poor to
reactionary, parochial, spontaneous collective actions.[38]

However, it will be useful to give some examples of the cultural interchange
between the lower orders and élites in Co. Roscommon. The symbiosis
between great and little traditions involved a good deal of conditional paternalism and deference, but also some shared conceptions. Keogh had written
without any hint of scepticism of St Bride's Well, five miles from Athlone,
'famous for medicinal waters whereby many cures are wrought'. Skeffington
Gibbon noted that landowners and middlemen expected tributes of fowl as
well as labour from their employees. This vertical reciprocity can also be seen
in relation to the Lyster family of Newpark. Gacquin noted that 'the natives
frequented the house and were welcome there'. The Lyster family were mentioned favourably in a 1786 vernacular poem in which their names were rendered in Irish, suggesting that in the late eighteenth century the Protestant
landowner and Gaelic rural poor lived in rather less hermetic cultural isolation
than Corkery believed. In 1828 the *Roscommon Journal* reported:

> Mrs Bowen Lyster, wife to Col. Bowen, has visited her estate at Ath-
> league, in this County, after an absence of nearly thirty years. She was

37 McCabe, 'Social order' (1987), 109; Clarke, *Christopher Dillon Bellew* (2003), 7, 59.   38
OS Letters, vol. 2, 251; Burke, *Popular culture*, 58, 60; Connolly, ' "Ag Déanamh *Commanding"* '.

met by her numerous and respectable Tenantry, who paid her off with the respect due to so amiable and good a Lady. The town was a scene of joy and merriment for the whole of the night, with illuminations, bon-fires, music &c. Mrs Bowen was so pleased with the reception, that she ordered some Barrels of Porter on the occasion.

As late as 1837, the *Journal* reported that:

> Upwards of one hundred fellows (preceded by musicians) passed through this town, from Fairymount, to cut down the crops of that just-ly esteemed Gentleman James LYSTER ... a distance of ten miles. They cut down upwards of twenty acres of corn, and previous to their returning home they assembled at Mr Lyster's hall-door and heartily cheered that Gentleman and his amiable lady, on presenting themselves at the windows to thank the poor fellows for their voluntary and unso-licited conduct.

It will be seen that such events did not prevent the beating by whiteboys of a bailiff who came to distrain cattle on the Lyster lands in lieu of rent arrears.[39]

The withdrawal by the upper and middle strata from shared conceptions of the world, when magic and mystery, duties and rights were gradually replaced by more prosaic commercial relations, legitimized violent collective resistance on the part of the rural poor. Aspects of the little tradition such as the Wren Boys' use of costume, which were well-known in Co. Roscommon, then found their way into the repertoires of resistance used by agrarian collectives. This coincided with the increasing proscription by the Catholic church of manifes-tations of popular religion. By the 1840s the Kilronan pattern still attracted thousands, but the Brideswell pattern (involving several days of hard drinking) had been denounced by the clergy. The hostility to 'non-Christian manifesta-tions of supernaturalism', manifested in the attack on 'venerable old customs' like patterns and wakes, was part of a tightening of discipline by the Catholic church.[40]

The rural poor of Roscommon were participants in the cultural interchange between traditions, but their involvement with élites did not mean that their cus-toms were uncomplicatedly deferential. Traditional culture could also be rebel-lious. The county was, along with Co. Sligo and Co. Mayo, the centre of the most serious anti-militia resistance in 1793 (and it was among the last places

39 Keogh, *Statistical account*, 120; Gibbon, *The recollections*, 167; Gacquin, *Roscommon before the famine*, 20; RJ, 9 Aug. 1828, 23 Sept. 1837.   40 Beames, *Peasants and power*, 99; Coleman, *Riotous Roscommon*, 12; Connolly, *Priests and people*, 143, 113.

where the militia remained established). The Defenders were also present in the county during the 1790s, and a well-known ballad celebrates a battle at Crossna in 1793. The leader of the Defenders in the county, John McDermot, had been 'no humble tenant' and had once been a member of the militia and converted to Protestantism (this is startling, given the sectarian reputation of the Defenders). The ballad says he led 1,500 men at Crossna against paying rent, although Gibbon reported that it was to support the abduction of a Miss Tennison. Again, it is possible to speculate about the presence of an underground gentry that retained enough authority to rally a significant number of followers through the strength of a vertical attachment. Whether the notion of an underground gentry is sustained or not, it is apparent that there was still an interchange in eighteenth- and early nineteenth-century Ireland between great and little traditions that was quite independent of Corkery's conception of the determining loyalties of race, language and religion. This interchange co-existed with an awareness of mutual obligation that could be the source of antagonism when one party abrogated its role.[41]

The contrast between the Ireland of Corkery's account and the changes taking place in the first half of the nineteenth century are captured in O'Donovan's wry story of a well said to have been blessed by St Patrick. It was at the point where St Patrick had divided the 'deep and impassable' River Boallus to get across, 'as neither boat nor vessel was available'. O'Donovan wrote that the well had 'latterly lost a great portion of its sanctity, its water is now made use of in the town of Boyle for every purpose required'.[42]

Another incident, reported in the press and the Outrage Reports, illustrates dramatically the ways in which the forces of change were confronted by a rebellious traditional culture. As the remains of a Miss McDermott Roe were brought to the family burial ground at Kilronan, a crowd tried to prevent the hearse from going to the church, saying the body should be conveyed directly to the burial ground, as was usual with that family. A scuffle ensued and,

> as the coffin … was carried into the church yard some Roman Catholic clergymen shut the gate, and by using their whips rather freely, prevented the people from going into the church.

A large quantity of spirits had been distributed to the people before the body was removed from the house. The McDermott Roes were the descendants of a minor native gentry family, potentially members of the underground gentry. It is reasonable to assume that the immediate family had given the instructions for

41 Bartlett, 'An end to moral economy'; Broeker, *Rural disorder,* 72; Mattimoe, *North Roscommon,* 143.   42 OS Extracts, 244; OS Letters, vol. 2, 242–3.

the non-traditional funeral procedure, demonstrating the break with the past by such families as they re-emerged, now possessing modernizing values, as a Catholic middle class. The *Gazette* lost no time in attacking 'the peasantry to whom conciliation is extended', narrating dramatically the fracas between a Mr Dodwell and the bearers on one hand and the tradition-bound peasants on the other. According to the *Gazette* the coffin and its bearers were hurled into a ditch, 'where renewed punishment awaited them'. Two weeks later Dodwell and a number of magistrates wrote to complain about the report, saying that only a few 'foolish persons' tried to stop the hearse going into the church, and that the Catholic priest had intervened to help. The alignment of the Catholic clergy with such a break with tradition illustrates that one of the most important groups of mediators between élite and popular cultures had, in the first half of the nineteenth century, distanced itself from popular religious observance.[43]

It is apparent, then, that Co. Roscommon is suitable for an investigation of Irish agrarian conflict. From the late eighteenth century it experienced a number of characteristic economic and social developments. Additionally, its social, cultural and historic background complies with general accounts of Irish society until the early nineteenth century. However, the earlier caveat about regional variation ought to be recalled. Local studies will always reveal local exceptionalism. Co. Roscommon is offered here as a viable case study reflecting aspects of the consciousness of the Irish rural poor, a customary consciousness that would be refracted through variable social and economic contexts in other regions.

Charles Tilly has examined events that 'other historians ... found routine, redundant or trivial. That is the point: to include both the sensational and the routine'. Agrarian conflict in Co. Roscommon has been studied closely for similar reasons. There are relatively few references in this study to events like the Mahon murder (privileged as they have been in the existing historiography of social conflict in pre-famine Ireland – for whatever purpose) because it is as important to study the apparently trivial matters reported in the seemingly endless stream of correspondence between the county's law enforcers and Dublin Castle. Roscommon provides a reasonable basis for conducting such a study. The next two chapters proceed with that detailed examination.[44]

43 OR 1838/79, James Reed, chief constable; Boyle, to Warburton, 14 June 1838; Arthur Crossley, resident magistrate, Elphin, to under-secretary Thomas Drummond, 31 July 1838; RLG, 16 June 1838; 30 June 1838.   44 Tilly, *Popular contention*, 68.

4

'The affliction of the poor'

The focus of this study is not on a chronological narrative of whiteboyism, but on historiographic themes. For this reason, the evidence adduced below will not be presented chronologically. Instead, social conflict in pre-famine Co. Roscommon will be considered in terms of particular kinds of actions, threats or notices. This chapter, however, covers broadly the period from the turn of the century until about 1830.

Furthermore, any attempt at a computation of popular collective action is of little value. The documents in the primary sources for this study do not constitute a comprehensive statistical account of agrarian conflict. A nocturnal raid on a house by a whiteboy band might include beatings and the administering of an oath, yet might be reported merely as 'administering an oath' or a 'house attack' by constables and magistrates. A night-time abduction involving disguise and the swearing of a woman to marry one of her abductors would be a relatively minor statistic. Yet it could be of immense interest in respect of the customs and consciousness of the rural population. An anonymous letter written to the *Roscommon and Leitrim Gazette* suggested that 'few of these [outrages] are reported even by the Police'. There are some years with no extant reports. It is apparent that these are lacunae, rather than evidence of tranquillity. For example, there are only five outrages reported in the 1821 papers for Co. Roscommon. It is not sustainable, however, after reading the reports from 1820 and 1822, that there were only five outrages in the county during 1821. It seems likely that most of the papers for 1821 have been lost. A number of reports for 1828 to 1831 can be located in George Warburton's correspondence with Dublin Castle in the Chief Secretary's Office Registered Papers. Local newspapers cannot fill statistical gaps, but they have some use in terms of understanding attitudes towards whiteboyism. The amateur nature of law enforcement and the rudimentary bureaucracy during much of the period under consideration in this chapter mean that correspondence from gentlemen, magistrates and the military was often confined to general statements of fears of widespread rebellion (frequently to justify requests for military reinforcements and personal protection). This means that many papers speak generally, rather than enumerate outrages. For example, Sir Edward Crofton of Mote Park, one of the county's major land-owners, reported on 9 December 1810 that he had 'heard of a vast many meetings and outrages that would be too tedious to mention'. This broad statement was written in a letter which did not list any single incident. The only attempt to provide outrage statistics for Co. Roscommon found in the State of the Country Papers is in the 1828 papers, when an attempt to be rather more systematic was made through the submission of monthly crime returns for the county. Given the notorious difficulty in distinguishing between private and public crime, the individual and the collective, these figures should be treated cautiously, but nevertheless they suggest that the source materials in the State of the Country Papers and Chief Secretary's Office Registered Papers are the tip of a statistical iceberg. The source of the Co. Roscommon returns was George Warburton, inspector of constabulary for Connacht, who collated them from reports submitted by constables across the county.[1]

Further, incidents that a person who was close to the events in 1828 might have considered in a particular way, might obscure as much as illuminate collectively-held attitudes and beliefs about rights and duties, the proper ordering of society and about legal authority. Contemporary attitudes to and explanations of whiteboyism have been explored earlier, but they should be borne in mind when considering the sources. The disciplining of members of the rural community according to customary expectations could suggest a different explanation of actions that may have been reported as *prima facie* a sectarian, national, intra-family or neighbour dispute. It is apparent, for example, that the Threshers of 1806 and 1807 objected to both the levels of tithes and the dues charged by Catholic priests, not to the payment of tithes or dues *per se*. For this reason, many anti-tithe actions need to be re-evaluated, rather than explained in terms of any sectarian or national impulse. The intention here is to arrive at a closer understanding of the consciousness of the rural poor, at the ways that social conflict was refracted through a customary consciousness which manifested itself most clearly on the occasions when customary expectation of fair economic dealing was challenged or disrupted.[2]

Although this study focuses not on specific movements but on a broad chronological span, it is nevertheless worth recalling initially some specific whiteboy movements in Roscommon. Michael Beames identified three movements there during the first half of the nineteenth century: the Carders, 1813–16; Ribbonmen, 1819–20; and the Molly Maguires, 1844–7. However, not only was unrest in the county not confined to those periods, but also it was legitimized by a remarkably coherent and rational consciousness throughout the period under consideration. A year-by-year computation of the number of offences reported in the State of the Country Papers, Chief Secretary's Office

1 RLG, 31 Jan 1846; SOCP1 1278/20, Sir Edward Crofton to unnamed, Dublin Castle, 9 Dec. 1810.   2 Fitzpatrick, 'Class, family and rural unrest', 44, has pointed out that 'the unsystematic character of the outrage reports renders statistical analysis inadmissible'.

Registered Papers and Outrage Reports would indeed demonstrate that there were more agrarian 'outrages' during the years suggested by Beames. That economic stimuli provoked collective responses among the rural poor is not especially surprising. What is at issue in this study is the underpinning legitimation, and how the actions of whiteboys were affected by their beliefs about the way society ought to be ordered.[3]

Conflict and nationalism

When considering the evidence in terms of how it relates to popular nationalist historiography, it has been necessary to consider instances of conflict on the basis of perceived religious and national grounds, as well as contrary instances of conflict within a national or religious group.

In 1808 a man was carded four miles from Strokestown (carding involved the tearing of flesh by a comb used for carding wool). His crime was having given evidence against seven or eight 'Thrashers'. Whether the communal law of the rural poor was upheld through consent or fear is in a sense irrelevant here. The point is that a collective justice was imposed. The correspondent relating this incident was Lord Hartland of Strokestown Park. It was in the same letter that he added that the origins of the disturbances were in complaints about fees for clerical duties, adding that 'these thrashers complain much and swear every one not to comply … nor give more than what was usual'.[4]

Hartland's words illustrate that the whiteboys did not discriminate on the grounds of confessional affiliation. Nor did they, in targeting the Catholic clergy, evince any particular nationalist consciousness. What is interesting here is the invocation of customary norms as a benchmark for reasonable fees. In the winter of 1806 and 1807 a campaign against tithe levels and priests' dues had been waged across Connacht. The marquis of Buckingham had noted that 'the systematic plan of swearing whole parishes to give only four shillings per acre tithe money, and to diminish to one-half the dues of the priests, and to obey Captain Thrasher, spread without check of any sort through Sligo and Roscommon' in 1806. In February 1807 Harlow Knott of Battlefield, near Boyle, reported that six stacks of tithe oats belonging to Lewis Irwin had been scattered and a notice posted on a chapel door, telling the curate that he had paid too much for a piece of land. Major General Robert Taylor reported from Athlone on 1 October the same year that the Thresher activity was caused by 'opposition to tithes' and 'church money'. Later that month Robert Lloyd of Elphin reported to the under-secretary, James Trail, that Creeve and Aughrim

3 Beames, *Peasants and power*, 43.   4 SOCP1 1192/9, Hartland to Mahon, 7 Dec. 1808.

parishes in Co. Roscommon were 'greatly disturbed' by 'the oppression of Tythe farmers and the exactions of their Priests'. Indeed, in Creeve the priest and people were at 'open war' with each other. The rural poor appear to have made little distinction between tithes and Catholic priests' dues, viewing both as economic impositions which they sought to regulate. There is no suggestion that they opposed tithes on the grounds that they were collected for the maintenance of the established church, but rather because the sums levied were too much. Francis Blackburne told the 1824 select committee that opposition to tithes arose not from the view that they were an unjust demand but from an inability to pay. Customary expectations of reasonable prices for clerical duties lay behind the oaths

Table 2: Crime returns, Co. Roscommon, June and July 1828

Offence	June	July
Murder	2	1
Robbery	2	0
Burglary	1	0
Malicious burning	1	0
Common assault	94	123
Assault 'connected with Ribbonism'	2	4
Illegal notices	3	0
Livestock theft	1	3
Rape	4	2
Riot	5	1

Source: State of the country papers

that were being sworn. Sir Edward Crofton also reported in December 1810 that 'there was an immense number at the Chapel of Fuerty this day to proclaim Captain Thresher's laws to the priest'.[5]

5 Fortescue MSS, NLI, 463; SOCP2, 58/4047, Harlow Knott to William Elliot, chief secretary, 16 Feb. 1807; SOCP1 1121/53, Taylor to unnamed, Dublin Castle, 1 Oct. 1807; SOCP2, 158/4451, Robert Jones Lloyd, Elphin, to James Trail, under-secretary, Dublin Castle, 21 Oct. 1807; SC 1824, 35, evidence of Francis Blackburne.

It should also be noted that Crofton believed that fairs were becoming places where the lower orders were meeting under the pretence of being merely parish factions, but in fact to ascertain their numbers and strength. Crofton appeared to imply a belief that factions were relatively harmless but that these assemblies signified something more sinister. Open rebellion could only be kept down in this 'most desperately disturbed country' by a display of military force, Crofton concluded.[6]

The Catholic clergy evidently shared the belief that whiteboy organization was qualitatively more serious than factional dispute. While whiteboys were less frequently excommunicated for their crimes in the nineteenth century than previously, in the Kildare and Leighlin diocese they were still refused absolution for their sins until after they had done penance for a year. In the adjacent diocese of Cashel, faction fighting, on the other hand, required only a three-week act of contrition. Indeed, it appears that in the first two decades of the century there appear to have been more protests over dues to Catholic clergy than over tithes or tithe farming. Further examples of conflict with Catholic clergy arose. Some years after Hartland's observations, notices fixing fees for performance of duties by Catholic clergy in Co. Roscommon were still being posted, although less frequently. For example, in 1820 rates included 11s. 4½d. for marriage and 2s. 8½d. for anointing of the sick.[7]

Nor did Catholic members of the judiciary make any special allowance for their co-religionists. Colonel William Doyle reported in December 1809 that a magistrate named Burke on the borders of counties Roscommon and Galway was anxious to demonstrate to 'the lower orders' that Catholic magistrates were as ready as those of the established church to call out the military to quell disturbance. It is clear from this small handful of incidents that, while not at the centre of the disturbances attributed by Beames to Threshers in the adjacent counties of Leitrim, Longford, Mayo and Sligo, in the first decade of the nineteenth century the movement had spread across most of Connacht and into Leinster. Later, unrest was to spread from Roscommon to neighbouring counties. While it is doubtless fruitful to consider the movements at their peaks, according to Beames's approach, these examples demonstrate a more general conception of how the poor perceived the correct ordering of the world, in which Catholic landlords and clergymen could be the object of popular protest.[8]

A Catholic farmer called John Fallon, of Runnamoat, near Roscommon town, also revealed, in a letter of 19 October 1811, that agrarian protesters

6 SOCP1 1278/20, Crofton to unnamed, Dublin Castle, 9 Dec. 1810.   7 Connolly, *Priests and people*, 229–30; SOCP1 2188/10, notice enclosed with letter from Col. P. Brown to Gregory, 27 May 1820.   8 SOCP1 1229/7, Col. William Doyle, assistant adjutant general, to unnamed, Dublin Castle, 11 Dec. 1809.

made no concession to his denomination. He wrote that the Threshers, among whom his own shepherd was most active, had turned him out of his chapel on the Sunday before last and that the priest had been turned out at the same time.[9]

An 1822 notice demonstrated a continued antipathy towards Catholic farmers. On this occasion the farmer was warned to be a better neighbour, for General Springlawn had heard of his bad temper, and that he must leave the neighbourhood or lose his life. The correspondent who sent this notice to Dublin Castle commented that the man was instead 'a highly respectable and humane character; having done numerous acts of kindness among his poor neighbours during the winter. He is of the Roman Catholic religion.' In a similar vein, the 1824 Lords select committee was told that rent campaigns did not discriminate between Catholic and Protestant landlords. Thomas Costello, a parish priest in Co. Limerick, told the 1825 select committee hearings that the whiteboy oath made no mention of religion – in contrast to the sectarian ribbon oaths.[10]

In February 1824 the *Roscommon and Leitrim Gazette* reported the imprisonment of two men for assaulting the parish priest of Creeve while he was 'remonstrating with his congregation on the late outrages in the County Roscommon'. The *Roscommon Journal* reported in January 1830 that another parish priest had been 'most active in putting down nightly meetings'. George Warburton told the 1824 parliamentary enquiry that whiteboys did not discriminate between Catholics and Protestants in their campaigns 'against property'.[11]

The nationalist *Journal* distanced itself from whiteboyism. Attacks on houses near Grange were described as being 'on pretence of looking for arms'. The sensitivity of élites to arms raids because of the imputed national and rebellious character of such actions should be recalled here. The *Journal* appears to have been suggesting that the attackers were criminals who were discrediting nationalism. The following week it described how 'party feelings' (which should be understood as referring to political conflicts between Ascendancy and emergent Catholic élites) were put aside at a series of meetings 'in the great question of preserving the public peace and tranquillity of the county'.[12]

However, there were also instances where correspondents attributed sectarian motives to agrarian rebels, and indeed there were a number of instances where bloodcurdling ribbon oaths were relayed to Dublin Castle. There appears to have been a systematic attempt to boycott Protestant shops in Strokestown for

9 SOCP1 1388/34, John Fallon, to unnamed, 19 Oct. 1811.   10 SOCP1 2363/4, Sir John Elley to Lt. Col. Thomas Sorrell, 27 Mar. 1822; SC 1825, 420, evidence of Revd Thomas Costello; SC 1824, 203, evidence of Sergeant Lloyd.   11 RLG, 28 Feb. 1824; RJ, 30 Jan. 1830; SC 1824, 136, evidence of George Warburton.   12 RJ, 20 Dec. 1828, 27 Dec. 1828.

about a month during the summer of 1813. The first complaint about this was made by a particularly partial source, the Protestant bishop of Elphin. On 4 August 1813 he complained that notices had been posted in Strokestown saying no one should deal with any shopkeeper who was an Orangeman, and that the Threshers had sworn all the people in the neighbourhood not to work for Orangemen. Men who disobeyed had been carded. As noted previously, a letter to the bishop from a magistrate named Devenish revealed that all Protestants were to be murdered the following Thursday in a general rising of the rebels.[13]

The following day the bishop wrote again, saying four Protestants had been named in a notice posted in Strokestown. One, a shopkeeper called Boyd, had written to him saying that another shopkeeper, Egan, had removed his usual window display and replaced it with coffin mountings, 'as there would be a great demand for them again'. The bishop's letter also enclosed a threatening notice that said:

> we bid no person or persons whatsoever to buy any commodity from any of the villainous crew calling themselves Orangemen ... now Depend on it that there will be a proper watch set for to mark all those that will Dare to attempt to go inside the Doors of the persons herein mentioned First that upstart orange scoundrel Boyd.

It would be reasonable to suppose that the movers of such a campaign against Protestant shopkeepers were men like Egan, and it is quite likely that such sectarianism prevailed more among shopkeepers than among the rural poor. Indeed, it is possible to speculate that such sectarianism among shopkeepers prefigures the confessional exclusivity of later nationalism, which found much of its support and cadres among the shopkeeper and 'strong farmer' strata in rural Ireland. This possibility is further corroborated by a copy of a catechism found in the house of a man named as a 'very comfortable farmer called Hynes', espousing the Catholic cause and the tree of liberty that was planted in Irish soil. The catechism asked: 'What is your intention? It is destroy Protestant kings of Erin – to burn churches – to destroy heretics.' Exclusive dealing has been found to be a common tactic in threatening notices from other parts of Ireland that were overtly anti-Protestant. The contrast of this with the loyalty to the king of the whiteboy 'Captain Farrell', who will be encountered shortly, is remarkable. It is also apparent that sectarian notices such as the one found at Hynes's house tended to express individual motives, rather than collective legitimation.[14]

13 SOCP1 1538/19, Trench to Gregory, 4 Aug. 1813, enclosing letter (same date) from G. Devenish to Trench.   14 SOCP1 1538/20, Trench to Gregory, enclosing letter from Boyd

On 7 August the bishop's horse was hit in the eye by a stone thrown from behind a wall while the bishop was returning from a visit to Athlone and an old woman living two miles from Elphin was 'much abused merely for the crime of being a Protestant'. Furthermore, the bishop reported that the homes of two Protestants were attacked and a prominent landowner remarked that Catholics were being prevented from working with Protestants who had 'in any manner been obnoxious to them'. A notice forbidding people to work on a Protestant church under construction was posted on the structure, and a man was carded for having bought shoes from a Protestant. Windows were broken in a house where a Methodist service was being held. Yeomanry commander James Kemmis, stationed at Boyle, reported that a general rising and the carding of all Protestants was planned. However, Kemmis concluded:

> danger to the country as represented frequently does not exist ... The wretchedness of the poor and consequently the vicious state of their morals, arising from oppression, is a strong and I think principal cause of those disturbances, for which the remedy rests with the landlord to apply.

The system of non-cooperation with Protestants had subsided by the following month, September 1813. A correspondent from Co. Sligo wrote to the chief secretary, Robert Peel, that there had been attempts to spread the boycott into that county and notices had been posted on Catholic churches in two baronies bordering Roscommon by men who came from there, wearing white shirts. He commented that the notices were ridiculed by everyone. One of the notices stated:

> We do forthwith Caution all Romancatholicks in future to have no Communication with Orangemen or with any prejudiced Protestant thats known to be a bad man in the country also we do caution them to purchase no tithes from any jobber only serve him with due notice to take the tithes unless the proprietors settles with the people we do further caution any man that attempts to cant any land in the possession of another.

The anti-Protestant 'system' (more accurately, perhaps, a boycott of certain Protestant businesses) which occurred in Strokestown during August 1813 was one of a few rare instances of anti-Protestant sentiment emerging from Co. Roscommon in the early years of the nineteenth century.[15]

to Trench, 5 Aug. 1813; SOCP1 1538/17, R. Cuppiadge to Gregory, 4 July 1813; Gibbons, *Captain Rock*, 34.   15 SOCP1 1538/22,23, Trench to Gregory, 8 Aug. 1813, 12 Aug. 1813;

A catechism submitted to Dublin in August 1815 by a magistrate from Drumsna, just over the border in Leitrim, expressed similar sentiments to those in the document recovered from Hynes's house. It promised an endeavour to recover lost rights usurped by tyrannic and oppressive Protestants and Orangemen, and professed an ability to swim three leagues in Orange blood. It also talked of the tree of liberty, of America and of France. The anti-Protestant sentiments sit strangely alongside the enlightenment language and imagery of brotherhood. In early 1820 a similar catechism talked of swimming nine leagues in Orange blood. These oaths and catechisms seem to have been standard and widespread, and may be connected to a national ribbon confederacy. They certainly appear to be derived from the standard Defender oaths and catechisms of the 1790s, but their relation to whiteboyism has not been verified. Similarly mixed sentiments have been noted among other Ribbon materials.[16]

Evangelical Protestantism was the target on one occasion in 1819, when 'Ribbon-men' served notices on several people not to send their children to a Sunday school, after which the bible was allegedly torn up on the road and called the devil's book. The vicar of Roscommon town wrote to the Castle in 1819 that the local Catholic priest had warned people about sending their children to the school 'with all the terrors of priestcraft'. The partiality of the vicar's language may not be surprising, and serves to reinforce the point made earlier about the sources' structural prejudices.[17]

An oath sent to Dublin Castle early the following year bound anyone taking it thus: 'You will not buy anything from a Protestant unless you get either better or cheaper than from a Catholic.' This amounts to little more than self-help for the Catholic shopkeepers. Another, recovered from a man committed to Roscommon jail two months later, reveals more generalized anti-Protestant sentiments. It promised to help the French or anyone else endeavouring to liberate the downtrodden, to be ready to collect money or arms to further the cause, only admit Catholics (or worthy Protestants) to membership, and wade knee-deep in the blood of Protestants and others who despise 'our blessed communion'. Its particular displeasure was reserved for 'those who feed on the tenth part of our

SOCP1 1538/25, Trench to Gregory, 14 Aug. 1813. SOCP1 1538/27, Brigade Major A. Lyster to Littlehales, 24 Aug. 1813; SOCP1 1538/28, Trench to Gregory, 29 Aug. 1813. SOCP1 1538/29, W. Kemmis to Lt. Col. Murray, Boyle, 3 Sept. 1813; SOCP1 1538/31 Lt. Gen. G.V. Hart to Peel, 7 Oct. 1813, enclosing information from Edward Wilson, magistrate, 24 Sept. 1813; SOCP1 1544/95, Brigade Major Bridgeham, Ballymote, to Peel, 3 Oct. 1813. 16 SOCP1 1713/12, enclosed with letter from Francis Waldron, magistrate, Drumsna, 4 Aug. 1815; SOCP1 2175/23, enclosed with letter from unknown to Denis Browne MP, 1 Feb. 1820; Clarke, *Christopher Dillon Bellew*, 55. 17 SOCP1 2074/8, Revd Thomas Blakeney, vicar of Roscommon, to Gregory, 12 June 1819.

labour'. This reveals some tendency towards general political conspiracy, some sectarianism and the familiar grievance of tithes. The exclusive dealing imperative, the general opposition to tithes, the enthusiasm for the French and the national politics suggest that this proto-nationalist oath originated from a shopkeeper rather than from among the cottiers and agricultural labourers, and that it was a characteristic Ribbon oath, descended from Defenderism.[18]

John Wills, a stipendiary magistrate, summarized his views on the disturbances in a long letter responding to questions put by Peel's successor, Charles Grant, in June 1820. He suggested that there were no economic justifications for the disturbances that had afflicted the county, that tithes had not been collected in a vexatious manner (indeed some had not been paid for two years), and that rents and tithes were only a pretext for disturbances that were in fact intended to overthrow the established church and government. However, he admitted that 'they have attacked the house of both Protestants and Catholics'. Wills added that during the disturbances of 1813 to 1815, when the disaffected had assumed the name of Threshers and Carders, Catholic priests' dues had been an issue, although they were no longer a major grievance. Catholic priests could have worked harder to persuade their flocks such activities were wrong, but they had lost influence. Grant had asked whether farmers and gentry could have resisted the rebels more determinedly, which is a revealing question. For Grant clearly perceived the farming stratum as quite separate from these lower orders. Wills, however, suggested that the farmers were too scared to come forward 'in consequence of their property being open to depredation'. He did not suggest the same was true of landlords, revealing by omission that the gentry and head landlords, being further removed and rather better protected from agrarian rebels, were relatively immune from direct attack, but that intermediate strata might be more effectively disciplined.[19]

On another occasion a threatening notice expressly disavowed any sectarian intent:

> some malitious and ill disposed person has circulated reports that our intention is to destroy our country Protestant men but they are mistaken we abominate such barbarity.

However, in another case some men called on a publican called John McNulty in Loughglynn. McNulty swore (whether willingly or not is unclear) 'not to buy two pence worth from any other religion but the Roman Catholic, that is

18 SOCP1 2176/9, enclosed with letter from Wills to Grant, 6 Feb. 1820; SOCP1 2176/37, Ribbon oath submitted by unknown to Dublin Castle, April 1820; see Clarke, *Christopher Dillon Bellew*, 54.   19 SOCP1 2176/49, Wills to Grant, 8 June 1820.

from any heretick, to pay no tithes to the parson, to throw down or level Protestant Houses and New Churches, if any invasion arise to aid and assist against the king'. It is apparent that national and religious sentiments were frequently expressed by such men as McNulty and stronger farmers like Hynes, confirming that such ideologies prevailed more among them than among the rural poor, whose objects tended to be more overtly economic. Indeed, Warburton told the 1824 select committee that anti-Protestant Ribbon oaths came from sources in Dublin and were not local or spontaneous. The lower classes had never thought about emancipation until the Catholic Association was formed and emancipation 'would not quiet the people'.[20]

In December 1823 Wills reported a horse being maimed and two attacks on its owner's house, saying that the man's Protestantism was the only reason that could be assigned for the outrages. Thus it can be seen that during the first three decades of the nineteenth century, the period when the alignment between confessional and national identities were supposedly becoming embedded in Irish society, the sum of sectarian feeling in Co. Roscommon was a month-long call for a boycott of Protestant shops in Strokestown and some other isolated instances of sectarian sentiment. It also seems clear that these were associated with a more prosperous social group within the Catholic population than the whiteboys, as the sources reveal them to be motivated by retail and lease competition. There are no further mentions of religious antipathy in the Co. Roscommon papers under consideration in this chapter.[21]

Hostility towards Protestantism must be seen in a broader Irish context, at the point of intersection of confession and class. For, as is often mentioned in the sources, Protestants in Co. Roscommon were almost exclusively not of the lower orders. They were a tiny minority in the county, yet owned much of the land, held many of the important positions as middlemen and agents, magistrates and police, ran shops and services and farmed tithes. It is therefore not altogether surprising that there were manifestations of an anti-Protestant consciousness when the rural poor's subsistence equilibrium was disturbed. The 1824 select committee was particularly concerned about opposition to tithes. However, it is apparent that the rural poor more frequently objected to the amounts demanded by farmers and proctors than to the payment of tithes.

Some of the witnesses understood that the appeal of Catholic solidarity was rather limited. Henry Newenham, a magistrate from Co. Cork, suggested that disturbances did not commence because of religious antipathy but that 'it is

20 SOCP1 2188/10, enclosed with letter from Brown to Gregory, 27 May 1820; SOCP1 2363/10, information sworn by William Swift, submitted by Wills to Gregory, 29 May 1822; SC 1824, 140, 141, 142, evidence of Warburton. 21 SOCP1 2502/53, Wills to Henry Goulburn, chief secretary, 16 Dec. 1823.

one of the strongest handles the ill-disposed can make use of to turn to their own purposes'. Richard Willcocks, Warburton's equivalent in Munster, believed that Catholic emancipation would not end outrage. The 'better class of farmers and professional men' were the only ones who mentioned the state of the law in respect of Catholics and they enlisted the help of the Catholic clergy in trying to pacify the lower orders. Insurgency was directed as much against them as against Protestants. He added:

> I do not think the lower class of the peasantry of Ireland care two pence about emancipation.

A Sligo magistrate told the 1825 enquiry that Catholic peasants cared little about emancipation, but that the clergy and some other Catholics had told them it would be a great benefit. The function of Catholicism as a solidarity mechanism was threatened whenever the people often seen as brokers of influence among the Catholic rural poor – for example, the clergy and the underground gentry – spoke or acted against secret associations. Another witness, William Becher (also a member of the committee), said that shopkeepers were anxious about their religious 'disabilities'. His comments articulated the changes taking place and the process of erosion of vertical and communal ties within Catholicism:

> the Catholic, having acquired property, and having been admitted into professions, became ambitious and anxious to participate in all the privileges of the constitution ... though perhaps the lower orders may not be so much benefited by any political concession, yet they may be easily led to think that they have a common interest with the Catholic body in endeavouring to effect the object of a full enjoyment of the privileges of the constitution.

The evidence from Co. Roscommon suggests that conflict among Catholics was so significant as to mean the lower orders were not easily led into any pan-Catholic solidarity. Daniel O'Connell acknowledged in his evidence to the 1825 committee that the removal of disabilities would remove only the 'double aspect' of oppression and that he had never attributed all Ireland's ills merely to 'the want of emancipation'. William Despard, a magistrate in Queen's County, said in his evidence to the 1831 parliamentary investigation into the state of Ireland that there had been 'a complete separation' since 1828 between the lower orders and gentlemen. It is perhaps not surprising that this separation occurred at the same time as the reform of 1829, which granted the privileges of the constitution to a limited number of better-off Catholics. Despard added that Catholic farmers were ill-treated as much as Protestants, and the Catholic clergy were doing everything in their power to stop outrages.[22]

Primitive rebels?

In August 1808 a report from the border between Co. Mayo and Co. Roscommon suggested that an attack on his majesty's government never was the object of this mob' and that 'jealousy from one faction to another for taking a farm caused the haughing of some cattle'. In 1810 there were reports of hundreds gathering at night, wearing white shirts and organizing outrages. One major general believed that such assemblies were not significant and 'frequently originate from family feuds'. Jealousies over coveted farms and reports of family disputes appear to confirm David Fitzpatrick's view, considered in an earlier chapter, that the agrarian outrages of pre-famine Ireland reflected family-orientated solidarities among Irish peasants. A number of instances which may, to follow Fitzpatrick's suggestion, be interpreted as kin or communal conflicts, occur through the papers and can be considered at this point. The use of disguise was also evident. Viscount Lorton wrote of a skirmish with a party of men wearing white shirts near Castletenison in December 1806. The following December an encounter with 'thrashing rebels' near Lough Key, 'all dressed in white shirts & white handkerchiefs in their hats with straw bands around their waists' was reported to Lorton. These incidents could be understood as evidence of the solidarity function (and practical use for identification purposes) of a common uniform. There were therefore sound reasons for the agrarian rebels to wear disguise and uniforms, reasons that were not confined to any pre-modern era.[23]

The use of the word 'faction' is noteworthy. In this context it appears to confirm the suggestion that families or neighbourhoods could be equated with factions. However, faction conflicts may have been rather more complicated than merely recreational set-pieces for the playing out of pre-modern or vertical loyalties. Sir Edward Crofton remarked that:

> under the plea of one parish being challenged by another, or one leader's part by another's, they frequently meet both at fairs and dances, much more to shew or find out the strength of their parties than to fight.

22 SC 1824, 300, evidence of Henry Newenham; SC 1824, 101, 117, evidence of Richard Willcocks; SC 1825, 695, evidence of Colonel John Irwin; SC 1824, 185, 204, evidence of William Becher; SC 1825, 127, evidence of Daniel O'Connell; SC 1824, 37, 43, evidence of William Despard.   23 SOCP1 1192/7, Brannick to unnamed, Dublin Castle, 7 Aug. 1808; SOCP1 1278/19, Major General Montresor, Athlone, to Littlehales, 4 Oct. 1810; SOCP2, 157/3941, Lorton to unnamed, 27 Dec. 1806; SOCP2 158/4568, Molloy McDermott to Lorton, 26 Dec. 1807.

There was an implication in this remark that the factions were perfectly conscious of the effect their counter-theatre may have had, and that something
potentially more threatening than a primitive or pre-modern group squabble
was latent in such a rendezvous. Wills made a similar suggestion in 1814:

> several hundreds assembled during day time at Fairymount under the
> pretence of fighting but from every information I have been able to col-
> lect it was for the purpose of shewing there numbers and administering
> a new oath.

It may be that these meetings were not for the purposes of agrarian conspiracy, but non-violent ritual confrontations. However, there was apparently some
connection between factions and agrarian movements, rendering it sometimes
difficult to distinguish precisely between faction fighter and whiteboy. The Co.
Limerick parish priest, Thomas Costello, believed that faction fighting and
whiteboyism were unrelated. This prefigures Beames's assessment, although it
would be surprising if there were no overlap in membership between factions
and whiteboy groups. Roberts's study of the Caravats and Shanavests, however, demonstrates the ways in which the two kinds of organization could have
divergent ideological tendencies. The belief that whiteboy organization was
qualitatively more serious than factional dispute was evidently shared by the
Catholic clergy. Later in 1814, the suggestion that faction meetings disguised
something more worrying was made again when a magistrate reported a meeting of between 2,000 and 3,000 men at Cavetown, near Boyle, on Sunday 10
July 'under pretence of fighting but nothing of that kind took place'.[24]

It seems apparent that factions were often led by descendants of the dispossessed land-owners who had maintained a local presence and some authority. The 1824 parliamentary enquiry into disturbances heard a number of
witnesses testify in such terms. Willcocks reported that a man who led a faction in Co. Tipperary boasted of the blood of his ancestors. Indeed, such loyalties may have been behind family-based disputes over land, as a Cork parish
priest suggested in his evidence to the 1825 parliamentary enquiry:

> I mean by clanship factions for fighting and carrying the object of a par-
> ticular family or a particular set of persons.

---

24 SOCP1 1278/20, Crofton to unnamed, Dublin Castle, 9 Dec. 1810; SOCP1 1558/24,
Wills to Gregory, 10 Jan. 1814; SC 1825, 419, evidence of Revd Thomas Costello; Roberts,
'Caravats and Shanavests'; Connolly, *Priests and people*, 229–30; SOCP1 1558/34, magistrates McMahon and Harrison to Wills, enclosed with letter from Wills to Gregory, 23 July
1814.

John Irwin told the 1825 select committee that on his Co. Sligo estate two men with the same surname had fought for the lands on which one of them lived, both claiming that they were the descendants of a family Cromwell had dispossessed. James Lawler, a Catholic who was an agent and a magistrate at Killarney, Co. Kerry, told the 1824 select committee of a dispute over land that had been confiscated after the Williamite wars. He noted that the dispossessed family 'particularly venerate the memory ever since'. The heads of factions were people who had command of people with the same name or family, or were in some way connected with them, the Co. Limerick landlord Richard Bourke told the following year's parliamentary enquiry into Irish disturbances.[25]

There are some further examples of conflicts that appeared to be based on family or other loyalties. A merchant from Roscommon town who was also an extensive farmer re-let land, a farm and offices after the previous tenant surrendered the tenancy while still owing eighteen months' rent. The night before the incoming tenant took up residence, all were burned down. The magistrate William Bowles deduced that 'all those outrages have been committed on people who have taken land that was thrown up by other tenants'. The outrages were attributed by Stephen Mahon to 'private resentment'. Lieutenant General Thomas Meyrick reported that a house at Ballagh, near Slieve Bawn, recently out of lease and taken by a new tenant, had been set fire to by some friends of the old tenant. Actions on the basis of private resentments, however, could be legitimized by reference to collectively accepted views on rights to land. The Roscommon merchant's previous tenant clearly believed he had a right to the land that was superior to the contractual one that required him to pay a certain rent.[26]

Such private resentments could be related to family or community conflicts. The case of the O'Haras of Castlerea was mentioned earlier, and the dispute resulted in murder on 14 October 1816. Private grievances were considered a major cause of disturbances in Co. Roscommon in 1820. Michael Dunne wrote from the head office of police to Grant:

> The disturbances in this county appear to have originated in private grievance (not religious ones) by the taking of land over each other's heads.

25 SC 1824, 114, evidence of Richard Willcocks; SC 1825, 397, evidence of Revd John Kelly; SC 1825, 696, evidence of Colonel John Irwin; SC 1824, 450, evidence of James Lawler; SC 1825, 325, evidence of Richard Bourke.   26 SOCP1 1767/44, Bowles to Peel, 20 July 1816; SOCP1 1767/46, Mahon to Peel, 28 July 1816; SOCP1 1408/27, Lt. Gen. T. Meyrick to unnamed, 7 Jan. 1812.

Dunne appears to have assumed that because he could find no religious (and by implication national) cause for the disturbances, they were merely private. However, the collectively-held views of subsistence rights that legitimized these actions were public and social. On 1 November 1822 notices were posted on the houses of Patrick Connor and Christopher Carley in Kilteevan parish, 'threatening vengeance against them, or any other persons, who may set lands or tenements to a man named Cadigan of that place'. Cadigan's house had been set alight on 28 October. Such disputes may indeed be the consequence of family or neighbourhood disputes over desirable parcels of land, but they reflect widely held principles of rights and justice. They may have been the values of a community, encompassing different social strata in vertical ties connected with the underground gentry, but whiteboyism in the early nineteenth century appears to have occurred most often when such community principles were becoming the exclusive property of the rural poor. However, the legitimation of conflict still referred to the upholding of traditional notions of fairness.[27]

Further, it is unclear whether these disputes were between more substantial farmers who might not have had access to the communal disciplinarians (indeed, may have been in conflict with them) and therefore had to pursue their vendettas individually. The threats made to Connor and Carley suggest that they were indeed tenant farmers who were letting land to the rural poor. Likewise, the case of the Roscommon merchant's farm appears to relate to the tenancy of a substantial holding. This is not to suggest that such private resentments or family disputes might occur only between substantial tenant farmers, although it does stimulate further reflection on the issue of agrarian social stratification. For example, private grievance was behind the burning down of two houses in Kilgefin parish on the night of Sunday 1 June 1823, after two men took joint possession of a piece of ground which had formerly been rented collectively by them and others. It appears that such a dispute, involving rundale, would certainly have occurred between poorer landholders and some of their number who appear to have broken from the collective discipline of the rural poor. The sources reveal only two further cases in Co. Roscommon of disputes attributed to private causes, which may have been occasioned by disputes between or within families over land, during the period covered in this chapter. It is thus apparent that private grievance could not be regarded as the primary source of collective mobilization of the rural poor. There also appears to have been a distinction between the collective means the rural poor used to further

27 SOCP1 1776/97 Brannick to Mahon, 25 Oct. 1816, enclosed with letter from Mahon to Peel, 2 Nov. 1816; SOCP1 2188/15, Michael Dunne to Grant, 11 Oct. 1820; SOCP1 2363/20, Wills to Goulburn, 1 Dec. 1822.

individual interests and the factional or family-based mechanisms deployed by farmers.[28]

At this point modernization and nationalist explanations of conflict both tend to converge at a conceptualization of social relations between agrarian social strata in pre-famine rural Ireland which suggests that vertical solidarities led to a confession-based identity. If vertical loyalties to the descendants of the dispossessed native landowners persisted, however, these were under increasing strain as both native and upstart middlemen, farmers and landlords withdrew from cultural reciprocity with the rural poor. It is evident that social and economic relations between the rural strata beneath the land-owners became increasingly conflictual from the time of the Whiteboys onwards. The withdrawal of farmers and middlemen from popular culture and the decline of vertical mutuality was the concomitant of economic reorientation by the farming and land owning élites.

Community solidarities could also find expression in hostility to strangers. A notice was posted on a door in Kilcooley parish warning all strangers to quit lands taken in the district. On another occasion notice was served on a man to give up 'the widow Gounleys ground ... and if you go to the said land you will rue the day you first thought of coming there'. On 29 March 1820, four days after the notice was served, the house it was posted on was burned down. This warning may have been to a stranger or to someone who had moved in on a coveted piece of land. In April 1822 a notice from 'General Rock' was served on John Carr in Athlone barony, warning him to return to his own country, and in the same area the following year a Co. Galway man was beaten for working in the neighbourhood. Francis Blackburne noted hostility to the hiring of strangers in his evidence to the 1824 select committee. However, just as family-based factions could close ranks when faced by a common enemy (usually police), so on one occasion Co. Galway and Co. Roscommon people who were fighting at Mount Talbot fair united when the police became involved. The police opened fire and killed two people.[29]

However, actions against strangers were not confined to Ireland. The *Roscommon and Leitrim Gazette* noted that 'Captain Rock' appeared in England in 1824, when a number of Irish labourers sought work in Lincolnshire. The indigenous workers 'drove off' the Irish migrants. This demonstrates that there was nothing peculiarly Irish in the protectionist measure of seeking to secure employment by excluding others. It should also be noted that there is nothing inherently pre-modern in such tactics.[30]

28 SOCP1 2502/32, Wills to Gregory, 2 June 1823.   29 SOCP1 2176/30, Wills to Gregory, 3 Apr. 1820; SOCP1 2502/27, Wills to Gregory, 15 Apr. 1823; RLG, 4 May 1822, 30 Aug. 1823; SC 1824, 8, evidence of Francis Blackburne; RLG, 19 June 1824.   30 RLG, 28

It may be sustainable that the root of some agrarian actions, in addition to those just considered, was private (or even family or neighbourhood) but only in an abstract sense, because agrarian crime habitually involved communal discipline and such discipline was invariably salutary and public. Whether an action was against someone of the same or higher social status, it could be justified by a public sense of custom. One of the major sources of conflict was the disengagement of certain strata in the Catholic population from such notions of fairness and duty. The rural poor believed that it was wrong to evict, and it was also wrong to take land from which someone had been evicted.

The sense that agrarian outrage was conservative, irrational, spontaneous and resisting technological and modernizing processes, may also be considered. Conflict ensued as landlords (whether owners, agents, middlemen or farmers) in Ireland increasingly adopted the ethos of improvement and disturbed customary equilibria, as the intrusion of commerce brought change to the subsistence-orientated community. However, the conservatism and violence of such conflicts did not necessarily signify that the protesters were reacting blindly and spontaneously to external stimuli. Randall's discussion of the Wiltshire outrages of 1802 notes that social historians have equated violence with organizational immaturity but suggests that the violence was directed specifically, as the shearmen believed employers were breaking both statute and custom. Nocturnal visits, threatening letters, the exclusion of strangers who came from Gloucestershire, supra-regional links with Yorkshire, subscriptions for parliamentary campaigns and the attacks on blacklegs rather than employers all characterized these outrages. Indeed, the use of the same descriptive term – 'outrages' – that has been employed to describe Irish disturbances is noteworthy in itself. In the absence of institutional or associational forms for collective bargaining, new ways of asserting the validity of custom were added to Irish repertoires of resistance. The parliamentary sources also repeatedly emphasize the success of agrarian movements in achieving reductions in prices and especially in lowering rates for conacre. The O'Conor Don told the 1831 parliamentary enquiry into disturbances of occasions when Co. Roscommon landlords had agreed to reduce rents.[31]

Politics and the rural poor

Having considered the extent to which whiteboyism reflected confessional and national sentiment or pre-modern social relations, the question of political

Aug. 1824.   31 A. Randall, 'The shearmen and the Wiltshire outrages' (1982); SC 1831, 32, evidence of the O'Conor Don.

motivation may now be profitably examined. The idea that whiteboyism belonged to an era in which solidarities were with family or neighbourhood is closely aligned with the view that it was pre-political. These perspectives have been considered earlier, particularly in relation to the work of Rudé, Hobsbawm and Fitzpatrick. Indeed, the close connection between pre-modern and pre-political appeared to be confirmed by Matthew Wyatt, a landlord and magistrate from near Castlerea. His letter to Peel, referred to in chapter one, discussed the case of the O'Haras, which concerned the murder of a man by his son-in-law. Wyatt was relieved that there was no political motivation behind the outrage (political, in the sense used by Wyatt, inevitably meant the high politics of parliament and nation). Parliamentary enquiries were particularly interested in whether the leaders of unrest were men of a higher social status. In the aftermath of 1798, combination was always investigated because of the fear that it was the forerunner of nationalist rebellion. Edward Mills, the county sheriff, linked the nocturnal agrarian activities with the high political causes of the time, suggesting that 'they are growing more haughty every day, thanks to my Lords Grey and Grenville'. Religious disaffection was also taken to be a similar indicator, though it was evidently much less apparent to agrarian rebels themselves.[32]

A number of attempts were made to discern whether whiteboyism was pervaded by any party spirit, which reward detailed examination. The Church of Ireland bishop of Elphin spoke of 'open rebellion'. Thefts of arms were always seen as potentially political, doubtless due to the memory of 1798, especially when combined with acts of insubordinate counter-theatre like the group of men who styled themselves 'Captain Thresher's men', who met in a pub and then proceeded to Boyle to throw mud at the statue of William III on the town's bridge.[33]

The raising of political issues around election times was believed to inflame passions and, however obliquely, influence the disposition to outrage of the rural poor. This connection between the public political sphere and the shady world of whiteboyism (for example, the relationship between the O'Conellite mass movement and agrarianism) has proved notoriously difficult to research. It may be that any scheme which entirely separates the two is unsatisfactory. It is certainly the case that the Castle's correspondents failed to distinguish between Ribbon confederacy and whiteboyism. The parliamentary enquiry held in 1831 was told that agrarian disturbances were not connected to the emancipation campaign. William Despard suggested that emancipation meet-

32 SOCP1 1767/52, Wyatt to Peel, 21 Oct. 1816; SOCP1 1408/36, Mills to Saxton, 24 Mar. 1812.   33 SOCP1 1538/25, Trench to Gregory, 14 Aug. 1813; SOCP1 1956/23, information of Longford carriers Denis and Peter Rush, sworn 6 Feb. 1818.

ings provided an 'organized machinery of operation' which was appropriated
by 'other people' who harangued people after the emancipation rallies were
over. Irish agrarian rebels were not 'pre-political' unless 'political' is defined
narrowly, in terms of parliament and parliamentary parties. The marquis of
Sligo reported in early 1820 that:

> the whole thing as far as I can judge arises from the vile extortions of
> the gentry in the county of Roscommon whose system of letting land in
> conacre at exorbitant rents drives the people to despair, famine and mis-
> ery of the highest degree. In addition to this they feel the tythes are very
> oppressive to them, as they are collected out of the fag end of their
> means after rent and other taxes have been extorted from them, proba-
> bly in not the most lenient way.

He believed that such a situation could develop into a general political revolt
and warned ominously that pike manufacture had commenced in Co. Roscommon (this, like the arms raid, was regarded as another sign of political conspiracy and imminent rebellion).[34]

A riot in Strokestown in 1819 – after a 'misunderstanding' between the
parish priest and his parishioners – was related to elections, one commentator
suggesting that 'the party spirit that has been consequently excited ... does not
appear to have subsided yet'. A magistrate named Strickland wrote the following year that 'the general impression they give is that their conspiracy is dif-
fused over every part of Ireland'. He also claimed shortly afterwards that
bodies of men numbering three to four hundred were meeting nearby at night,
armed with pikes and guns, that they exchanged oaths and catechisms, and that
'their object is nothing short of rebellion'. He believed 'the secret association
of the Ribbonmen to be spread very generally over Ireland'. This may also
reflect an undiscriminating associating of all protest with national rebellion, of
whiteboys with Ribbon conspirators. Strickland's warning about the extent of
the perceived conspiracy was contained in an enclosure submitted to the Castle by the Mayo MP, Denis Browne. Browne's own letter explicitly referred to
the 1798 rebellion; he also understood that disaffection might be translated into
political terms (his homily on the state of the county may be recalled) and considered that the troubles that had started in Co. Roscommon were spreading all
over Ireland. He called for the re-enactment of lapsed 1798 legislation and concluded, 'I fear you must prepare for a general rebellion'.[35]

---

34 SC 1831, 40, evidence of William Despard; SOCP1 2175/7, Peter Browne, marquis of
Sligo, to unnamed, Dublin Castle, 20 Jan. 1820.   35 SOCP1 1963/32, unnamed, general
office of yeomanry, Athlone, to Dublin Castle, 1 Aug. 1818; SOCP1 2074/20, J.C. Strick-

Another correspondent near Castlerea suggested in a communication to the Castle in January 1820 that each village or townland had a captain, who received orders from officers commanding parishes, who in turn received orders from barony commanders and county generals. A general rising and attack on Castlerea was planned for the following night, but if that failed to materialize they would at least set free a man named Moran, who was due to be whipped publicly for an unspecified misdemeanour. The contrast in the scale of the potential outcomes forecast by this writer may at first seem rather ludicrous, and needs to be explained in terms of the writer's own beliefs and fears, expressed in this instance by an explanation that 'after getting arms and ammunition a general massacre of Protestants is to take place'. The anticipated rising did not take place, but Wills nevertheless asserted that 'a competent system of organization exists, not only in this neighbourhood but throughout this and the adjoining counties'.[36]

Wills's belief may have been based partly on his own perceptions and political outlook, but also on notices such as one he forwarded to Dublin in February 1820. This notice, from Captain Right, instructed the recipient not to allow a particular man called Studders to stay in his house, or it would be destroyed. The captain threatened to punish 'as far as the United Powers directs'. Such grand titles may have provoked Wills to believe general conspiracies were afoot, but they may more profitably be explained in terms of a counter-theatrical language of dissent, which will be considered further in chapter six. However, the connection between a local objective and a language of general conspiracy reveals once again the problematic relation between the local and the political. One of the most useful manifestations of this relationship was provided by Stephen Mahon. He wrote:

> Notices in writing have been lately posted on the doors of chapels and other conspicuous places fixing the prices of labour and the rent of land directing all herds and shepherds of the large farmers to cease from attending their flocks and herd and requiring the abolition or diminution of tythes and a general division of land among the labouring class.

Mahon's letter reveals the connection made in threatening notices between the local and particular on one hand and general solutions to the rural poor's political, economic and social predicaments on the other. Utopian visions may be

land, Loughglynn, to Gregory, 2 Dec. 1819; SOCP1 2176/10, Strickland to Grant, 7 Feb. 1820; SOCP1 2175/1, Strickland to D. Browne, 16 Jan. 1820; SOCP1 2175/8, D. Browne to unnamed, Dublin Castle, 23 Jan. 1820.   36 SOCP1 2176/6, information of H. Caldwell, Castlerea, 28 Jan. 1820.

part of the political programme of the rural poor. Millenarianism has indeed been identified as a product of agrarian social movements, and has been noted in Ireland during this period, particularly in the 'Pastorini prophecies'. However, evidence of millenarianism is almost entirely absent from Co. Roscommon in this period. On one occasion an unknown correspondent told Denis Browne that a preacher called Thomas Dixon had appeared, proclaiming that the hour of peace was approaching. He was also said to have been seen at the head of two parties of Ribbonmen across the border in Co. Galway. This seems an unlikely millenarian tale, as Dixon was a Maynooth-trained Catholic priest who had been converted to Protestantism two years after taking up a curate's position in Killala, Co. Mayo, and who testified about the dangers of popery to an 1825 Lords enquiry into Irish disturbances. There are no further references in the State of the Country Papers to millenarian movements touching the county. The Threshers' support for Bonaparte 'who is to set all this right' in 1806 and 1807 may perhaps be understood as expressions of abstract millennial desires. Peter Burke has suggested that millenarianism was one of the available cultural responses to perceived injustice among the peasants of early modern Europe (see discussion in chapter 7 below. It will become apparent that, in the absence of associational expressions of their custom-based politics, the poor could at times transfer their abstract political desires on to figures like O'Connell, who was usually ready to provide some demagogic expression of those abstractions, without ever having to take steps to fulfil them. At this juncture in Co. Roscommon, it appears that millenarianism had a limited resonance and that more concrete political responses were forming during this period of rapid change. The co-existence of general political visions and concrete local demands renders questionable the suggestion that the rural poor were incapable of moving beyond the specific and the local.[37]

Wills attempted some detailed answers about possible political ends in a lengthy reply to questions put by Grant. He suggested that this 'Ribbonism' was no more than the continuance of the agrarian movement that had been known a few years earlier as the Threshers and the Carders. However, some people had been led further, to believe that the established religion and government were their bitterest enemies, that they were slaves and that by overturning both their situation would be improved.[38]

Such statements lead to the question of leadership. There was a general assumption among the magistracy and politicians that agrarian rebels needed

37 SOCP1 2176/7, Wills to Grant, 31 Jan. 1820; SOCP1 2176/24, Mahon to Grant, 7 Mar. 1820; SOCP1 2175/23, unnamed to D. Browne, 1 Feb. 1820; SOCP1 2175/28, unnamed to D. Browne, 1 Feb. 1820; HL 1825, 504–12, evidence of Thomas Dixon; Fortescue MSS, NLI, 464; Burke, *Popular culture*, 174.   38 SOCP1 2176/49, Wills to Grant, 8 June 1820.

external leadership in order to merit the designation political, so there was a particular sensitivity to whether there were men of a 'better sort' pulling the strings. This was mistaken. It is a similar assumption to the one underpinning the approach that sees the rural poor as pre-political. Thus the only political substance available to whiteboys was nationalist, fed from above by O'Connell. In the next chapter it will become apparent that whiteboys had their own leaders, 'organic intellectuals' who could make political generalizations. However, it seems that there must also have been intermediaries between whiteboys and the literate, monoglot anglophone world. There were a number of occasions when the chimera of agitators or Catholics of the 'better sort' in leadership rôles haunted political and judicial élites, but rarely any concrete evidence of leadership by other groups. John Kelly, the parish priest at Mitchelstown, Co. Cork, believed that whiteboyism 'could not have been devised by the lowest order of the peasantry'. However, the lord lieutenant wrote to London in 1814:

> Nor is there any evidence at all conclusive that they act under the guidance of leaders of respectability either in point of talents or property.

Lieutenant General Sir Edward Paget reported that there was no positive proof that 'political incendiaries' were fomenting revolt during the disturbed months of early 1820, although it was likely that 'some such miscreants have been thus employed, and have contrived to convert the just grievances of this indigent and oppressed peasantry, to their own diabolical purposes'. Paget believed that some amelioration of poverty was required in order to prevent insurrection. He added that all his colleagues believed poverty resulting from exorbitant rents and the cheapness of labour were 'the main ground of the present disorders'. Another military man opined the following year that 'much local mischief may be contemplated, but I do not apprehend therefrom, a general and simultaneous rising'. In 1824 the Co. Roscommon magistrate Arthur Browne expressed anxiety at 'a disposition on the part of the lower orders to purchase fire arms', although he was 'not disposed to impute this inclination to any aims of a political nature'. Another Roscommon magistrate reported that 'men of wealth and prosperity' were aiding those who committed outrages. However, by the following year there was 'great activity in collecting the Catholic rent'. This accords with the more plausible evaluations of Richard Willcocks and George Warburton. Willcocks believed that increasing clerical influence on the people was due to the priests' connections with the Catholic Association, and Warburton that the Association 'produced the tranquillity of the country in combination with the clergy'. Such evaluations confirm that the rather hysterical assessments of O'Connell's subversive intentions offered by the Castle's local correspondents should be treated with great caution. Fergus O'Ferrall has

noted that it took some time for the government to realize that the Catholic
Association was a different phenomenon to Captain Rock and not to be dealt
with similarly. Such exaggerated fears of the extent of O'Connellite radicalism
may thereby be explained more satisfactorily. Such fears among the élite's
backwoodsmen reflect also the continued entrenchment of the notion that any
Catholic political mobilization was disturbing as it represented a threat to their
property. This 'great activity' suggests that where O'Connellism did penetrate
the rural poor, it may have been most successful in periods of hiatus in agrarian disturbance, when the poor may have looked for deliverance to élite leadership rather than their own efforts.[39]

Indeed, O'Ferrall has described O'Connell as belonging to a 'messianic tradition of political leadership'. At such times, O'Connell 'displaced Captain
Rock as the focus of popular hopes'.[40]

If millenarian abstractions were largely absent in Co. Roscommon during the
period in question, it may be because during periods of downturn and defeat
such abstract aspirations were transferred to O'Connell, who proved adept in
appearing to address the real concerns of his lower-class audience, while offering no solutions other than that somehow, generally, things would improve after
emancipation or, later, repeal. Such, it will be recalled, was O'Connell's evidence
to the 1825 parliamentary enquiry when he spoke of emancipation removing
only one aspect of the poor's 'double oppression'. Thus, during the emancipation campaign, for example, his speeches could address the many local concerns
that formed the majority of the 'grievance letters' sent to the Catholic Association, by expressing what has been described as the 'ill-defined demand of the
Irish people for justice and good, representative government'. This lack of definition corroborates the suggestion that O'Connell operated in such a way as to
appear to address the concrete concerns of the poor while offering no more than
the vaguest strategies for the satisfactory resolution of those anxieties; 'hence ...
his numerous contradictions and inconsistencies'. One critic of O'Connell suggested that the 'great Liberator, amongst his other liberations, set words free
from all precise meaning'. Furthermore, the Catholic Rent itself was collected
most successfully from two key groups – discontented Catholic townsmen and
the rural middle classes. One of O'Connell's biographers has concluded that the

---

39 SC 1825, 401, evidence of Revd John Kelly; SOCP1 1567/1, Whitworth to Sidmouth,
5 Jan. 1814; SOCP1 2189/12, Lt. Gen. Sid Edward Paget to unnamed, Dublin Castle, 5
Apr. 1820; SOCP1 2291/11, Lt. Col. Farquharson to Elley, Boyle, 2 Dec. 1821; SOCP1
2625/26, Arthur Browne, magistrate, Roscommon, to Goulburn, 20 Dec. 1824; SOCP1
2832/34, James Keogh to unnamed, undated (1827); SOCP1 2730/23, Joseph Tabuteau,
Ballinasloe, to Gregory, 14 June 1825; F. O'Ferrall, *Catholic emancipation* (1985), 75, 82.   40
F. O'Ferrall, *Daniel O'Connell* (1981), 136; O'Ferrall, *Catholic emancipation*, 73.

'poor man' was only sporadically involved in subscription to the Catholic Rent. A more complex picture thus emerges of the O'Connellite movements for emancipation and repeal than the nationalist portrait of a homogeneous people united behind their liberator.[41]

It has often been assumed that O'Connell's campaigns for emancipation and repeal reached far among the lower orders, but the evidence for homogeneous national consciousness among whiteboys is flimsy. Indeed, there appears to be little evidence of the appeal of the two campaigns to whiteboys other than the size of attendances at his mass rallies, and Sean Connolly has suggested that 'it remains doubtful how far down the social scale either movement really penetrated'. The evidence from Co. Roscommon during the emancipation campaign confirms that the penetration of O'Connell's confessionally exclusive nationalism was indeed limited. If the clergy were his footsoldiers, they met a fierce opposing army in Co. Roscommon whiteboy organizations.[42]

As a possible alternative leader to O'Connell, the rural poor might perhaps have acknowledged the descendant of a dispossessed local lord (as suggested by Whelan's account of the underground gentry) or indeed one of the upstarts who adapted to local mores (according to Barnard's view). Having also established that these other potential leaders of Catholic Ireland were disengaging from customary and vertical cultural ties with the rural poor in the early nineteenth century, the fascinating references to other kinds of outside agitation may now be considered.

In the period of hiatus between the political movements of the 1790s and the birth of the emancipation movement, it is possible to detect the subterranean continuation of radical political impulses among the lower orders, and it is in this sense that it becomes possible to speak of a secret Ireland. Many correspondents perceived that there was some connection between radicalism in England and Ireland, although again most presumed that its character in Ireland would be separatist. Denis Browne was one of the few correspondents who perceived the social dimension of the disorder as a threat.

In 1812 the return of a man who had lived in England for a number of years aroused suspicion. One magistrate believed he had been deeply implicated in disturbances in England and his return to Ireland was not for the best purposes. In 1820 Wills wrote that Englishmen and Scots had been among the people in Co. Roscommon and 'talked a good deal about the distresses and grievances

41 O'Ferrall, *Daniel O'Connell*, 75, 51; Report of a lecture delivered by Isaac Varian to the Desmond Confederate Club, Cork, *United Irishman*, 12 Feb. 1848; O'Ferrall, *Daniel O'Connell*, 48–9.   42 For the continued assumption of O'Connellite hegemony, see, for example, Gibbons, *Captain Rock*, 36, and Clarke, *Christopher Dillon Bellew*, 59; Connolly, *Priests and people*, 30.

of the people'. They had pretended to be pedlars. Hedge school masters have been considered as possible intermediaries between whiteboyism and the literate world. Interestingly, the pre-famine recollections of the Fanad schoolmaster Hugh Dorian reveal how men would meet at night at houses in that remote part of Co. Donegal to discuss the affairs of the world. Possession of a newspaper ensured entry to such gatherings, at which someone would read from a newspaper bought in Letterkenny or that had been sent to them by a friend 'across the channel'.[43]

When an allegation was made that an Englishman (whose day job had been as a coachman to Sir Edward Crofton's brother-in-law) was relaying orders down a chain of command for the posting of Thresher notices on chapels, James Irwin, the Co. Roscommon magistrate, wrote, 'If this be true, an Englishman, a stranger, unconnected here, he must ... be the agent of others far above himself'. Another magistrate, Devenish, said he could find no connection with the Catholic dissent. In October 1816, but weeks before the Spa Fields mass meetings and riot in London, an anonymous informant in London wrote to Peel that there was a provisional government organized in every part of Ireland and Britain, exciting disaffection and fomenting disloyalty. It was connected with similar movements in Madrid, Paris and Rome, raising arms and ammunition. Denis Browne, writing in 1819, commented that the riots in England had been heard of but had caused no trouble, although all the mischief in Connacht was in Co. Roscommon. He was writing two months after Peterloo and three weeks after the procession that heralded Henry Hunt's entry into London, accompanied by Arthur Thistlewood and banners of green silk, emblazoned with Irish harps. A printed copy of Hunt's address on the eve of Peterloo had been distributed widely in Ireland. A Mayo magistrate reported 'that communication exists between the disturbers in England and those in this country ... swearing in Ribbon Men at the Chapels after the Priest goes away'. Two months later, Browne changed his mind, writing in December 1819, 'all depends on England if mischief there be put down'. Browne evidently believed that the local disturbances could potentially be transformed into some kind of social crisis, and the prospects for the importing of political radicalism from England could be the spark to the agrarian tinder. Another correspondent entertained the spurious notion that a sportsman was the go-between in this revolutionary scenario, suggesting that 'Donnelly the great Boxer is acting secretary for the rebels of both England and Ireland & that the correspondence is carried on through him.' One correspondent claimed that there was certainly an 'active correspondence' between English and Irish radicals, another that

43 SOCP1 1408/22, Hart to Saxton, 17 May 1812; SOCP1 2176/49, Wills to Grant, 8 June 1820; H. Dorian, *The outer edge of Ulster* (2001), 142.

there were 100,000 guns in Roscommon, Mayo and Sligo, and that rebels were meeting near Boyle at night under Protestant leadership. The weight of evidence makes it seem likely that there was some connection, although it may be that any formal communications were with the nationalist Ribbon societies. Here the opaque relations between agrarian rebellion and Ribbonism frustrate attempts to be more precise about the connection. For English radicals the espousal of Irish nationalism was a means to oppose the British political élite (O'Connell endorsed the Charter in 1838, and it was broadened to demand repeal of the union in 1842, although he derided Chartism) as well as an end in itself. However, it may safely be supposed that the language of liberty had penetrated further merely than the farmers, shopkeepers and publicans who provided the organizational spine of Ribbonism, and that the notion of liberty had a different, egalitarian inflection among whiteboys, less prone to sectarianism and less devoutly Catholic. The 'Ribbonism' that prevailed in Connacht in 1819 and 1820 was certainly more agrarian than conspiratorial and nationalist, insofar as it was Ribbonism at all, and not merely a misnomer applied by magistrates, landowners and the military. The disturbances prompted a lengthy report from Peel's successor as chief secretary for Ireland, Charles Grant, to Viscount Sidmouth, the Home Secretary. Grant said there was 'no proof that they deserve the name of a radical insurrection'. Nor had he been able to establish that there were English emissaries to the Irish, or 'a connection between the Radicals and the Ribbonmen'.[44]

There was, however, an opportunity for radicalism to be preached in Boyle, and an audience. A correspondent wrote to the *Roscommon and Leitrim Gazette* to complain that that there was 'at our doors, an expatriated Yorkshire radical, and his protegée in this town'.[45]

It was after Peterloo that an 'address to Irishmen' was posted in Clonmel, Co. Tipperary, speaking of the 'murdered patriots of Manchester'. There were rumours that the ultra-jacobin Arthur Thistlewood (who was executed for

---

44 SOCP1 1775/4, 'Amicus' to Peel, 12 Oct. 1816; SOCP1 2074/12, D. Browne to Gregory, 7 Oct. 1819; SOCP1 2086/7, précis of correspondence between magistrates and Dublin Castle for all Ireland, Oct. and Nov. 1819; Thompson, *The making of the English working class* (1980 ed.), 746–7, quoting the *Cap of Liberty*, 15 Sept 1819; D. MacRaild, *Irish migrants in modern Britain* (1999), 131; SOCP1 2086/7, précis of correspondence between magistrates and Dublin Castle for all Ireland, Oct. and Nov. 1819. Sir S. O'Malley, Castlebar, had been informed of the connection between English radicalism and Irish disturbances on 2 Nov. 1819; SOCP1 2086/8, D. Browne to unnamed, Dublin Castle, 11 Dec. 1819; SOCP1 2086/10, Edward Kelly, Mote, to unnamed, Dublin Castle, 16 Dec. 1819; SOCP1 2086/11, unsigned letter, undated (late 1819); SOCP1 2086/12, G. Anderson, Dublin, to unnamed, Dublin Castle, undated (late 1819); J.K. Walton, *Chartism* (1999), 7, 27; SOCP1, 2188/11, Grant to Sidmouth, 30 May 1820.   45 RLG, 27 Nov. 1824.

leading the Cato Street conspiracy of early 1820) was in Ireland. Three hundred copies of a handbill talking of Peterloo and Hunt's triumphant procession were seized from a man at a fair in Thurles. In the embryonic, combined and uneven development of political consciousness among the Irish rural poor, the emblematic significance of Peterloo was grafted on to the Irish agrarian tradition. Thus might the developing consciousness of class appropriate motifs and emblems from France, Paine and now Radicalism, as social relations in rural Ireland were re-constituted according to different principles from those of vertical interdependence. A lawyer at the trial of two Co. Galway Ribbonmen in 1820 said that the lower orders had disengaged from the affinity that should exist between landlord and tenant. In the shifting language and emblems of agrarian rebels it is possible to discern the hardening of social polarizations after the withdrawal of élites from vertical affinities. George Warburton told the 1824 select committee that Thistlewood's son was believed to be in Ireland, distributing medals bearing the image of a tree or cap of liberty. His father had been a member of the Spencean group that had advocated a return to small farms and 'spade-husbandry', which may have accounted for his son's interest in Ireland. Thistlewood senior had also possibly been involved with an English man in Paris in raising funds, and had spent the time between the Spa Fields affair and the Cato Street conspiracy moving 'from one midnight meeting to another', building an 'underground chain of communication' across England. He had also been acquainted with Irish veterans of 1798 in London. The uprising he planned for London in the spring of 1820 was to be accompanied by the posting of bills proclaiming a 'Provisional Government'. Indeed, it has been suggested that there was continuity in personnel and ideology between the republicans of 1798, the Despard conspirators and Thistlewood's plot. There appears to be a connection between what Peel's informant told him in 1816 and the details of events in England between late 1816 and early 1820, so it may be that there was some extension of that network to Ireland. The informant presumably felt there was some reason to write from London to the chief secretary in Dublin, just as Grant and Sidmouth later corresponded about a possible connection between English radicalism and Irish agrarian disturbances. It should not be assumed that the same kind of effective intelligence-gathering was available to Grant as was available to Sidmouth, for agrarian collectives were notoriously hard to penetrate, unlike English conspiracies. They were particularly vulnerable, as a result, to the misconceptions of polit-

46 S. Gibbons, 'Rockites and Whitefeet' (1983), 204; S. Palmer, *Police and protest* (1988), 218; SOCP1 2188/11, enclosed with letter from Grant to Sidmouth, 30 May 1820; SC 1824, 139, evidence of Warburton; Thompson, *Making of the English working class*, 673, 761, 766, 772; A.W. Smith, 'Irish rebels and English radicals' (1955), 83.

ical élites. Even if Grant's information was accurate, it is evident that at the very least there was an interchange of motifs, emblems and ideas of liberty.[46]

The anxiety of a ruling élite about its position on both sides of the Irish Sea is readily discernible. The anxiety functioned in two paradigms. One was an anxiety about the possibility of social upheaval and the other was about the potential for nationalist rebellion and independence in Ireland. These were not exclusive. The privileges and position of the established church, for example, were common ideological components of each paradigm, but what is interesting in the case of Ireland is that the social upheaval paradigm has largely been obscured in by nationalist and modernization historiographies. In one, social conflict was subsumed into the cause of national liberation, and in the other the rural poor have been deemed incapable of acting beyond certain limitations imposed by their economic and cultural status before the widespread development of factory production and the associational forms that accompanied it. Some observers, like Denis Browne, were aware of the social dimension to this unrest. On one occasion, even the *Roscommon and Leitrim Gazette* could talk of the rural poor's 'revolutionary designs on property' without mentioning religion or nationalism, but habitually the *Gazette*, and élite sources generally, accentuated the national.[47]

Land, work, prices and law

A common theme in much of the recent historiography of agrarian conflict has been the relative immunity from attack of the head landlord class, contrary to the popular notion of struggle between rapacious Saxons and a homogeneous, oppressed Irish tenantry. The occasions when a landowner was directly attacked were usually made explicit in the State of the Country Papers. However, the papers offer a number of clues about the status of people who were more frequently attacked or disciplined according to customary expectations. For example, some physical description of a house that was visited is often given, which compensates to some degree for the shortage of information regarding farm size or occupation. This might be the mention of whether the building was glazed, the number of doors, the presence of outbuildings, how many floors there were, the presence of live-in servants and the type of roof. Mathew Simpson's information to a magistrate investigating a nocturnal visit to his home reveals that he and his father's servant were made to get up and swear to keep Captain Thresher's laws. Additionally, the use of the word farmer usually signified a more substantial tenant. For example, when thirty or

47 RLG, 23 Aug 1823.

forty people calling themselves Ribbonmen attacked a farmer's house in late 1818 and plundered it for arms, one of their number was shot dead by the farmer's son.[48]

There were further reports of attacks on middling farmers, such as Charles Tinsillant, who has already been encountered in this study. He was described as a wealthy farmer who took a farm of 180 acres on the estate he managed, built a new house and then had it burned down. A yeomanry officer reported the destruction of a farmer's hay and a shot being fired at a Mr McDermott's servant, while another report gave an inventory that could only signify the relative comfort of the victim's home. A man named McCawley fled through the back window of his house during a nocturnal visit and the attackers bayoneted his beds and chests. Then the 'captain' ordered the gang to fire into the lofts. On another occasion attackers were described as having broken down the doors of Thomas Mullins's house in Kilmeane parish, the plural 'doors' signifying comparative wealth. Another man claimed compensation for the burning down of his outhouse, saying it was because he had given evidence against Ribbonmen four years earlier. Similarly, it was reported that out-offices containing wool had been burned down near Castlestrange. The *Roscommon and Leitrim Gazette* noted that 'suspicion rests on some of those persons who were lately dispossessed for non-payment of rent'.[49]

In December 1823 an outhouse with a horse inside was burned down at the other end of the county, near Keadue, and on other occasions windows were broken and the inhabitants sworn not to prosecute Captain Rock's men. Three attacks accompanied by demands for weapons were mounted on the houses of better-off farmers in Moore parish. These examples give an impression of the nature of agrarian conflict in the county over the period. It would be possible to construct an inaccurate table reflecting crimes against members of particular social groups, but the examples considered here give a more valuable qualitative impression of the nature of such conflicts. Land conflicts tended to involve farmers on one side, and cottiers and labourers on the other.[50]

Evidence suggesting that strong farmers were frequently the object of attack does not, of course, prove that they were attacked by employees, conacre sub-

48 SOCP1 1408/34, information of Mathew Simpson, 18 Jan. 1812; SOCP1 1963/43, abstract of reports from general offices and brigade majors of yeomanry for Nov. 1818.   49 SOCP1 1767/42,44, Bowles to Peel, 14 July 1816 and 20 July 1816; SOCP1 1767/48, South to Mahon, 7 Oct. 1816; SOCP1 1776/88, information of McCawley, submitted by Mahon to Peel, 6 Oct. 1816; SOCP1 2502/26, Wills to Gregory, 15 Apr. 1823; SOCP1 2502/30, Wills to Gregory, 4 May 1823; SOCP1 2502/37, Wills to Gregory, 15 July 1823; RLG, 12 July 1823.   50 SOCP1 2502/53, weekly report from Wills to Goulburn, 16 Dec. 1823; SOCP1 2884/19, Warburton, statement of outrages for Nov. 1828; SOCP1 2832/33, information of Daniel Gurin, Moore parish, regarding attack on 5 Mar. 1827.

tenants or cottiers. On some occasions they may have been attacked by rivals for the substantial farms they rented, but there is a strong suggestion that attacks by other substantial farmers were often by people against whom they had given evidence in court or information to magistrates. Given the reluctance of many among the rural population to testify against agrarian rebels, through fear of the sanctions that might be imposed, this appears to confirm that the emergent strong farming class was becoming less likely to feel bound by such unofficial, communal discipline.

The evidence is also sometimes apparently contradictory. For example, when Co. Roscommon was at the periphery of the Thresher disturbances of 1807, it was suggested that the Threshers were 'by no means unpopular with the middling gentry'. On the other hand, a middling farmer called Thomas Sandford, 'a respectable farmer much above the common crop', gave evidence against men who called at his house to persuade him not to testify against one of their number. After his court appearance Sandford had soldiers stationed at his house at the public expense. The steps the authorities took to protect a witness also demonstrate the strength of the moral sanctions imposed by agrarian rebels. It has been suggested that the social composition of a movement could vary according to prevailing economic conditions, which led to the adoption of particular programmes. For example, the movement of 1806–7 was likely to appeal to a broader range among the rural poor, as it involved priests' dues and tithes.[51]

However, when the house of Peter Boland was attacked, the magistrate Devenish did supply the Castle with information about holding size, revealing that Boland was a farmer of forty acres who was shot for refusing to co-operate in punishing a man who had informed the authorities about an unlicensed still. Boland was described as a man with 'strong connections', and it was also suggested that someone in Boland's family might have been implicated in the attack. It may be that lurking behind this incident was a struggle within an emergent strong-farming family group over control of the distilling business in the Strokestown area.[52]

Other incidents that may be connected to economic change and shifts in rural social relations included attacks on graziers. Lieutenant General G.V. Hart reported to Sir Charles Saxton on 23 March 1812 that Co. Roscommon was now the seat of disturbance in the western district and that oaths were administered nightly 'to the lower orders of people and some farmers'. He also considered that the action against herdsmen was taken 'with a view, it is sup-

51 SOCP1 1120/61, Charles Burke, solicitor general, Roscommon, to unnamed, Dublin Castle, 17 Mar. 1807; Donnelly, 'The social composition of agrarian rebellions'. 52 SOCP1 1538/16, Devenish to Peel, 6 Feb. 1813.

posed, of compelling farmers etc to convert their pasture lands into tillage for the production of Grain instead of animal foods for exportation'. A substantial farmer, John Gifford, complained that hundreds were gathering to swear the herdsmen, ordering them to give up the stock in their charge on pain of death. His father had 41 bullocks and 90 sheep at the mercy of the whiteboys and not a night was passing without some new edict.[53]

Actions against grazing, and concerning the price and supply of land, especially for conacre, were a significant cause of grievance over a number of years. A number of incidents in the winter and spring of 1819–20 were typical. There were actions in December 1819 against graziers near Castlerea, when men calling themselves Ribbon men 'assembled by night ... and rode away the horses out of the pasture fields'. Wills reported six weeks later that:

> The Banditti ... swore all the herds belonging to the Gentlemen of the Country to drive the stock off the Lands in order to leave the lands bare, and such is the intimidation exited by their threats, that a number of the Herds actually drove the Cattle home to their Employers residence.

In March 1820 a group of men visited the house of a herdsman in Rahara parish and swore him to give up such work. On the same night a flock of sheep was slaughtered near Strokestown. On the night of Tuesday 28 March 1820 a party of 100 men delivered threatening letters to farmers and agents in the parish of Killinvoy, demanding that the price of conacre be reduced. In 1823, Martin Conway, from near Athlone, was sworn to obey Captain Rock and give up his job as a herdsman to Mr Kelly. The following year, James Knott's herdsman was visited and he was sworn to give up his job. The agrarian protesters were, in many of these instances engaged in disciplining members of their own order according to customs that accorded subsistence rights to all. It was a deeply entrenched notion that the primary use of land was to provide subsistence minima for its occupiers.[54]

A threatening notice posted in St Peter's parish, near Athlone, attacked landlords generally and held out the vague threat of revolutionary social change:

53 SOCP1 1408/39, Hart to Saxton, 28 Mar. 1812; SOCP1 1408/38, John Gifford, Rockhill, to Godfrey Burne, 23 Mar. 1812, enclosed with letter from Gifford to Saxton, 26 Mar. 1812.   54 SOCP1 2074/28, Capt. John Holden to Wills, enclosed with weekly report, 14 Dec. 1819; SOCP1 2176/13, Wills to Grant, 12 Feb. 1820; SOCP1 2176/29, Wills to Gregory, weekly report for proclaimed county of Roscommon, Mon 20 Mar. to Sun 26 Mar. 1820; SOCP1 2502/42, Wills to Gregory, 14 Aug. 1823; RLG, 13 Nov. 1824.

> Whereas by a late act passed by our legislature an act to suppress land-
> lord or landlords that will disposs their tenant or tenants or cant his or
> their effects Now we the Knight of St Patrick's Rock ... do hereby warn
> the inhabitants ... that each and every of them will refrain from taking
> any lands the grass of said lands bid or cant any cattle destrained for rent
> without are severely under the sign of our law ... landlords' lands will
> be left desolate if they remove tenants ... it is the affliction of the poor
> that caused me to express myself in this way ... N.B. It is not in oppo-
> sition to king or country we are but in opposition to such landlords as
> will not lower their lands or such people as will deviate from the above
> act – we do not mean to disposs them of their properties but it shall be
> left in their own hands until the lower the rents.

In the terms suggested by Burke's conceptualization of five possible responses to wrongs, these sentiments are undoubtedly in the radical range. They are
more than the moralism that requires a return to customary relations, for they
demand significant changes in those relations. Yet they do not express the millenarian yearnings sometimes attributed to the crude political programmes of
whiteboys, for the demands made are concrete. Judging from the self-consciousness of 'it is the affliction of the poor that made me express myself in this
way', the writer of the notice was evidently aware that he was moving forward
from a customary outlook to make new demands that might provide a more
permanent solution to his problems. He was also therefore insistent that his
demands were only reformist, and that he did not want to turn the world
upside down. Such embryonic self-consciousness of class position illustrates
the way moral or customary demands were being shifted as a consequence of
structural changes.[55]

There were some attacks on head landlords, which tended to become more
celebrated (such as the assassination of Denis Mahon). Anti-landlord sentiment
was also present in attacks on people connected with substantial landlords, such
as William Guthrie, an agent at Ardmore. His windows and doors were broken
down and a gun was stolen. A threatening notice was left at Patrick Spearman's
house at Mount Cashel. Spearman was wood ranger to Stephen Mahon. Henry
St George, a substantial landowner, was murdered on leaving his brother's estate
near Ballinasloe, just across the river Suck in Co. Galway, and there was a further attempt to assassinate a 'gentleman' near Mount Talbot. In January 1827 a
carriage bearing Lords Churchill and Crofton was pursued for five miles along
the road from Athlone towards Crofton's house at Mote Park, near Roscommon

55 SOCP1 2502/49, threatening notice enclosed with letter from Wills to Goulburn, 13
Nov. 1823; Burke, *Popular culture*, 155.

town, with an unsuccessful attempt being made to stop it as it traversed Kiltoom parish. The attacks on head landlords, such as when the soldiers protecting Lord Hartland's house were pelted with stones, were infrequent. These attacks were doubtless more effective as counter-theatre than as moral sanctions, such as when Thomas McNaghten's evening meal was disturbed by a volley of stones flung through the windows of the room he was dining in. MacNaghten was the owner of a building at West Park, Drum parish, that was being converted into a police station.[56]

A man of 'good character' was murdered near Athlone for not complying with a threatening notice to quit his house and land in the spring of 1820. A band of men forced their way into Michael Kilroy's house in the spring of 1822 and swore him to divide a farm he had recently rented. Almost a year later a nearby house was burned down because a new tenant had taken the property. The same year three more properties were attacked and the occupiers ordered to give up their holdings. When hay was burned, animals maimed and an empty house knocked down in Moore parish, Wills explained that the victims all lived on the estate of Captain Thomas St George and the lands had been surrendered the previous May by the occupying tenants. Suspicion for the attacks on the new tenants' property rested on the former occupiers. It is notable that the lands had been surrendered, not repossessed. The implication was that the former occupiers believed in a right to occupy the lands that was bestowed by custom. The rights thus conferred were more important than their ability to fulfil contractual rent obligations.[57]

Also in 1823, a band of 100 men attacked the houses of seven men who had taken land from Colonel French. The new occupiers were sworn to surrender their holdings. In another similar case a house was burned down in consequence of the occupier taking lands from which defaulting tenants had been evicted. In late 1826 an agent was shot at for driving [distraining] cattle in lieu of rent, and two drivers on the estate of Morgan Crofton near Boyle lost a barn, an outhouse and cattle in an arson attack. A house at Ballyglass was burned down in consequence of the occupier taking lands from which defaulting tenants had been evicted.[58]

56 SOCP1 2176/3, Wills to Gregory, 14 Jan. 1820; SOCP1 2502/26, Wills to Gregory, 15 Apr. 1823; SOCP1 2074/15, inquest into death of Henry St George, 31 Oct. 1819; SOCP1 2766/49, Warburton to Goulburn, 19 Dec. 1826; SOCP1 2832/22, unnamed correspondent to Warburton, 4 Jan. 1827; SOCP1 1963/34, abstract of reports from general offices and brigade majors of yeomanry for Sept. 1818; RLG, 19 Oct 1822.   57 SOCP1 2176/32, W. Handcock to Gregory, 11 Apr. 1820; SOCP1 2363/9, Wills to Gregory, 27 May 1822; SOCP1 2502/27, Wills to Gregory, 16 Apr. 1823; SOC1P 2502/29, Wills to Gregory, 29 Apr. 1823; RLG, 3 May 1823; SOCP1 2502/47, Wills to Goulburn, 18 Oct. 1823.   58 SOCP1 2502/51, Wills to Goulburn, 21 Nov. 1823; SOCP1 2832/23, chief constable John

Such examples, and the number of people involved in enforcing the collective mores of the rural poor, demonstrate amply that land and its occupation were significant causes of conflict. However, agrarian rebels sought to impose a customary control on all aspects of economic life in order to ensure the satisfaction of subsistence needs and provide future security. As Richard Bourke told the 1825 select committee, 'I think they only require security.' Threshers, Ribbon men, Rockites and the variously named agrarian protesters (those are merely the three main whiteboy appellations in the county during the thirty years between 1798 and 1828 – other names like Lamplighters, Steel Boys, Hearts of Steel and Finishers also occurred) acted in defence of their more widely perceived collective economic interests.[59]

For example, in July 1807 Brigade Major Ninian Crawford wrote from Strokestown that whiteboys were 'swearing the People who have Potatoes & other articles for sale not to demand (or take) above a certain price, on pain of being carded'. An innkeeper near Knockcroghery was reported to have been carded in December 1811 for not selling whiskey at a stipulated price. Lieutenant General Meyrick reported from Athlone that several sheep belonging to a farmer in St John's parish had been killed because he had taken land at an increased rent. However, Meyrick concluded:

> the views of these people seem to be to regulate the prices of provisions and liquor, to prevent farmers taking ground over the heads of old tenants and to deter new settlers from coming into the county.

This assessment is not consistent with the familiar view that land and rents were the sole focus for agrarian protest in Ireland, contrary to the price-fixing riot and other mechanisms designed to operate in a market economy such as England's. On 22 February 1817 a crowd took meal and potatoes from several stores at Athlone market and set prices for the sale of the goods. E.P. Thompson suggested price-fixing was known in Ireland, and these Co. Roscommon instances do reveal a blending of Irish tradition with functional responses to economic developments. Eoin Magennis has investigated eighteenth-century price-fixing actions in Ireland, noting that the 'Irish crowd ... continued to right perceived wrongs where they found them'. The examples already described show that the range of grievances encompassed many aspects of the rural poor's economic life and security. A further example of such comprehensive prescriptions for a return to economic stability is contained in a threatening notice:

Browne to Warburton, 5 Jan. 1827; SOCP1 2766/49, Warburton to Goulburn, 19 Dec. 1826; SOCP1 2832/28, chief constable D. Winslow to Warburton, 7 Jan. 1827; SOCP1 2832/23, J. Browne to Warburton, 5 Jan. 1827. **59** SC 1825, 318, evidence of Richard Bourke.

March 11th 1812. God bless the King. Gentlemen and farmers of the parish ... We will not allow any priest but 11 shillings and 4 pence half pence for publick marridge and 1/– for anointing and 1/7 for baptism. No man or woman shall lay offerance only one Crown for Mass and we will not allow any Proctor on any account. Let the parish minister come forth and set his Thydes as usually in the year 1782 any man that asks more than £6 per acre for dunged ground woe be to that man any man that gives more shall share of the same fate any whose lease is up no man shall bid for it till three years after date we were waiting in this parish this many years back Woe be to any man that take this down for 21 days. No more at present but we desire that ye Land Holders and priest and minister of the parish ... to take warning by this we will not allow any publican but 4/– Noggin for spirits, 6 for punch and 4 for brandy. So fare well for a short time. James Farrell, Captn.

The notice was posted again four days later, and is a fascinating glimpse of the consciousness of the rural poor. It prescribed reasonable prices for land, drink and the clerical duties of both the established and Catholic churches, as well as professing loyalty to the crown. In a further notice this Captain Farrell declared 'every man according to his Mens'. It is apparent that land was not the only cause of conflict, and indeed shopping was a significant part of the rural poor's financial calculations. It also looked back to enforce customary rates for tithe collection. This notice demonstrates exactly where the moral response to per-ceived wrongs shaded into the radical response.[60]

In early 1812 Meyrick reported that levies were being collected at night to fund legal defences of accused Threshers, although Co. Roscommon appears to have been one of the few places in the western district, Meyrick's command, which continued to be disturbed. Regulation of food prices was again men-tioned as a cause of such combinations. Prices fell during the summer and rel-ative calm prevailed, according to a subsequent yeomanry report. A farmer who had sold potatoes at market in Ballaghadereen was murdered nearby. This act suggests that the assassin or assassins were among the very poorest and had no cash to buy provisions. They fed and sheltered themselves from the produce of conacre gardens that they paid for in labour. It had been preceded by a

---

60 SOCP2, 157/4233, Brigade Major N. Crawford to Sir Arthur Wellesley, chief secretary, 1 July 1807; SOCP1 1401/7, report of Meyrick, 1 Jan. 1812; SOCP1 1838/19, abstract of reports from general offices and brigade majors of yeomanry for Feb. 1817; Thompson, 'The moral economy reviewed' (1993), 295–6; E. Magennis, 'In search of the "moral econ-omy"' (2000), 207; SOCP1 1408/39, enclosed with letter from Hart to Saxton, 23 Mar. 1812; Burke, *Popular culture*, 155.

notice posted nearby in March which threatened people who sold provisions at market. The notice claimed:

> This is no Thrashing, burning nor Defenderism but seeing that we are all in a state of starvation ... we will gut them and burn them and their proportys to ashes. from Mr 'Fair Play'.

It is significant that the notice expressed a sense of anger that the writer (and his like) were in desperate straits because potatoes were being sold while people were struggling against starvation. This reflects the writer's belief in a right to subsistence, aside from any law of the marketplace. It also appears to be, like the murder of the farmer, an attempt to stop the sale of potatoes, rather than merely regulate prices.[61]

Rather more typical were the notices posted near Ballaghadereen at around the same time which reflected the encroachment of the market. They attempted to regulate prices, rather than abolish markets completely. One warned that:

> Any person that charges a penny more than half a crown here for potatoes and two shillings a stone for meal ... shall be made an example to the whole country,

while another was slightly more generous:

> This is a general notice to all those pitiful rascals that has ... potatoes or meal to sell dare demand or receive no more than three shillings per hundred and two shillings per stone for meal. Now you parcel of devils ye would see your fellow creatures starve for one stone of meal but now let it be known to you ... any man that dare go beyond these rules shall suffer death ... Thomas Costello, [a local magistrate] I expect youl have nothing to do with this notice of mine because I dont meant to harm King and or Country but shivering to prevent starvation ... God Save the King.

The writers of these notices were anxious not to be associated with any more widespread conspiracy and to make clear that their ends were economic, not political. The professions of loyalty to the crown may have been sincere or may have been rhetorical stratagems. The declarations of loyalty were widespread

61 SOCP1 1401/7, report of Meyrick, 1 Jan. 1812; SOCP1 1401/32, Brigade Major Synter to Dublin Castle, undated.

enough for Thomas Drummond to tell the 1839 Lords investigation into Irish disturbances that one of the most common forms of oath used by agrarian protesters declared allegiance to the monarch. This contrasts starkly with the sectarian and nationalist tone of Ribbon oaths. The belief that the king was badly served by ministers and gentry and that if he knew about these injustices they would be rectified (or alternatively that he was not the true king) has been noted in other societies, and recurs in the Co. Roscommon sources. For example, during the Cossack rebellion of 1773 many peasants in Russia saw the gentry, not the monarchy, as the cause of their distress and sought protection from a just monarch; the 'good tsar' motif was a vital ideological component of Pugachev's rebellion. Similarly, 'Blacks' in eighteenth-century England declared their loyalty to the house of Hanover. Such stratagems were not confined to the rural poor, and appeared during the agitation in favour of Queen Caroline as a means to attack the corruption of the Hanoverian court when George IV acceded to the throne in 1820.

The discourse of Irish agrarian rebels bears comparison with the common radical theme that it was ministers or landlords, rather than the crown, that were to blame for the people's woes. There was no intimation of a desire for liberation from the crown.[62]

Comprehensive notices dealing with many aspects of economic life continued to appear, although at certain times with different emphases. Catholic clergy fees were a central complaint in 1813, but in 1820 Wills mistakenly reported:

> In the years 1813, 1814 and 1815, when they assumed the name of Carders and Threshers such a practice prevailed but under the Ribbon system I have never known it to exist in this county.

As noted earlier, dues to Catholic clergy were indeed mentioned in March 1820, in notices posted from one end of the county to the other. These fixed prices for crops, set the fees for Catholic clergy of 11s. 4½d. for marriage and 2s. 8½d. for the last sacraments, as well as tithes to be paid to the minister at 6d. per acre, tilled or untilled, no proctors to be allowed, no vestry money to be paid by Catholics and 'no man whatsoever to bid, propose or demand anothers ground or land'. The comprehensiveness of the economic prescriptions of the whiteboys is again striking.[63]

62 SOCP1 1408/24, notices enclosed with Charles Costello, Ballaghadereen, to unnamed, Dublin Castle, 30 Mar. 1812; SC 1839, 1,127, evidence of Thomas Drummond; P. Longworth, 'The Pugachev revolt' (1974), 243; Thompson, *Whigs and hunters* (1990), 146; Thompson, 'The patricians and the plebs' (1993), 92–3.   63 SOCP1 2176/49, Wills to Grant, 8 June 1820; SOCP1 2188/10, enclosed with Brown to Gregory, 27 May 1820.

Concerns associated with industrial conflict and rudimentary versions of industrial tactics could also arise. For example, on the night of 2 June 1823, 30 to 40 perches of a ditch were destroyed alongside a new road being built near Strokestown. The cause was apparently that the workers on the road had been insufficiently diligent, and as a result their employers had suggested that they might be paid, henceforth, a fixed fee for completion of the project. Wills explained:

> it appears that a combination exists amongst the workmen employed to prevent the work being undertaken by contract in order to protract its performance that employment might be afforded the longer to the labouring classes.

There were a number of other cases of industrial conflict. The owner of the Lissdiernan mills, Roscommon town, was attacked on 25 November 1821, and on 14 January 1823 windows were broken and threatening notices posted at Daly's mill near Athlone. Twenty people broke into Gonville French's stable at Ballyforan, assaulted his servants and told them to tell French to raise the wages of the men.[64]

The memory of perceived wrongs or past defeats could also stimulate whiteboy activity. In January 1812 Samuel Hodson of Hodson's Bay reported an attempt by Threshers to compel people to build a road and bridge at a point where some had been killed while fleeing from the army in 1795. Hodson reported:

> in the year 1795 after burning Mr Mills's house their flight was interrupted and a considerable number of their body, then called Defenders, killed and drowned.

It is worth noting that the Threshers had, according to this source, been related to the Defenders. This appears to demonstrate a continuity in the perception of agrarian protest by some members of non-farming élites. Hodson, like most of his peers, erroneously saw a straightforward continuity between Defenderism and the Threshers, saying that in 1795 they were 'then called

---

64 SOCP1 2502/36, Wills to Gregory, 9 July 1823; SOCP1 2363/2, Wills to Gregory, 23 Feb. 1822; SOCP1 2502/22, Wills to Goulburn, 23 Jan. 1823; SOCP1 2884/16, statement of outrages for May 1828; SOCP1 2886/12, statement of outrages for Apr. 1828.

Defenders'. However, Denis Browne saw a dimension to the 1798 rebellion that has perhaps been obscured by other events of that year, when there was only a handful of United Irishmen in Boyle: he explicitly linked the participation of the poor in the 1798 rebellion to social injustice, rather than a developed sense of national oppression, writing that 'the people burst from those tramels and this misrule into Rebellion'. Matthew Lyster, a Co. Roscommon magistrate, had written to the Castle in the autumn of 1798 to request the assistance of troops to put down Houghers and defend jails. It is interesting to note that Lyster had also given the movement the name attached to the earliest outbreak of agrarian violence, that which afflicted Connacht in the second decade of the eighteenth century. This appellation, importantly, located whiteboyism in a tradition of agrarian rebellion and not necessarily in one of nationalist revolt. Nevertheless, these reports demonstrate the impossibility of making absolute distinctions between the agrarian movements and the nationalist Defender-Ribbon political current.[65]

Alongside the link suggested by Browne was a continuity in the legitimizing consciousness of the agrarian rebels. Indeed, while the rural poor continued to perceive social relations in terms of custom, the disengagement of élites from paternalist notions of social relations remained incomplete, despite the embracing of improvement. It is apparent that people like Viscount Lorton sent such mixed messages, and it ought to be noted that changes in outlook were gradual, rather than irruptive. Echoes of paternalism and deference may be found in the threatening notice posted on an estate gate in Drum parish in August 1823, which said that if it was not for the kindness of the mistress to the poor, 'the plantation would be consumed to the hall door'. Another landlord reduced conacre rents to £1 an acre after hearing of a potato crop failure in 1828. The previously-mentioned Studders would not be hurt out of respect for Mrs Armstrong, 'as she been a good Gentlewoman in the place'. Dr John Church gave evidence to the 1824 parliamentary enquiry into Irish disturbances of a parish priest's gratitude for a one-third rent abatement and the provision of almost constant employment by Lord Headley. Warburton spoke of people's attachment to the landlord if he was considered a gentleman. Richard Griffith, a civil engineer, told the same hearings that the lower orders respected the higher gentry more than their immediate landlords. A Catholic civil servant, Anthony Blake, expressed similar views:

65 SOCP1 1408/28, Samuel Hodson, Hodson's Bay, to Major Gen. Doyle, 10 Jan. 1812; Mattimoe, *North Roscommon*, 145; SOCP1 2175/9, D. Browne to unnamed, Dublin Castle, 23 Jan. 1820; SOCP1 1017/45, Matthew Lyster to unnamed, 19 Oct. 1798.

> I do not think that the man who sub-lets, has that sort of feeling towards the person to whom he lets, that the proprietor of the land would have.

What was being described to the parliamentary committees was the emergence of landlords who viewed land as a commercial proposition and who were not custom-bound, after the comparative laxity and indulgence of eighteenth century landlord and tenant relations. However, the poor did not accept such paternalism without conditions and, also, paternal care may have been an example of a 'studied technique of rule'. The Revd Michael Collins suggested such an approach, telling the 1824 select committee that looking after the poor would make them 'feel an interest in the continuance of the existing order of things', much as Archbishop Kelly had suggested emancipation might have 'a soothing effect', even if it had little material benefit for the rural poor.[66]

A long complaint from a magistrate to Dublin Castle on 18th March 1807 was an example of the frustration felt by crown servants at the solidarity displayed in the court room between jurors and the accused. A respectable farmer had been forced to swear an unlawful oath after a search for arms at his house during the night. Three defence witnesses provided fabricated alibis, contradicting each other, and the conduct of a member of the jury was particularly remarked on as 'a curious instance of the casuistry by which men can reconcile themselves to doing what they know to be wrong. He required the juror's oath to be repeated, and exclaim'd, "I knew it was so, our oath is to find according to the evidence".' Another complaint was of 'would-be legislators' who, on 18 June 1807, carded a man near Ballaghadereen. He was found guilty on two counts, one of being a herdsman and another of selling potatoes above the price the Threshers allowed.[67]

These two examples demonstrate the ambivalence, if not outright hostility, felt by the rural poor towards the official law when it did not concur with custom. The second complainant used the language of law to describe the norms asserted by the poor against a particular transgressor. Further examples

66 SOCP1 2502/46, enclosed with letter from Wills to Goulburn, 25 Sept. 1823; RLG, 23 Aug. 1828; SOCP1 2176/17, threatening notice enclosed with letter from Wills to Grant, 24 Feb. 1820; SC 1824, 422, evidence of John Church; SC 1824, 161, evidence of George Warburton; SC 1824, 232, evidence of Richard Griffith; SC 1825, 38, evidence of Anthony Blake; Thompson, 'The patricians and the plebs', 64; SC 1824, 363, evidence of Revd Michael Collins; SC 1825, 245, evidence of James Doyle, bishop of Kildare and Leighlin. 67 SOCP1 1120/63, Burke to unnamed, 18 Mar. 1807; SOCP1 1120/47, Seymour to unnamed, 15 July 1807.

of this can be found throughout the sources and, indeed, threatening notices and agrarian actions often adopted a counter-theatrical legal language, suggesting a customary outlook at odds with the official legal system. The very acts of swearing oaths, serving notices and punishing wrongdoers can be seen as parallel legal actions defined by a customary consciousness, one that was increasingly in conflict with the official legal system. In such opposing conceptions of justice, one based on the rights of property and the other on customary balances of rights and responsibilities, social antagonisms were becoming ever more sharply defined. Threatening notices across Ireland in the 1820s were frequently written in terms of a legal code applied to anyone who interfered with age-old custom. John Kelly, the parish priest from Mitchelstown, told the 1825 parliamentary enquiry that there was a widespread lack of confidence in the justice system and that one of Ireland's greatest blessings would be to have an equal distribution of justice to all classes. Kelly added:

> I do not here make distinction of classes as it regards religion, but I mean the poor and the rich.

Some other aspects of the 'counter-theatre' of agrarian combinations may be considered alongside these specifically 'legal' ones, and illustrated by a number of examples.[68]

John Wills reported that nightly meetings of men in uniforms of white shirts were taking place in Oran parish during early 1814. The men were being sworn to obey Captain Thresher's laws. The sense of a parallel, customary authority, is expressed here in the costumes (which also had the practical value of disguise), the oath and the rank attributed to the leader. Such meetings were reported frequently at this time, from Co. Longford, to the east, through Co. Roscommon, to Co. Mayo. A notice reported in the *Roscommon and Leitrim Gazette* in 1822 warned that 'General Springlawn will not allow paper servers in his dominion'.[69]

In 1820 Wills again noted aspects of counter-theatre when a battle took place between the police and a body of about 400 men between Ballintober and Oran. The rebels were formed into divisions and had an advanced guard. After the confrontation, two hats with badges on them were recovered. It may be noted in passing that Wills was also keenly aware of the value of theatre. He ordered that the body of a whiteboy killed in the confrontation be taken to Roscommon town, where it was market day, and there exhibited, 'which I think

---

68 Gibbons, *Captain Rock*, 22; SC 1825, 397, evidence of Revd John Kelly.   69 SOCP1 1560/3, Brigade Major D'Arcy, Longford, to unnamed, Dublin Castle, 1 July 1814; SOCP1 1560/6, Hart to Peel, 1 Jan. 1814; RLG, 4 May 1822.

may have a good effect'. Similarly, a week later, Wills suggested that 'where the punishment is capital ... it should be carried into effect at such places as the outrages occurred and their bodies not given up to their friends'. The parallel with the approach taken by the Tyburn authorities is striking.[70]

On another occasion the men who collected money in Tibohine parish 'for the alleged purpose of relieving their brethren' described themselves as the police. Such titles were designed to bestow authority upon men who might otherwise have appeared merely criminal, and legitimized their actions as being according to a legal system, however unofficial.[71]

So, conflict was expressed in a language of law, justice and legislation. This was recognized by Sir Edward Crofton in bitter anticipation of a forthcoming nocturnal gathering. Seeking advice from the Castle on how to proceed, he remarked that, whatever happened, 'I shall have the fiery ordeal of the Irish parliament to pass'. This 'parliament' legislated that no-one should co-operate in the prosecution of alleged whiteboys, a problem complained of frequently by magistrates. For example, Wills complained that at assizes in early 1814 the jury had resolved to acquit nine accused men if capital indictments had pro-ceeded. Although the nine people were sentenced only to transportation, the houses of those who gave evidence were attacked and burned down shortly afterwards. Whitworth had noted the disproportion between the number of committals for agrarian crime and the number of convictions, which he took to be proof of a disordered society. It can be observed that it was proof of the rural poor seeking to impose their own order on society, and their adherence to their own conception of justice.[72]

Other aspects of agrarian conflict might also illustrate the customary con-sciousness of the Irish rural poor. The attacks on men who took land given up by others illustrate the belief that the fundamental right of a tenant (and oblig-ation upon the landowner to provide) was the means of subsistence. It has already been noted that men who gave up land nevertheless felt embittered and often attempted to impose sanctions upon incoming occupiers. The Church of Ireland bishop of Elphin complained that agrarian protest was 'occupied in removing the property of every person whose landlord has it under seizure for rent'. The tone of the bishop's letter betrayed that he did not understand how the whiteboys failed to share his straightforward sense of contract law. The response to distraint of cattle for arrears of rent illustrates the tenacious attachment to custom that created a solidarity among the poor. More than 200

70 SOCP1 2176/15, Wills to Grant, 12 Feb, 1820, 19 Feb. 1820; P. Linebaugh, 'The Tyburn riot' (1975).   71 SOCP1 2176/30, Wills to Gregory, 3 Apr. 1820.   72 SOCP1 1538/, Crofton to unnamed, Dublin Castle, 13 Aug. 1813; SOCP1 1558/27, Wills to Gre-gory, 13 Mar. 1814; Whitworth, *statement*, 1.

people turned out to help recover cattle when Roger O'Connor, Patrick Dyer and others drove cattle in lieu of rent in January 1815. The cattle were forcibly rescued. Similarly, in October 1822 around 200 people assembled near Carrick-on-Shannon, tied up a guard and carried off oats and potatoes that were under seizure for arrears of rent. There is a real sense here of a community's norms (and an acknowledgement of a right to a livelihood) being enforced. These norms could be upheld in surprising ways, as on an occasion when whiteboys were accused of compelling people to repair roads.[73]

It will be recalled that workers on a road-building project combined against contracting out the work so that they could prolong their employment. Workers also believed that job opportunities should be distributed fairly. A notice was posted which claimed that 'any man taking a task shall suffer punishment for so doing Because the Country at large is against it without giving every man his chanch'. The notice demanded work opportunities equal to those enjoyed by Lord Hartland's tenants.[74]

It is clear that whiteboy activity reflected beliefs about fairness and justice that cannot be easily accommodated within the historiographies of nationalism or modernization. Yet the repertoires of resistance were being transformed as the rural population became increasingly socially and economically differentiated. To borrow the terms used by Peter Burke, the moral response was being transformed into a radical response. The next chapter will trace the continuing conflict in Co. Roscommon as far as the great famine, again seeking to consider such conflicts in terms of the historiography of popular protest.

73 SOCP1 1767/56, Trench to Peel, 10 Dec. 1816; SOCP1 1956/26, information of constable Roger O'Connor, Boyle, 20 Jan. 1815; RLG, 19 Oct. 1822; SOCP1 2074/29, Lt. Col. John French to O'Loghlin, undated (Dec. 1819).   74 SOCP1 2502/36, notice enclosed with letter from Wills to Gregory, 9 July 1823.

5

Repertoires of dissent

There were a number of significant ways in which Irish society changed as the first half of the nineteenth century proceeded. These changes included land-lord improvements, economic integration into the United Kingdom and the well-known demographic explosion. There were also significant changes in the tactics of whiteboys, although the persistence of conflict legitimized by refer-ence to custom, tradition and subsistence rights is notable. Despite changes such as a decrease in night time agrarian activities, in the use of disguise and, significantly, increasingly direct conflict with landlords and the state, the Irish rural poor's views of rights and obligations continued to be informed by a cus-tomary consciousness. Can the shift towards direct conflict that did occur be ascribed either to the emergence and hegemony of O'Connellite nationalism from the late 1820s onwards, or to any progressive modernization of political, economic and social life?

'The foolish and disgraceful conduct of the peasantry'

There were few instances of popular protest that might be interpreted as expressing national sentiments. These included disturbances at election times, such as when the O'Conor Don was elected MP in January 1835. Before polling day, six ewes belonging to John Heague of Strokestown were killed in Lisanuffy parish, Chief Constable Thomas Blakeney attributing this to Heague's inten-tion to vote for Barton, the O'Conor Don's opponent. Two notices posted in Strokestown the following month warned Heague, 'take Notice if you dare to sow the land you took from Mr Conry that was held by the tenants for four years you will be sorry for it.' The second notice declared 'if you attempt to deprive the poor Tenants that got the trouble of reclaiming the Field that you took from Mr Conry you will repent it'.[1]

Thomas Conry was an agent to the Mahon family, the major landowners in the Strokestown area, and it appears that Heague had been installed in a consolidated farm after the removal of rundale partners or a number of small farmers from the lands in question. From the second of these notices

---

1 OR 1835/7, Thomas Blakeney, chief constable, Strokestown, to Warburton, 15 Jan. 1835; OR 1835/10, enclosed with letter from Blakeney to Warburton, 20 Feb. 1835.

may be derived a sense that rights to occupy land were held by those whose toil had made it viable, rather than the contractual right conferred by a lease. The slaughter of ten sheep belonging to Lord Hartland in the Strokestown demesne was possibly related to this dispute. Chief Constable Blakeney's attribution of the slaughter of the ewes to Heague's support for one candidate against the Catholic aristocrat in the election was erroneous, and illustrates the problems posed by sources that rely on the interpretations of police and state officials. Similarly, Blakeney attributed an action intended to intimidate another landlord, Gilbert Hogg, as a consequence of Hogg voting for Barton in the election. This was in March 1835, when three roods of conacre land at Culbeg in Kilglass parish, which were stripped for burning, were turned back. A grave and a cross were erected at the site 'for the purposes of intimidation'. Another explanation may be found in the Hogg family's tough attitude to its tenants. Gilbert Hogg's exploits had appeared frequently in the pages of the *Roscommon Journal* after he faced two murder charges, and his father Godfrey was habitually among the hardliners when the magistracy met to condemn whiteboyism and call for government action. Such ongoing conflicts between farmers and their sub-tenants, sustained over a number of years, were instances of endemic social conflict in the pre-famine Irish countryside. Indeed, stipendiary magistrate Samuel Vignoles told the Lords 1839 committee hearings that not one person in prison for collective agrarian crime had stated that separation from England had been his or her objective.[2]

Antipathies based on religion might also be indicators of an emergent O'Connellite nationalist consciousness (this being the period when the United Irish rhetoric of universal fraternity was being replaced by more confessionally exclusive senses of nationality). These, too, are infrequent in the sources. There is an 1835 reference to an armed party being assembled near Keadue one night in the hope of encountering Leitrim Orangemen, whose meeting night it was (although O'Connell's nationalism was avowedly non-sectarian, it assumed the Irish nation to be a Catholic one). In November 1837 two windows were smashed at James Brown's house in Tibohine parish. Chief Constable Frederick Carr reported that Brown attributed this to his having 'cast some reflections on the Catholic religion some time ago in the hearing of two of his neighbours'. In December 1840 Chief Constable Daly reported a piece of counter-theatre. Gowns, religious books and cupboards belonging to Sir Gilbert King had been burned in the school room at Charlestown, Kilmore parish. It seems likely that these items were the object of a symbolic

2 OR 1835/20, Blakeney to Warburton, 25 Mar. 1835; RJ, 30 Jan. 1830; HL 1839, 302, evidence of Captain Samuel Vignoles.   3 OR 1835/22, Robert Curtis, chief constable, Boyle,

attack because of their association with a Protestant attempt to evangelize among the children of Catholics.[3]

This was also the period when manifestations of popular religion were being replaced by a more ultramontane version of Catholicism, although before the famine its success in dispelling this rival popular belief system was 'remarkably unimpressive'. This process might be seen as a concomitant of the abandoning by the Catholic middle class of customary attitudes to social and economic arrangements. The Catholic Church was attempting to break the hold of customary religious beliefs in pursuit of its own agenda at the same time as landlords were disengaging from customary social relations with the rural poor. Instead of appearing as the steadfast friend of the oppressed, as suggested in nationalist historiography, the Catholic clergy were more often found sternly admonishing whiteboys. From the 1820s onwards, summoned by O'Connell, the Catholic clergy became political agitators, but their agitation was not aligned with the primitive politics of the rural poor. The Catholic priest 'was … taking sides in a conflict within his congregation'.[4]

In 1845 the Revd Edward Dillon spoke out from the pulpit after an angry crowd forced a police officer to take refuge. He said that the officer was only doing his job. Constable Robert Buskerville reported to Frederick Carr, the Castlerea chief constable, that the Revd Dillon 'deprecated the system of wight boys and that it was calculated to marr the prospects of men of foresight and of talent who were labouring for their country's good'. The implied approval of the constitutional methods of O'Connell was contrasted with the hostility of the crowd towards a representative of the state. Some historians have assumed that hostility to the state means hostility to a colonial state, and have taken it as evidence of nationalist consciousness. Michael Beames made that assumption when claiming that agrarian rebels rarely attacked state officials. He took this to mean there was no nationalist consciousness among the rebels, but might have come to the same conclusion by considering whether the whiteboys considered the state to be a colonial one. It is not the case that attacks on state officials were rare in Co. Roscommon in the first half of the nineteenth century. However, Beames also asserts, correctly, that the police were objected to not because they were representatives of a colonial regime but because they were obstacles to the administration of whiteboy justice. Clark and Donnelly suggested that Catholic farmers could be the objects of local, economic antagonism but that generalized outlooks viewed Protestantism and the state as ene-

to Warburton, 13 Apr. 1835; OR 1837/145, Frederick Carr, chief constable, Castlerea, to W. Miller, deputy inspector general of police, 13 Nov. 1837; OR 1840/30151, John Daly, chief constable, Elphin, to James Shaw Kennedy, inspector general of police, 3 Dec. 1840.
4 Connolly, *Priests and people*, 272, 239.

mies. Yet, the state could be viewed as an enemy without it being seen as a colo-nial or Protestant state. Indeed, the Roscommon sources for the study of white-boyism suggest that state officials like the police were seen as oppressors of the poor, rather than as deniers of religious or national freedoms.[5]

One of the county's bastions of Catholic opinion, which was becoming coterminous with nationalist opinion, was the *Roscommon Journal*. It passed comment on the Saturday after Fr Dillon had opined from the pulpit that 'this county has never been in so disturbed a state, owing to the wretchedness of the peasantry'. The publisher, Charles Tully, reminded readers of his previ-ous warning that there would be a reaction from the poor if there were wide-spread evictions to make way for graziers, but he added, 'we deprecate as much as others the foolish and disgraceful conduct of the peasantry.' Tully's approach to agrarian violence thus had two elements. One, highly critical of some landowners, believed the worst excesses of landlordism had to be con-trolled. The other was equally critical of the rural poor when they took direct action against those excesses, however legitimate their grievances. Tully was aware of the potential for social upheaval inherent in challenges to those rights – rights that the emergent Catholic commercial class was striving to share. This approach foreshadows that of later nationalist writers like Sullivan, sym-pathizing with their co-religionists' wretchedness but not condoning any action the poor might take for themselves if it appeared to contest the prin-ciple of the rights of property.[6]

In April 1846 there was an attack on a house where a Catholic priest had dined and was reposing. The priest called out to tell the attackers who he was and was told 'to mind his own affair'. Glass was broken in the hall door. The detail about the hall door suggests that the priest was staying with someone of fairly substantial means. The whiteboys were certainly not impressed by the fact that there was a Catholic priest within the house they were attacking. Nor were they impressed when the Revd M. Walker preached against Molly Maguire at the chapel of Elphin, members of the congregation reportedly laughing aloud. This detail suggests the laughter was a ritual humiliation of the priest, not unlike the rough music deployed to show up transgressors against customary norms in other societies.[7]

In January 1848 joint resolutions penned by the Catholic parish priests of Lisanuffy and Cloonfinlough were submitted to Dublin Castle, proclaiming:

5 OR 1845/6723, Robert Buskerville, constable, to Carr, 17 Mar. 1845; Beames, *Peasants and power*, 144; S. Clark and J.S. Donnelly, 'The tradition of violence: introduction' (1983). 6 RJ, 20 Mar. 1845.   7 OR 1846/9631, David Duff, resident magistrate, Roscommon, to Richard Pennefather, under-secretary, 21 Apr. 1846; RLG, 16 May 1845.

we hold in horror & detestation the detestable crimes of Assassination by which this County has been recently afflicted ... while hundreds of our unfortunate neighbours were – as they *now* are – famishing around us, not a half dozen of individuals were found to disturb the rights of property by the commission of Petty Larceny.

The priests, like Tully, condemned whiteboyism, but sympathized with the lot of the poor. They believed that the Castle ought to be impressed by the lack of ordinary crime in such a desperate situation. However, the phrase 'rights of property', used so often by landowners like Lorton, had found its way into the lexicon of Catholic clergymen, even when such rights might perhaps have been reasonably mitigated by the extraordinary circumstances of the famine. In July the same year the Catholic parish priest of Roscommon was commended to the under-secretary for keeping his flock 'in very good order'. The priest, who was also chaplain to the county prison, specialized in using the dying recantations of condemned men against whiteboyism. In 1849, when resident magistrate John Kirwan suspected renewed agrarian activity in his district, he reported that he had denounced it at the Boyle petty sessions and that the 'Priests from the Altars have done the same'. It is apparent that, despite some exceptions, the popular nationalist image of religious oppression and the solidarity of clergy and oppressed along confessional lines is a significant distortion. Indeed, the separation between priests and the poor continued until the famine as the 'devotional revolution' gathered pace and as the clergy became increasingly identified with the farming, shopkeeping and professional classes.[8]

Families, factions and strangers

The historiography that places agrarian conflict on a linear continuum that pre-dates the development of associational forms based on social and economic distinctions suggests that solidarities and conflicts before such a development were based on parochial and kin networks. There are a number of examples that suggest such loyalties and divisions, but these are many fewer than those suggesting collective antipathies and actions. However, intra-family disputes, abductions, and factional loyalties reflect the survival strategies of farming families. Use of disguise and hostility to strangers may

8 OR 1848/41, resolutions of Roman Catholic parish priests of Lisanuffy and Cloonfinlough, 9 Jan. 1848; OR 1848/443, M.C. Browne, Roscommon, to Thomas Redington, under-secretary, 31 July 1848; OR 1849/412, John Kirwan, resident magistrate, Boyle, to Redington, 8 Nov. 1849.

be seen as having a practical logic in the concrete circumstances of the time. The anonymous threatening letter, the oath and the use of disguise might be associated with societies of clientage or dependence, when associational class forms like the trade union and friendly society were as yet unknown. Such a society might be expected to persist longer in a rural setting, where the strength of the collective discipline of the workplace was less likely to bind workers to each other. However, the collective identity of class organizations was prefigured by the communal discipline located in the customary consciousness of the rural poor. Threatening letters, oaths and disguise continued to be used throughout the period under consideration, although they do appear to have been less frequent as the mid-nineteenth century approached. It was certainly much less common for whiteboys to display paraphernalia such as ribbons (which had been considered evidence of surviving Jacobite affiliation in early nineteenth-century reports of agrarian conflict), although as late as November 1828 Thomas and Johnston Morton described witnessing a gang wearing white ribbons on their hats attack a group of police officers. Similarly, the 'tree of liberty' image that was associated with Paine and Jacobinism no longer appeared in the second quarter of the nineteenth century. In October 1836, men armed with pitchforks, with blackened faces and wearing white shirts over their coats, robbed a woman in Kilronan parish of money her husband had been given by the master at the Arigna iron works. Similarly, a group of men with straw fixed around their hats and wearing their coats inside-out removed distrained furniture from a house in Boyle parish. In January 1841 seven men with blackened faces swore John Maguire of Clonaff half-parish not to serve any more 'law papers'. The reversed coats may have provided a sense of uniform and collective solidarity for these groups, as well as being, on their part, a sensible precaution against recognition by constables. Indeed, these examples suggest responses to concrete social and economic circumstances, rather than evidence of a pre-modern place in a meta-narrative of modernization.[9]

Disputes among or between kin groups also occurred. John Dunican of Ballinamene was murdered on the way home from drinking in December 1835. At the inquest into his death Edward McKeane and Pat Flynn were blamed. Chief Constable Robert Curtis suggested that 'some spite' had

9 CSORP 1828/W108, information of Thomas and Johnston Morton, enclosed with letter from Warburton to marquis of Anglesey, lord lieutenant, 22 Nov. 1828; OR 1836/112, Curtis to Warburton, 28 Oct. 1836; OR 1837/64, Curtis to Miller, 3 June 1837; OR 1841/1077, information of John Maguire, enclosed with letter from Daly to inspector general of police, 26 Jan. 1841.

existed between these men and Dunican because he had mistreated his wife, who was a relative of theirs. In February the next year Peter Cunningham of Ballinafad, just over the boundary in Co. Sligo, died after his brother-in-law, Owen Sharket, poisoned him. Sharket's object 'was to be possessed of property that would be left to the deceased by his father'. In May 1836 Peter Kelehar died after he was beaten by Patrick Lennan of Mount Talbot. The two men had been drinking whiskey and had quarrelled over payment. Chief Constable Edward Sparling noted that they were near relatives. On 22 December 1837 Sally McGreevy, aged 80, was murdered by her daughter-in-law Mary, in Ardcarn parish. The two women had lived together for several years, 'but on the most unhappy terms'.[10]

These murderous incidents reveal some interesting aspects of agrarian crime. It appears that when family or neighbour disputes arose, they tended to be more violent than collective conflicts. It is a weakness of David Fitzpatrick's argument that agrarian disputes were based on the loyalties and antipathies of family and neighbourhood that he used findings from only one parish, one that was notorious for its violence. Fitzpatrick has also used a relatively narrow period. It is possible that Fitzpatrick's reliance on the reports from Cloone, Co. Leitrim, distorted his view of the reasons for conflict. It is also apparent that such disputes were recorded most frequently in Co. Roscommon in the late 1830s, the years when the reports for the county appear to be most comprehensive. Indeed, it is questionable whether some of the reports, particularly from this period, can be considered reports of collective crime at all. The label 'outrage reports' might be changed to 'crime reports'. It also reveals that family disputes were just that. Disputes between or among families over land were never conducted by large assemblies of people turning out to enforce one person's claim against a member of their own family or a neighbour; nor did they ensure the enforcement of the mores of the community, although the participants might want to persuade people they were doing that. A number of examples illustrate this. In September 1836 John Finnerty of Kilglass parish claimed his mearings had been thrown down by his brother, although the reporting police officer was not inclined to believe him because the two brothers were in dispute over land. In the same parish the following August Bernard Donohoe found his potatoes and cabbages cut down. He blamed Patrick, Michael and James

10 OR 1835/51, Curtis to Warburton, 17 Dec. 1835; OR 1836/16, William Galbraith, sub-inspector of constabulary, to Drummond, 14 Feb. 1836; OR 1836/60, Edward Sparling, chief constable, Roscommon, to Galbraith, 9 May 1836; OR 1837/149, Reed to Miller, undated (Dec. 1837).

Donohoe, whom Blakeney described as relatives of Bernard. Blakeney con-
fided in the deputy chief inspector of police that the tale appeared doubtful
and that a family dispute over a pig was behind the allegation. In February
1839 there was a 'riot' between two related families named Kean in Kilgefin
parish after one man tried to remove potatoes from the land of another without paying the due rent. Such family disputes may be the point where faction fighting and agrarian combination appear most closely connected. The
brother of John Hanly, the Catholic parish priest in Kilgefin, believed it was
relatives who stole £400 from the priest's house in November 1839. In June
1840 houses were attacked in Kilronan parish in an attempt to compel a
family member to supply potatoes to a relative. A Catholic priest was suspected of posting a notice on the chapel wall and, at Cootehall, advising people not to frequent John Bruen's public house because of a dispute between
the priest and Bruen, who was married to the cleric's niece. In February
1852 the Catholic parish priest of Termonbarry, James McNally, complained that a parishioner, Constantine Maguire, had entered the chapel and
broken into pieces a pew McNally had just erected for members of his own
family. The new pew had been erected where Maguire's used to be. These
instances demonstrate the ways in which the forms of communal discipline
could be appropriated to pursue private grievances.[11]

Faction fights may be seen as part of the culture of the Irish countryside,
but as one characteristic, rather than a paradigm, of the customary consciousness of the rural poor. These set-piece battles seem to have been partly
recreational routine, partly the communally-legitimized expression of family
tensions and antipathies. They happened most frequently on fair and market
days after drink had been taken, or after funerals and other solemn or festival
occasions. In December 1835 a party of men returning from a funeral in Co.
Leitrim gathered and attacked a pub at Crossna, near Cootehall, where some
men belonging to another faction were drinking. It is apparent that most factions were bound together by a neighbourhood or family loyalty, and that fairs
and drink were almost essential elements, although two groups of ten men
were arrested for fighting after mass one Friday in March 1836 at the chapel
of Aughamore, Ballaghadereen. A faction fight based on family loyalty took
place at Elphin in May 1842 between the Feenys and the Byrnes. Similarly,

11 OR 1836/106, Blakeney to Warburton, 10 Oct. 1836; OR 1837/96, Blakeney to Miller,
7 Aug. 1837; OR 1839/1000, Sparling to Miller, 21 Feb. 1839; OR 1839/9728, John Blake,
resident magistrate, to inspector general of police, 17 Nov. 1839; OR 1840/10689, Reed to
inspector general of police, 11 June 1840; OR 1842/8847, outrage report, 15 May 1842,
Crossna, Ardcarn parish; OR 1852/60, Blakeney to Carr, 1 Mar. 1852.

police dispersed the Giblin and Dowd factions after they assembled to fight in January 1843. As noted earlier, as late as 1850 a resident magistrate reported having prevented a faction fight that was due to take place at Cootehall races, and another at Killukin races. On some occasions the factions made peace hastily to attack the police, and on others they appeared to be cover for more sinister combinations, as noted in the previous chapter. In 1845 one resident magistrate welcomed faction fights as an alternative to agrarian combination. After dispersing a faction fight in Elphin on St Stephen's Day, John Blake wrote:

> One good result that may be anticipated from this disposition to riot on the part of the Country People will be, viz, that it will lead in a great measure to knock up the system of Outrage, as it will much shake the confidence they had in each other, and informations may be more easily obtained.

The fact that the fight occurred on St Stephen's Day suggests also the recreational or quasi-ceremonial nature of such collective conflicts. Blake's view reflected widely believed élite perceptions that factions were a welcome and relatively innocent distraction from the serious business of agrarian conflict. The 1824 select committee had been told that 'some people think it a good thing to set the lower classes at variance'. It is possible that even until the great famine, factions reflected continuing loyalties to local pre-confiscation élite families whose descendants had become the underground gentry, and who were reappearing among the nationalist strong farmer stratum.[12]

Family-centred disputes were often ostensibly about marriage. Such disputes were frequently accompanied by the abduction of a woman whose dowry included a piece of coveted or desirable land. They arose most frequently among the better-off farming and retailing families. In December 1835 a group of men abducted a widow called Mary Berne from a house at Ballykilcline, Kilglass parish, to compel her to marry one of the group. The following month five men

12 OR 1842/8847, outrage report, 15 May 1842, Crossna, Ardcarn parish; OR 1836/21, J. Ireland, Castlebar, to Drummond, 2 Apr. 1837; OR 1842/9591, outrage report, 25 May 1842; OR 1843/1723, outrage report, 20 Jan. 1843; OR 1850/3, John Duckworth, resident magistrate, Boyle, to unnamed, Dublin Castle, 10 Jan. 1850; OR 1851/1, Duckworth to unnamed, Dublin Castle, 31 Dec. 1850; OR 1845/29807, Blake to Pennefather, 28 Dec. 1845; For example, T. Bartlett, 'An end to moral economy', 218, quotes a letter from Captain James Plunkett to Lord Minto, 28 Sept. 1800, recalling a time when 'they would fight at fairs until they got bloody heads and afterwards drank and were friends, but now murder and depredation is become the order of the day'; SC 1824, 113, evidence of Major Richard Willcocks.

abducted 16-year-old Rose Hart from her home at Ardmore, Boyle parish. Her father told the police where to seek her and they did indeed find her, nine miles away. They arrested two men, one of whom had wanted her to marry him. In April 1836 Catherine Hanley was snatched from her house (a two-storey building) in Cortober, on the Co. Roscommon side of the Shannon opposite Carrick, and taken over the bridge into Co. Leitrim. The police pursued the cart she was in and traced it to William Betheridge or Bertridge. Betheridge and his brother, plus two accomplices, were arrested. Thomas Lloyd JP observed that 'the Bertridges are of a very respectable family and no doubt but their relatives will exert themselves to prevent prosecution'. The same month 'an abduction of a very respectable girl, a farmer's daughter near Hillstreet took place'. Police rescued the girl and arrested five men. When Philip Murphy of Tibohine parish let down a woman and married another, his house was burned down. In October 1837 Anne Seally was forced from her house in Termonbarry parish by a neighbour, John McNamara, accompanied by his brother and other people, and compelled to swear that she would marry none but he. Chief Constable Blakeney noted that Seally's mother was a widow. In February 1838 four men attempted to abduct Margaret Bannon from Monksland, St Peter's parish, but were prevented by a servant boy. Four similar examples were reported in the first fortnight of February 1838, including the abduction of Mary Anne Kelly in Kilmore parish, as she was known to have a fortune. In February 1840 chief constable Daly reported the abduction of a farmer's daughter who was worth £400. Thirteen windows were broken at the house she was taken from, indicating the residence of a better-off farming family. The status of the people involved in these conflicts suggests that the tactic of family alliances was among the strategies adopted by farmers to ensure the family's fortunes rose and to secure future economic vigour. At the point where people became desperate for a particular alliance, abductions might occur.[13]

Hostility to strangers might be seen as another aspect of pre-modern loyalties in the Irish countryside, and indeed such hostilities were occasionally evi-

---

13 OR 1836/2, Blakeney to Crossley, Elphin, 1 Jan. 1836; OR 1836/8, Curtis to Warburton, 26 Jan. 1836; OR 1835/45, Curtis to chief secretary, 9 Apr 1836; Thomas Lloyd JP to Drummond, 9 Apr. 1836. Name of suspect given as Betheridge elsewhere; OR 1836/51, Carr to Warburton, 8 Apr. 1836; OR 1836/91, Galbraith to Miller, 17 Aug. 1836; OR 1837/124, Blakeney to Miller, undated (Oct. 1836); OR 1838/11, M. Knight, chief constable, Athlone, to inspector general of constabulary, 3 Feb. 1838; OR 1838/19, T. Johnston, chief constable, Elphin, to inspector general, 14 Feb. 1838; OR 1838/17, Blakeney to inspector general, 1 Feb. 1838, describing the abduction of Bridget Cox in Kilbride parish, who swore to marry Michael McDermott but instead married another on the same day; OR 1838/18, Johnston to inspector general, 10 Feb. 1838; OR 1838/16, Blakeney to Crossley, 8 Feb. 1838; OR 1840/2857, Daly to Kennedy, 19 Feb. 1840.

dent, most frequently in connection with taking work or land that was considered to belong by right to local people. In September 1840 Michael Fallon's hay was burned after he rented a meadow. Chief Constable Blakeney explained in his report on the incident that Fallon was 'a stranger and not connected with the land on which the hay was cut. The tenants it is supposed committed the injury, considering that they had the best right to the meadow'. The language of connection with the land is again significant. In January 1836 Robert Begley of Athlone was warned by a threatening notice posted at the crossroads at Fairymount not to buy land in that part of the country, about 23 miles from Athlone. A notice was posted in May the same year near Keadue, warning people against countenancing a grazier from Co. Sligo named Simon Mulvany. As a result, several people who had sent their cattle to Mulvany for grazing withdrew their stock from his care. Although the reporting constable believed hostility to Mulvany as a stranger was the reason for the notice, the notice may have been occasioned by hostility to the use of land for grazing instead of producing subsistence crops. Perhaps Mulvany's offence as a grazier was compounded by being a stranger. A notice posted on a door in Cloontuskert parish in June 1837 warned people not to give lodgings to strangers, and not to work for less than one shilling a day. Given the context of conflict over wages in which this warning against strangers was delivered, the hostility to strangers may be seen as the operation of economic protectionism. This is hardly evidence of pre-modernity. The same impulse was suggested to chief constable Johnston by a notice put under Gilbert Gannon's door in Kilmacumsy parish later that year. Johnston wrote: 'the reason assigned by Gannon his having workmen from another part of the country who work at a lower rate.' The rural poor's apprehension of social relations was revealed in the diction employed by the writer of this notice. He warned the strangers they would be 'civilised' by Captain Rock, suggesting that a customary view of labour was the proper way to ensure subsistence and security, not the free contract of master and employee. During construction of the Roscommon poor house in October 1840 a notice was posted on the door, warning:

> We the labouring class of the town of Roscommon and its vicinity do early apprise you that it is our fixed determination to stop all further employment being given to strangers from distant parts of this and other counties.

Two men from Co. Mayo were attacked in St Peter's parish and compelled to swear not to work for Malachy Naghton of Drum. The attackers might have been enforcing expectations that Naghton would give work to local men. As an employer Naghton presumably did not want to be bound by customary obligations that might affect his costs. However, the employees required reciprocity in social and economic relations. Language, consciousness and tradition provided a formal framework that evolved to reflect changes in the social and economic relations between groups such as employers and workers, landlords and tenants. As Thompson suggested, 'Custom may also be seen as a place of class conflict.' A language of hostility to strangers was employed to justify the class antipathy that was expressed in a threatening notice sent to a land agent named as Hugh Doogan. The notice, posted in September 1839 in Taughmaconnell parish, ordered Doogan to return to his native county on account of his 'perpetual annoyance to Mr Omoore's tenants' and to surrender his turbary rights and a piece of land he held. Analogously, a parliamentary enquiry heard that Welsh workers left their jobs at Drogheda dock after 'combinators frightened them'. While this antipathy to strangers may appear pre-modern, the authorities prosecuted the combinators under thoroughly modern trade union legislation. Elements of identities and organization that have been considered pre-modern may have existed among the rural poor of pre-famine Co. Roscommon, but these were not confined to particular times or locations. They were aspects of an uneven consciousness that adapted traditional forms to pursue conflicts in circumstances that were evolving continually.[14]

One examination of peasant movements that has been written within a modernization paradigm notes that the rural poor were like English industrial workers in the early nineteenth century in making reactionary demands about regulation of wages and the supply of labour. Similarly, James O'Neill suggested that agrarian unrest in Ireland was a reactionary response to economic change in the development of English capitalism. To term such demands reactionary is to say no more than that they impeded the accumulation of capital and the re-organization of production in non-traditional ways.[15]

Land, work, prices and law

Any analysis of the customary consciousness that informed pre-famine agrarian conflict must necessarily examine attitudes to the legitimacy of struggle and

14 OR 1840/16201, Blakeney to Kennedy, 11 Sept. 1840; OR 1836/7, Galbraith to Warburton, 10 Jan. 1836; OR 1836/61, Curtis to Galbraith, 12 May 1836; OR 1837/70, enclosed with letter from Sparling to Warburton, 19 June 1837; OR 1837/136, Johnston to Warburton, 25 Oct. 1837; OR 1840/17103, enclosed with letter from Blake to inspector general, 2 Oct. 1840; OR 1837/140, Sparling to Miller, 28 Oct. 1837; Thompson, 'Custom, law and common right' (1993), 110; OR 1839/8617, enclosed with letter from Knight to inspector general, 4 Oct. 1839; SC 1839, 239, evidence of Sir Francis Hopkins.   15 H. Landsberger, 'Peasant unrest: themes and variations' (1974); J. O'Neill, 'Popular culture and peasant rebellion' (1984), 1.

to the impositions of local élites (landlords, employers and retailers, for example) and the state. A sense of legal authority derived from a conception of rights that preceded modern contract law continued to inform the activities of agrarian protest as the third decade of the century closed. There was a striking contrast between agrarian rebels' respect for the unwritten authority of custom and their unwillingness to co-operate with the law. Donnelly has suggested that 'they were trying to replace the legal system which they detested with an unwritten but more just code of their own devising'. Hobsbawm noted that 'the social bandit is the very opposite of the criminal, in the public mind. He represents morality.' His moral authority was greater than that of the official law. De Tocqueville summarized the situation thus: 'in Ireland nearly all justice is extra-legal'.[16]

Indeed, the evidence from Co. Roscommon is of a pervasive sense of solidarity that militated against co-operation with the state when it acted against those perceived as defending the rural poor. Police officers and Dublin Castle officials frequently misinterpreted such unwillingness to co-operate with the official law as simply the consequence of intimidation. For example, in December 1835 a party of men, some armed, entered Michael Farrell's house in Termonbarry parish and demanded arms. Farrell, like others, attempted to conceal this from the authorities, prompting the reporting police officer to grumble that 'several persons whose houses have been entered endeavoured to deny their having been so'. When a wanted man named John Kelly was recognized and seized by police outside the Catholic church in Dysart parish under a pre-existing arrest warrant in May 1833, the party was followed from the church by a mob, which assaulted the police and rescued Kelly.[17]

Robert Atkinson, a police officer at Strokestown, reported to Warburton that men took money to James Regan's house in Bumlin parish in May 1828 to hand over cash collected for the benefit of Captain Rock's brother, whom they believed to be imprisoned in Longford jail. When Regan declined to take the money they replied that they had sworn to leave it with him and would be perjured if they did not. Constable Atkinson also reported the swearing of people not to prosecute any of Captain Rock's men. The scene is intriguing: two unknown men handed over cash, rather than absconding with it, and another man declined to take money freely offered. Given the poverty that generally prevailed in the county at this time, it is a remarkable example of customary consciousness affecting the behaviour of the rural poor. Instead of merely

16 Donnelly, *Landlord and tenant*, 27; E.J. Hobsbawm, 'Social banditry' (1974), 143; Larkin, *Alexis de Tocqueville's journey*, 21.   17 OR 1835/49, Blakeney to Crossley, 19 Dec. 1835; CSORP 1833/84, Alexander Lowrie, chief constable, Athlone, to Warburton, 13 May 1833.

obeying economic instincts, custom and a sense of obligation affected their actions to the degree that they did not merely see the money as a means to private enrichment.[18]

Captain Rock posted a notice in July 1838 on a house in Aughrim parish ordering levies to be delivered to Martin Cooney's home. Similarly, fifteen houses were visited in the Elphin district in March 1831 to raise cash to appoint counsel for some prisoners. A group of seven or eight men (some armed) compelled each of twenty different households in the parishes of Kiltrustan and Kilmore to hand over 1s. 6d. in April 1836. The fact that the same amount was demanded in each house suggests a levy, rather than a straightforward theft. A gang of robbers would presumably have taken as much as it could from each house. In November 1838 a party of around ten men, some armed with guns, visited sixteen houses in Termonbarry parish between 8pm and 10pm, demanding money to send a young man out of the country. They raised 1s. from each of ten of the houses visited. It should also be noted that Rowan, the anti-Catholic witness to the 1839 Lords enquiry, believed that the whiteboy associations frequently funded defences in criminal cases. This suggests a widespread, if primitive, form of associational activity.[19]

Hostile attitudes to the official law were also demonstrated in the opposition to the seizure of illicit stills, involving ferocious pitched battles with the revenue police, which frequently involved firearms. The sanctions of a community against a thief were expressed by someone styling himself Captain Macentire, who left a notice for Thomas Costello of Ardcarn parish in November 1840, telling Costello to flee the house he was staying in: 'Besides not paying for what you eat … you are impeached with amany atheft and you would not be let live so long in that … House.' The captain did not leave the alleged offender to the official law, instead judging Costello by standards seen as more important.[20]

The manager of the Arigna iron works, Thomas Cox, had been shot dead in the early morning of 23 February 1828. In August 1832 the watchman at the works, who was a principal witness for the prosecution in the case against the

18 CSORP 1828/W35, enclosed with letter from Warburton to Gregory, 25 May 1828; CSORP 1828/W89, Robert Atkinson, constable, Strokestown, to Warburton, 21 Oct. 1828. 19 OR 1838/86, Johnston to deputy inspector general of police, 30 Aug. 1838; CSORP 1831/W38, Warburton to Lt. Col. Dorset, 10 Mar. 1831; OR 1836/47, Carr to Galbraith, 5 Apr. 1836; OR 1838/108, Blakeney to Miller, 1 Dec. 1838; SC 1839, 166, evidence of H.W. Rowan.   20 CSORP 1833/649, a report in a letter from an unnamed police officer of a gun battle between revenue police and country people over the seizure of illicitly distilled spirits near Ballaghadereen reported in a letter from an unnamed police officer, Ballaghadereen,17 July 1833; OR 1840/19405, enclosed with letter from Reed to inspector general of police, 27 Nov. 1840.

men accused of Cox's murder, received a notice forbidding him from testifying, accompanied by a hyperbolic warning that 10,000 men were at the sender's command. The protection the law might afford those who testified against whiteboys involved the breaking of a solidarity that commanded greater loyalty among the rural poor than any to the state. It is too easy to see such notices, and the violence that precipitated it, as indicating a primitive form of struggle. Given the circumstances of illegality and the traditions of protest in rural Ireland, the Arigna iron works incident may be seen more profitably as an economic conflict in specific historical circumstances, rather than as a primitive struggle that can only be explained by referring to pre-modern solidarities. While social historians have tended to link violence with primitive rebellion and organizational immaturity, its presence may be reinterpreted as a symptom of organization, particularly in the specific circumstances of Ireland.[21]

However, the apparatus of the courts was readily made use of when it appeared there might be some gain to be made for those opposing the established order. When Daniel Egan of Bumlin parish refused to testify against a special constable suspected of poaching, he was stabbed in the thigh for not taking an opportunity to exact some retribution on a police officer. This incident, reported in January 1835, demonstrated a significant degree of antagonism between the rural poor and the apparatus of the state. In the willingness of the rural poor to use the official law when it suited their ends, it is possible to discern that appeals to customary notions of right, when made, were legitimizing means and not necessarily ends in themselves, much as customary demands were often of rather more recent origin than claimed. The actions of whiteboys were underpinned by the tactical approach perceived as most likely to succeed in specific circumstances. Punishment was also meted out to those who sided with the state, as when James Kenny's house was burned down the following month, after his prosecution of men who had committed murder. Similarly, in January 1835 a man named O'Donnell received a threatening notice after he prosecuted people who attacked his labourers while they were working, and in July the same year the house of a man living near Ballyfarnon was burned down. The cause attributed on that occasion was that the occupier had testified against a man for stealing carts from the Arigna mine company.[22]

21 RLG, 23 Feb 1828; CSORP 1832/1674, Reed to Warburton, 1 Sept. 1832, enclosing copy of threatening notice sent to Glynn. Resistance to technological advance in England during 1802 bore similar features. See Randall, 'The shearmen and the Wiltshire outrages'.
22 OR 1835/4, Blakeney to Warburton, 20 Jan 1835; OR 1835/6, Warburton to Sir William Gosset, under-secretary, 13 Feb. 1835; OR 1835/7, letter from Blakeney to Warburton, 15 Jan 1835; OR 1835/14, Crossley to under-secretary, 18 July 1835.

Although sanctions against those among the poor who had been seen to break their moral and customary codes continued to be used frequently and the legitimizing consciousness that allowed such attacks continued to be ostensibly traditional, landlords, agents and representatives of the state were increasingly the victims. This demonstrates the co-existence of a customary, backward-looking consciousness with changed material conditions. Pre-eminent among these was the vigorous assertion of property rights by some landlords and agents through the ethos of improvement (and the landlord and tenant relationships established in this process, unencumbered by middlemen) as well as the increasing professionalization of the legal and state mechanisms. The results were reflected in a combined and uneven consciousness in which the traditional and the new co-existed. The protests of the rural poor were parochial and filtered through tradition but at the same time demonstrated a consciousness of new egalitarian notions derived in the early nineteenth century from the image of the 'tree of liberty' and, as the century wore on, other cosmopolitan developments like Peterloo, Radicalism, Reform and Chartism. It is in this sense that custom as a legitimation of rebellion was modified. Thompson saw in Luddism a similar moment of transition, looking back to customs which could not be revived, but also using ancient rights to establish new precedents. These new precedents were significant articulations of the processes whereby change was apprehended and attempts made to regulate it. One historian of popular mobilization in Ireland has suggested that the Irish lower classes did indeed have 'political interests' and that whiteboyism can not be dismissed as non-political because it does not conform to later conceptions of politics. Indeed, agrarian unrest had a 'formative political potential'. After the French revolution the language of popular protest changed to talk of systems of liberty and equality. These changes are apparent in threatening notices from Co. Roscommon. However, social historians have tended to adopt a template for social conflict that requires the development of trade union gradualism, mild political reformism and its comfortable containment within the modern state as the natural form of development. Irish agrarian rebels should not be required to form a trade union, issue membership cards, appoint a bureaucracy and pay subscriptions before they can retrospectively be allowed political concerns.[23]

Thus law enforcers and revenue collectors could be the objects of attack as when, in March 1835, an excise officer's lumber boat was smashed up at its Shannon mooring. The cause assigned for this offence was that the officer concerned had encouraged a man to prosecute people for an assault on Godfrey

---

23 Thompson, *Making of the English working class*, 603; J. Smyth, *The men of no property* (1992), 34, 3.

Hogg's house the previous September, Hogg being athe well-known magistrate and landlord previously alluded to. Eight sheep belonging to a farmer named Owen Lynch of Moore parish were killed one night in the same month, 'injury to property having become prevalent in this parish'. In the same bundle of correspondence was a report that a party of seven men had visited fourteen houses in Bumlin parish, demanding money for the support of a prisoner held in Roscommon jail. What is common to both incidents is antagonism to the official law.[24]

The continued use of familiar tactics was evident also in a threatening notice posted in January 1836 on a house belonging to W. Lewis Morton at Bogwood, purporting to be from Captain Rock of Castlebar. This ordered Morton to comply with the laws of the country or be visited with severe punishment. The point here is the question of who made the laws. Indeed the very act of swearing people, and one reason why it was so vigorously proscribed by government, was that it raised directly the question of allegiance and legitimacy. In March the following year a threatening notice was posted where a new section of road was being built to Drumcormick. It said 'Notice that any person or persons found working on the new road without 10 pence per day will be dealt with according to law, Galway dated___.' This notice shows, like the notice sent to Morton, that legal authority was vested in the whiteboys and not in the state. It also demonstrated the way in which objectives which may, however loosely, be associated with trade union activity, increasingly co-existed with such tactics as the threatening notice. The Drumcormick notice also demonstrates that land was not the only concern of Irish agrarian rebels. A threatening notice posted in Taughmaconnell parish in September 1837 also concerned itself with employment, warning thus: 'Take notice that any person that will come to herd for Edward Naghton Esq[re] will be punished.' Chief constable Sparling noted that Naghton had sacked his herdsman for misconduct. Indeed it is apparent that land was only the most common issue provoking agrarian unrest in Co. Roscommon because of the specific significance it had in the subsistence economy of the rural poor. They legitimized their actions to defend or gain economic security in similar ways, whether the specific object was land, prices, wages or some other aspect of economic life.[25]

In February 1836, the month after the visit to Morton, five houses in Kilmore parish were visited by a party of around thirty men, who levied a total of

24 OR 1835/19, Blakeney to Warburton, 17 Mar. 1835; OR 1835/22, Lowrie to Warburton, 1 Apr. 1835; OR 1835/22, Galbraith to Warburton, 7 Apr. 1835.   25 OR 1836/7, Galbraith to Warburton, 8 Jan. 1836; OR 1837/37, Curtis to Warburton, 21 Mar. 1837; OR 1837/107, Sparling to Miller, 7 Sept. 1837.

five shillings from the occupants 'for a prisoner in Roscommon gaol', the sums involved suggesting that the subscribers were among the poor and might be most susceptible to the enforcement of this alternative jurisprudence. The same month sixteen houses in Termonbarry parish were visited and sums of between 1s. and 2s. 6d. levied at each for prisoners, although Strokestown chief constable Thomas Blakeney opined that 'the money is obtained not for the use of Prisoners, but for the purposes of dissipation'. However, numerous examples of the disciplined levying and collection of subscriptions for collective ends have already been encountered, and Blakeney's assessment should not necessarily be considered authoritative.[26]

Elphin Chief Constable Frederick Carr complained the following month that it was 'next to an impossibility to get any person to give us the slightest information' and requested that a reward be offered to Patrick Mooney, who had provided vital information enabling the police to arrest a man suspected of murder, 'as the services of such a person was never more wanted in this county'. Carr's comment confirmed the difficulty of persuading people to abandon their customary notion of justice in favour of the state's. This was demonstrated directly when Carr's colleague at Athlone, Alexander Lowrie, reported later the same year that an armed party attacked two men guarding corn seized for unpaid rent in Taughmaconnell parish. The chief constable reported that the keepers denied knowing their attackers, although Lowrie added, 'I am satisfied the contrary is the fact.' When a stack of oats belonging to Henry Roache, a farmer in Cloontuskert parish, was burned down, Roache said it was because he had paid his tithes 'and by that means incurred the displeasure of his neighbours'. In Fuerty parish in May 1837 a group of men locked up the sheriff's bailiff and took away property that had been seized in lieu of unpaid debts. A few days later two men attacked a tithe process server in Bumlin parish and destroyed fourteen processes he was serving in the neighbourhood. A number of people were reported to have stood by and offered no assistance to the beleaguered man. It is notable that a number of processes were destroyed, suggesting again that a shared conception of law was being enforced, rather than this being the action of a few unwilling individuals attempting to avoid payment. The following month a party of armed men swore bailiff Denis Swiney to destroy decrees under which a Mrs Croghan's goods had been seized in Lisanuffy parish.[27]

26 OR 1836/10, Carr to Warburton, 2 Feb. 1836; OR 1836/34, Blakeney to Galbraith, 28 Feb. 1836.   27 OR 1836/40, Carr to Warburton, 1 Mar. 1836; OR 1836/116, Lowrie to Miller, 1 Nov. 1836; OR 1836/119, Sparling to Miller, 17 Nov. 1836; OR 1837/65, Sparling to Miller, 5 June 1837; OR 1837/74, Blakeney to Miller, 20 June 1837; OR 1837/92, Blakeney to Miller, 21 July 1837.

In January that year ten men had visited Patrick Hagan at night and smashed a window in his house. They swore Hagan to surrender promissory notes and decrees he had obtained at the quarter sessions, leaving the settlement of his claims to the parish priest. In this instance the priest was seen as an arbiter. However, it is apparent that, while some clergymen, often curates, may-have still have been closely connected with the 'traditional' cultural practices of their parishioners, many others had moved towards a more modern acknowledgement of the rights of property and the state, encouraged by such concessions as emancipation.[28]

Memory played a significant role. Many assertions of claimed rights were derived from recollection of how things used to be and were attempts to restore an equilibrium perceived as disturbed. Conflict over conceptions of justice, for example, could thus be sustained for many years after the event that caused the disturbance. A man named Henderson took over Tully House in Moore parish in 1839 from the St George family. When he sacked an employee he was reminded in a threatening notice of the assassination of Henry St George twenty years earlier, which was considered in the previous chapter. At Deerpark, Boyle, in May 1840, Pat Boland was attacked and killed in an altercation about a dispute that had happened seventeen years earlier. A man named as Mattimo and two others were suspected of the crime. Robert Curtis, chief constable at Boyle, reported in August 1837 that a threatening notice had been put under Pat Concannon's door in Boyle parish. Concannon had 'some years earlier' informed on two men, who were then transported for robbery. The notice warned:

> To Pat Concannon, informer, Ballinamene.
> Take notice, I noticed you Patt Concannon about nine months ago to leave the neighbourhood of Ballinamene as there will be no informer or spy there … we listened no longer but will punish you … Signed Cap[n] Rock.

A notice posted on the chapel door in Taughmaconnell parish in June 1838 warned:

> To the publick at large. Prohibiting any person or persons whatsoever to take or propose for the lower Shraduff except the person or persons thereunto entitled by hereditary right lest it should enevitably inflict an insurmountable punishment or incur my displeasure pursuant to the Statute, in such case lately made and provided. Jeremiah Macubees.

28 OR 1836/128, Blakeney to Miller, 4 Jan. 1837.

The diction used in the notice was once again intended to convey a sense of legal authority. 'Jeremiah' was enforcing a customary right, held not through contractual tenure but by hereditary possession. Similarly, in December 1845 a farmer called O'Connor from Castlerea was sworn to give up his farm, as the children of the former tenant required it. O'Connor had leased the farm twenty years earlier after a previous tenant had been evicted. A man complained to the O'Conor Don in March 1846 that a group of men had tried to make his mother swear to give up four acres to the son of a man who had been dispossessed of them in 1831.[29]

The breaking open of pounds to release distrained livestock, attacks on process servers, the destruction of processes and the 'rescue' of property seized for debt continued for many years, frequently in daylight. This may be explained by the necessity of responding to perceived wrongs which could only be dealt with during daylight. This reflected the increasing professionalization of the workings of the state, precipitating formal changes in whiteboy organization and methods. Process servers and other officers of the civil law worked during the day. Daylight gatherings had occurred during the eighteenth-century Rightboy movement in Munster, when open evangelical marches were held before churches and mass assemblies elected committees of local leaders to draft resolutions. Broeker suggested that 1829 was a watershed, daylight actions becoming more common thereafter. Gibbons saw 1824 as a point after which agrarian conflict became less parochial, attributing the change to increasing communications by canal, rail, roads and newspapers. It is impossible to identify a date with such precision. As Tilly has observed of change in English 'contentious gatherings', there was no fixed point when one set of repertoires was exchanged for another. More than fifty years after the Rightboy movement, although daylight assemblies were increasing, they were still unusual enough for police officers in Co. Roscommon to think them worthy of special mention in reports to the Castle. A woman complaining of attempts to persuade her to surrender her holding in 1846 noted that her enemies assembled in open day and were permitted to go unquestioned by the country people. A landlord named George Lloyd complained in 1847 that the whiteboys 'walk *day* and night' and he had been warned that his life was in danger. The emphasis is revealing, suggesting that this was a comparatively recent or unusual development. Open assembly was clearly perceived as sig-

29 OR 1839/1034, Knight to Miller, 22 Feb. 1839; OR 1839/9389, Reed to inspector general, 13 May 1840; OR 1837/103, Curtis to Miller, 29 Aug. 1837; OR 1838/69, enclosed with letter from Knight to Warburton, 18 June 1838; OR 1845/29385, Duff to Sir Thomas Freemantle, chief secretary, 26 Dec. 1845; OR 1846/7267, B. Keon to the O'Conor Don, 18 Mar. 1846.

nificant, for a notice posted on a crane at a crossroads three miles from Boyle in June 1837 proclaimed:

> Take notice that any person working for the Tory's of the half Parish will suffer some, we are the Boys that's not afraid to come out in the day light, fight for freedom.

The notice displayed a collective self-consciousness and a belief that open organization was an advance on covert action. This accompanied a general opposition to those seen as the opponents of whiteboys, and a political understanding of the term 'Tory'. A primitive form of political generalization accompanied daylight mobilization.[30]

There is no suggestion that daylight made it easier to capture the rebels. For example, a large party of men armed with pitchforks, sticks and stones attacked Bernard Ginty at noon one day in March 1838, compelling him to destroy processes he was serving in Cloontuskert parish. The following month John Robinson and Michael Nugent were stoned early in the morning while serving processes for the Revd Thomas Caulfield in Cloonfinlough parish, but they refused to swear not to serve processes. Like process servers, bailiffs worked during daylight, creating the tactical necessity of daylight organization. In May 1838 the under-agent of Viscount Lorton and two bailiffs were attacked with pitchforks and sticks by tenants they were coming to dispossess of their holdings, while a number of women threw stones at them. Chief Constable Reed reported that the agent and bailiffs withdrew from the scene of conflict at Ardkina townland, Estersnow parish, and returned later accompanied by Reed and twenty men, when they accomplished their purpose. The evolution of the tenure arrangements on this townland were considered earlier. The conflict between Lorton and his tenants also demonstrates the increasing incidence of direct conflict between landowners and occupiers, as the owners increasingly became direct landlords of the occupiers of the land

---

30 There were many instances of such attacks, usually following a similar pattern to those described. See, for example, OR 1838/7, OR 1838/10 and OR 1838/41 for examples of a 'rescue' of livestock from a pound, an attack on bailiffs protecting goods seized to pay a debt and the swearing of men not to serve processes; Donnelly, 'The Rightboy movement'; Broeker, *Rural disorder*, 193; Gibbons, 'Rockites and Whitefeet', 62; Tilly, *Popular contention*, 48; For example, OR 1845/23471, G. Lloyd JP to under-secretary, 22 Nov. 1845. Lloyd emphasized that arms raids were taking place in daylight; OR 1846/18789, Gerard Barry, resident magistrate, Athlone, to under-secretary, 18 June 1846. Barry reported an attack on the house of a gentleman farmer in the early afternoon, noting that the attackers were 'in no way disguised'; OR 1846/7267, B. Keon to the O'Conor Don, 18 Mar. 1846; OR 1847/ 768, George Lloyd to under-secretary, 29 Nov. 1847; OR 1837/101, enclosed with letter from Curtis to Miller, 28 June 1837.

and sought to improve their estates. While other potential occupiers of the land could be disciplined within the community, the increasingly profession-alized mechanisms of the state had to be confronted by day. However, night-time attacks continued, as when, at the end of the following month, a bailiff's house in Ardcarn parish was visited at midnight and a number of outstanding warrants removed from the premises. In January 1841 seven men with black-ened faces entered John Maguire's house in Clonaff half-parish, ordering him not to serve any more papers for a law agent named Lawder.[31]

Landlords, tax collectors and law enforcers required protection to over-come this customary sense of law and exact compliance with the demands of the state for taxes and of the landlords for distress. In the autumn of 1842 poor rate collector James Sharkey of Elphin complained that the rate was only paid in Shankill parish when he was accompanied by police, and in the autumn of 1845 Michael Egan, a landlord near Tulsk, called for police pro-tection to execute distress warrants 'to enable me to obtain my rights'. While the rural poor may have continued to harbour a sense of rights based on cus-tom, reciprocity on the part of the landlord had apparently been aban-doned in favour of non-traditional conceptions of property rights and state mechanisms had been reformed to enforce uniformity in respect of taxation and law.[32]

While disputes concerning land were most frequently the subject of con-flict, whiteboys also acted to enforce customary attitudes to a wide range of economic and social arrangements. These arrangements included who was employed and on what terms. Actions could frequently take the form of threats against former employers, against people who had taken jobs after someone was sacked or against those accepting a rate of pay that was consid-ered too low.[33]

Warburton reported a threatening notice served on a 'respectable farmer' in March 1832 in the very south of the county. He noted that the farmer paid labourers no more than four and a half pence a day without food. In January 1834 several persons were sworn not to work for Mr Morton, and several sheep belonging to a Dr Lloyd had been shorn after Lloyd failed to comply with a notice demanding that he sack a particular servant. Several

31 OR 1838/34, Sparling to Miller, 24 Mar. 1838; OR 1838/41, Blakeney to Miller, 4 Apr. 1838; OR 1838/55, Reed to Miller, 15 Feb. 1838; OR 1838/84, Reed to Miller, 2 Aug. 1838; OR 1841/1077, Daly to inspector general of police, 26 Jan. 1841.   32 OR 1842/20041, undated memorial of Sharkey to lord lieutenant (autumn 1842); OR 1845/22049, undated memorial of Michael Egan (autumn 1845).   33 OR 1840/13775, Blake to inspector gener-al, 31 July 1840; OR 1840/14421, M'carty Colclough, chief constable, Athlone, to inspector general, 11 Aug. 1840.

houses in Kilglass parish were visited and the residents sworn not to work for Godfrey Hogg. A notice was posted at a forge on the border with Co. Sligo, ordering people not to work for the 'perjurer' who prosecuted Brennan. In August 1836 a threatening notice was served on Patrick Cummins in Creeve parish for having been employed as a herdsman following the dismissal of John Beirne.[34]

In July 1840 Pat Foley of Knockcroghery was sworn to give up his job after it emerged that he was working at a lower rate of pay than others. M'Carty Colclough, chief constable at Athlone, reported the following month that James and Walter Kelly of Taughmaconnell parish had received a threatening notice after sacking a herdsman for 'improper conduct'.[35]

However, many such disputes took 'traditional' forms but suggest a consciousness of collective interests beyond the family or neighbourhood. A notice that was removed from a gate at Cootehall in April 1837 ordered men labouring on public works to accept no less than 1s. a day. In June the same year a notice fixing a similar rate was posted in Cloontuskert parish after Longford men came to work there for 8d. a day. The following month around five men called on the steward of some public works in Lisanuffy parish and told him that men labouring on the new road from Curraghroe to Longford should earn no less than 10d. a day and a man and horse 3s. a day. A notice prescribing these rates was found posted the following day. In September several notices were posted in Ballinamene prescribing a rate of 1s. per day, one warning:

> You Paddy Moran James Henigan … and all others are not to work for Mr Patterson or for any other Tory less than one shilling per day or we will pay you another visit on another day.

The dismissal of Patterson and his like with the epithet 'Tory' demonstrates that the word was by then in use as a standard shorthand expression of class contumely. It is significant that the earlier construction of the word to describe the dispossessed landed Catholic losers in Cromwell's confiscations had now

34 CSORP 1832/501, Warburton to Gosset, 12 Mar. 1832; CSORP 1834/25, Warburton to Gosset, 20 Jan. 1834; Robert Grace, Kilglass, to Warburton, 3 Apr. 1834; Robert Grace to Warburton, 16 Apr. 1834; OR 1836/80, Blakeney to Miller, 7 Aug. 1836.   35 CSORP 1832/501, Warburton to Gosset, 12 Mar. 1832; CSORP 1834/25, Warburton to Gosset, 20 Jan. 1834; Robert Grace, to Warburton, 3 Apr. 1834; Grace to Warburton, 16 Apr. 1834; OR 1836/80, Blakeney to Miller, 7 Aug. 1836; OR 1840/13775, Blake to inspector general, 31 July 1840; OR 1840/14421, M'carty Colclough, chief constable, Athlone, to inspector general, 11 Aug. 1840.

evolved into a more modern political usage. Further notices were posted against other employers (and visits paid to employees) in the same area during the same month, thus constituting a general wages dispute. Pat Daly was warned not to work for Charles Peyton for less than 1s. a day and a notice posted on the chapel at Cootehall said:

> Take notice any person or persons who will work for Tobias Peyton or that Blind Brat Edw[d] Patterson unless they get 1[s] 3[d] per day let them look what may occur.

One of the Peyton family lodged informations against some men, who were arrested and bailed in Boyle. Warburton wrote to Morpeth that 'on our return from the Court House we were followed by a mob shouting that they were out in spite of us'. The official law and its representatives were the object of the crowd's defiance, as well as the employers whom the police and legal apparatus were perceived to serve. In the generalizations about the perceived collusion of the employers, the police, and the official justice system that were being drawn it is possible to see that 'formative political potential' already alluded to. In an 1841 outrage report from Strokestown that described the swearing of men not to work for less than 9d. a day, the dispute was labelled as 'combination'. In the eyes of the reporting police officer, at least, such disputes were evidence of some form of class organization. An incident at Roosky in February 1842 was likewise described as 'a case of combination ... intimidating labourers from working for the Road contractors under certain advanced wages'.[36]

There is some further evidence to suggest that the geographic extent of such wages combinations was greater than one employer's lands. Two notices posted on a farmer's house in Creeve parish purported to be from a committee attempting to enforce wage regulation at a shilling a day across the province of Connacht. One notice was addressed to the farmer and the other to employees accepting less than the rate prescribed by this 'Independent Committee'. It may be that the invocation of a committee title was merely a device to add authority to the notice. However, the shilling a day demand extended across the county, from the Peytons' and Patterson's workforces in the north-east through Creeve, a little to the south and to Bellanagare, further to the west. Chief Con-

36 OR 1837/46, Curtis to Warburton, 10 Apr. 1837; OR 1837/70, Sparling to Warburton, 19 June 1837; OR 1837/93, Blakeney to Warburton, 17 July 1837; OR 1837/109, 110 and 112, Curtis to Miller, 13 Sept., 12 Sept. and 19 Sept. 1837; OR 1837/114, 115, 116, Curtis to Miller, 24, 25 and 26 Sept. 1837; OR 1837/117, Warburton to Viscount Morpeth, chief secretary, 25 Sept. 1837; OR 1841/5079, outrage report, 8 Apr. 1841; OR 1842/2567, outrage report, 10 Feb. 1842.

stable Carr reported that several people in that district had been sworn to work for no less than 1s. a day. Similar demands were made in the south of the county the following May. In August 1838 road labourers went on strike for 9d. a day, their employer only being willing to pay 7d. In the December 1845 incident alluded to earlier, labourers in Ardcarn parish swore not to work for Lorton's agent, John Hackett, for less than 10d. a day in the summer and 8d. a day in the winter. Hackett sacked all who swore the oath and the situation hardened as all his employees stopped work to demand the reinstatement of those sacked. The *Roscommon and Leitrim Gazette* noted that this development coincided with sightings of large parties of armed men around the parish at night, including an encounter between police and around 40 men near Cootehall and shots being fired near a gentleman's house in that neighbourhood.[37]

One night in June 1837 a group of men broke into a barn belonging to a farmer named James McDermott in Cloontuskert parish and removed two wheelbarrows, which they smashed to pieces. Sparling explained: 'This outrage was committed in consequence of McDermott having taken a quantity of Turf to cut by Task, which prevents the Labourers of being employed by the day.' Furthermore, this action was part of a campaign, for ten days later newly cut turf belonging to George Beggs in the same parish was destroyed 'in consequence of the said Beggs having got his turf cut by Task, and not having employed labourers by the day'. This action could be explained as a trade dispute over piece rates and day rates, but articulated through a traditional action. It demonstrates the way in which old forms could be appropriated for the pursuit of new ends. Such apparent paradoxes reveal the limitations of modernization as an explanatory model for the complex, interacting shades of consciousness and culture that were fused within Irish agrarian protest.[38]

The tactics of whiteboyism could be put to use in other situations where there was a perceived right or need which ought to be satisfied, such as the construction of a direct line of road from a townland to the main road, as was the cause of disturbance in Kilglass parish in December 1835. On Christmas night in 1835 in Termonbarry parish several armed men with blackened faces recovered a flitch of bacon that had been seized under a court order. A horse was seized in August 1836 from the stable of a landlord named Bennison at Ballyfarnon after it was held there following its capture by the revenue police while the animal was carrying illicit malt. As many as 300 people were calculated to

37 OR 1837/128, enclosed with letter from Curtis to Warburton, 11 Oct. 1837; OR 1837/131, Carr to Warburton, 15 Oct. 1837, reporting incident three weeks earlier; OR 1838/59, Sparling to Miller, 18 May 1838; OR 1838/83, Sparling to Miller, 4 Aug. 1838; RLG, 20 Dec. 1845. 38 OR1837/80, Sparling to Miller, 28 June 1837; M. Hildermeier, 'Agrarian social protest, populism and economic development' (1979), considers the 'mixture of backward-looking and progressive forces' as typical.

have taken part in the dispersal of stones assigned for road repair into adjacent ditches and a bog in Ardcarn parish in the same month. Curtis commented that 'a combination in my opinion exists for the purpose of preventing competition in the contracting of repair for roads'.[39]

The customary culture of the poor was such that chief constable Sparling sought advice on the proposed moving of graves to allow an extension to a Roscommon town church, anticipating much opposition.[40]

Not only did land and trade disputes cause conflict. In Keadue one night in May 1837 a notice was posted on Michael Noon's door ordering him to return 6*d.* per hundredweight of the money he had charged for potatoes. Captain Rock said Noon should only charge 1*s.* 6*d.*, not 2*s.* The essence of this procedure is strikingly similar to the classic English price-fixing riot. Alan Booth has described how mealmen in the north-west of England were targeted, their wares sold at a price determined by the protesters and the 'just' price given to the mealmen.[41]

Like the English food riot, conflict over rights to food in the market might be seen as a locus of immanent class conflict. It has been suggested that there exists 'something of a consensus among historians that the English, Scottish and Welsh traditions of food rioting were not paralleled in Ireland'. Yet such actions were far from unknown in Co. Roscommon. In June 1839 Reed reported that three men had been attacked and oaths administered. He said the victims were sworn 'not to demand a higher price for their meal than 16*s.* per hundredweight, and 2*s.* 6*d.* for potatoes. Where they had sold the latter commodity at a higher rate they were to return the difference'. Similarly, the following week, around ten men fired shots into William Glynn's house near Keadue, and swore him to refund 2*s.* to a man to whom he had sold potatoes. Glynn was also sworn not to charge more than 2*s.* 6*d.* per hundredweight in future. The following month eight men set on a man they claimed had charged too much for meal. In Kilronan parish during August 1839 a man named Michael Tansy was visited and ordered to refund any money he had received for potatoes in excess of 2*s.* 6*d.* per hundredweight. At Buckhill in the west of the county two sheep were killed at much the same time because their owner, a comfortable farmer, had been selling provisions at a high price on credit, and had displeased some people by not extending such terms to them. This dispute between a 'strong farmer' and customers is an example of the conflict emerging between the strong farming class and the rural poor. Similarly, in November the previous year two turf ricks

---

39 OR 1835/47, Blakeney to Crossley, 7 Dec. 1835; OR 1835/52, Blakeney to Crossley, no date, (December 1835); OR 1836/85, Curtis to Miller, 11 Aug. 1836; OR 1836/88, Curtis to Miller, 13 Aug. 1836.   40 OR 1836/92, Sparling to unnamed, Dublin Castle, 19 Aug. 1836.

belonging to Patrick Mulanny of Boyle were set on fire and, when he rushed out to tackle the blaze, the windows and door of his house were broken. Reed reported that Mulanny sold meal, potatoes and other goods, 'which he generally gives on credit charging *exorbitant prices* and is in consequence obliged *to process many of his* debtors'. A Catholic called Michael Skevington or Skeffington received a threatening notice sent though the post office that chastised him for charging 25 per cent interest on loans, and ordered him to reduce the interest by 10 per cent. The notice observed:

> you have many desent people paying such damnable interest because they are distressed for money – but I will put a stop to such infernal usury'.

William Irwin, a constable based at Roscommon, reported a food riot in the town in May 1839, attributing it to a sudden rise in prices. Irwin said a crowd tried to stop carmen taking potatoes away from the market and threatened to cut their sacks. The police protected the carmen and there were no potatoes available by 2 p.m. Irwin commented that 'numbers of the poor people of the Town were not at that hour supplied nor could they get any to buy'.[42]

The food riot at Roscommon also demonstrated that integration into wider markets led to conflict. For several mornings in June 1837 a crowd assembled in the Curlew mountains north of Boyle to stop carmen taking potatoes out of the county to the market in Sligo town, another sign of resistance to change which should not be construed simply as spontaneous, conservative or reactionary. On the contrary, such actions reveal considered collective responses to perceived needs, appropriating traditional forms for use in actions undertaken to manage contemporary problems. A man in Boyle received a letter through the post office that ordered him not to send eggs to Dublin for sale, or they would be destroyed. In May 1840 a group of men, women and children knocked John Farrell of Co. Leitrim from his horse and took two hundredweight of potatoes he had bought at Ballyfarnon. Reed said the attack was to prevent potatoes being taken out of the county after a sudden price rise caused fears of impending scarcity. A few days later two carmen were attacked in Roscommon town

41 OR 1837/62, Curtis to Miller, 26 May 1837; A. Booth, 'Food riots' (1977). 42 Thompson, 'The moral economy reviewed', 287; R. Wells, 'The Irish famine of 1799–1801', 179; OR 1839/4577, Reed to inspector general, 23 June 1839; OR 1839/4703, Reed to inspector general, 28 June 1839; OR 1839/6387, Reed to inspector general, 19 July 1839; OR 1839/7577, Reed to inspector general, 28 Aug. 1839; OR 1839/6650, Carr to inspector general, 26 July 1839; OR 1838/106, Reed to Miller, 24 Nov. 1838; OR 1845/14169, information sworn by Michael Skeffington, Boyle petty sessions, 1 July 1845; OR 1839/3657, William Irwin, sub-constable, Roscommon, to inspector general, 21 May 1839.

after buying potatoes at Elphin. Their sacks were slashed and the potatoes taken. Carmen were attacked and a horse's ear cut off in a dispute over 'differences relating to the sale of Butter in the market of Boyle' in January 1850.[43]

The rural poor also believed they had rights to timber and turbary. In a May 1837 letter concerning Kilgefin parish, Denis O'Connor of Edgeworthstown, Co. Longford, complained of 'the habit the peasantry of that neighbourhood got of taking timber by night of a property ... I also got the Catholic clergyman to protest against these conduct but from long habit tis all of no use ... unless some aid is given we must give up all idea of improvement in that vicinity.' O'Connor's complaint is a fine example of improvement pitted against custom, and property rights against traditional use-rights. The assertion of customary rights was also apparent in September that year when three tons of hay were burned in Taughmaconnell parish. They belonged to a Captain Scott of Banagher in neighbouring King's County. Chief Constable Sparling said the attack occurred because 'Captain Scott took the land on which the hay grew from the tenants for his own use'. A great number of trees were cut down and removed from James Lyster's estate at Fairymount, Kilgefin parish, in January 1839. After the resulting prosecutions Lyster's wood ranger, Martin Mulligan, was attacked on his way home to Fairymount from Roscommon market. In July 1840 a notice was posted on Patrick McLoughlin's door in Kilglass parish, ordering him to stop prosecuting people for trespassing on Nicholas Balfe's lands, to whom he was bailiff and driver.[44]

Resistance to unwelcome change extended to matters as diverse as industrial espionage at a coal mine near Castletenison, and an 1837 proposal to move the location of Strokestown market from Brown Street to Church Street. The magistrate and land agent to the Mahons, Thomas Conry, had asked for it to be moved. Chief Constable Blakeney reported that the market had been held in Brown Street since it was established by a patent granted during Charles II's reign. Conry had in fact moved the market some time earlier. The traders had remonstrated and appeared determined to assert their rights. Blakeney believed it was 'a duty in which the police should be cautious, as interfering with a long established right and custom'. Blakeney was evidently uneasy about the move, discerning the tension between custom and progress, although he was resigned to supporting Conry's wishes.[45]

43 OR 1837/72, Curtis to Miller, 20 June 1837; RLG 19 Apr. 1839; OR 1840/10393, Reed to inspector general, 3 June 1840; OR 1840/10689, Michael Middleton, chief constable, Roscommon, to inspector general, 5 June 1840; OR 1850/9, outrage report, 10 Jan. 1850. 44 OR 1837/68, Dennis O'Connor to lord lieutenant, 27 May 1837; OR 1837/108, Sparling to Miller, 10 Sept. 1837; OR 1839/4, Sparling to Miller, 22 Jan. 1839; OR 1839/3756, Irwin to inspector general, 24 May 1839; OR 1840/13615, Blakeney to inspector general, 29 July 1840.   45 OR 1839/7450, Reed to inspector general, 26 Aug. 1839; OR 1837/125,

John Loughan, Lord Lorton's water bailiff, went to destroy three weirs built illegally on the Boyle river in November 1848. He said that the weirs were 'very injurious to the adjoining Lands and fishery', but Loughan was met by a party of more than thirty men who swore to kill him if he tried to remove them. James Mulhall exchanged shots with men he caught fishing for eels near his father's mills on the same river in September 1845.[46]

During the course of the first half of the nineteenth century direct conflict between the owners and the occupiers of the land became more common. The customary consciousness of the rural poor increasingly bore an overtly class inflection as whiteboy activity became less focused on disciplining members of the rural community and more on direct conflict with landowners and the state that enforced the landlord's rights to distress and eviction, in the context of the landowners' and farmers' disengagement from customary vertical and communal ties. The economic and social relationships between the rural poor and farmers, middlemen, retailers, agents, landlords and crown servants was evolving in to a more straightforwardly conflictual one as vertical and community consciousness slowly dissolved. The Co. Roscommon magistrates expressed this view when they agreed 'that the object of these disturbances is to interfere with the letting of lands – the amount of rents and the hire of Labourers etc'. The magistrates utilized the language of political economy, implying that interference in the free bargain of landlord and tenant or master and labourer was unwanted. It was precisely the conflict between such freedoms and the rural poor that caused conflict. Warburton noted a class distinction between the farmers, who were more inclined to give information, if protected, and the cottiers and labourers. The latter warned others to give up land they had recently taken and attempted to lower rents through intimidation, he added.[47]

Direct attacks on landlords and their agents continued to increase. An agent was 'murdered by some of the nightly unpaid Police of the Country' at Cranagh, some two miles from Athlone, in December 1828. Henry Gardiner was struck on the back of the head on his way home to Boyle one day in October 1837, confiding in Chief Constable Curtis that he had been warned by his own workforce that he was a marked man. A man named Thompson was threatened near Athlone over his plan to evict tenants at Knockanyconor, St John's parish, in 1843, while threatening notices were on occasion addressed to landlords as a class. Godfrey Hogg was ordered to let conacre at a cheap rate on his land at Ballymartin, Kilglass parish, in May 1843. A police officer in Roscommon town warned in early 1847 that 'the Peasantry here are as well

Blakeney to Miller, 1 Oct 1837.   46 OR 1848/605, information of John Loughan, 10 Nov. 1848; RLG, 4 Oct. 1845.   47 CSORP 1829/W40, Warburton to Gregory, 23 Apr. 1829.

Armed as the Police'. A landlord named Harrison reported that his out-offices at Cloonara were burned down and guns taken in April 1845. He added that 'this county is in a state of open rebellion & all the valuable fire arms of the gentry are at this moment in the hands of the pesantry'. Landlords clearly felt that the possession of arms by peasants was still a measure of their inclination to take up arms in a national rebellion. However, these observations, made in the context of whiteboy activity, confirm that caution must be exercised in assuming that agrarian rebels were acting out of a consciousness of national antagonism.[48]

One tactic that was still frequently employed was incendiarism. In April 1830 a house from which a man had recently been evicted for non-payment of rent was burned down. A house in Creeve parish was burned down in May 1834, prompting the reporting police officer, Frederick Carr, to observe that 'the Tenants on those lands are at law with their Land Lord Mr Aitcheson none of whom have paid their rent with the exception of Vaughan'. All had been served with notice to quit and had raised cash for their legal expenses. John Dolan's house in Moore parish was burned down in March 1835 'in con-sequence of Dolan being about to take some land held by other people'. In September the same year an unoccupied house near Elphin was burned down after it was rented by Samuel Goodman following the eviction of the former tenant for non-payment of rent. In December 1835 a house was burned down at Kilmacross, leading Boyle chief constable Robert Curtis to note in his report that the occupier had 'some time ago taken this house and some land from which another man was ejected for non payment of rent'. A family bought the interest in a house and four acres in Drum parish in April 1837 when the ten-ant emigrated to the United States, but it was burned down before they could take up residence. Although no reason was assigned for this action, it may be supposed that someone else had coveted the holding. When a horse, a cow and two heifers belonging to Thomas Killian of Taughmaconnell parish were maimed in July 1837, Chief Constable Lowrie explained that Killian had recently bought the interest in a farm 'and it is supposed some persons in the immediate neighbourhood wished to get the land'. In March 1838 an empty house near Roscommon town that belonged to a woman called Hall from Dublin was consumed by fire. Chief Constable Sparling at Roscommon town observed that 'the cause appears to be in consequence of the former tenant,

48 RLG, 20 Dec. 1828; RJ, 20 Dec. 1828; OR 1837/123, Curtis to Miller, 4 Oct. 1837; OR 1843/8650, undated outrage report (1843); OR 1843/7059, for example, a notice posted at Carrownaskagh, near Strokestown, 9 Apr. 1843; OR 1843/8729, outrage report, 1 May 1843; OR 1847/38083, George Knox, chief constable, Roscommon, to chief secretary, 1 Jan. 1847; OR 1845/10413, C. Harrison, Cloonaray, to unnamed, Dublin Castle, 15 May 1845.

named Denis Grealy, having been dispossessed for non payment of rent and the house let to another'.[49]

Threatening notices and illegal oaths also continued to relate to land. When land held in rundale was parcelled out to individual households, the resulting conflicts over who had been given what could be among the former partners, rather than between tenants and landlords. Further, when one person took a tenancy of land that had formerly been held in rundale partnership, he was taking a substantial physical risk. Ten perches of a new ditch were levelled on land in Kilglass parish in April 1836 because two of the former partners did not approve of the way in which it was laid out. A stack of turf belonging to John Moran was burned down in Cloonfinlough parish in October 1836, prompting Blakeney to observe that Moran had taken land formerly held jointly, and that eviction proceedings had begun against his former partners, who were still in possession. Lowrie reported that a cow shed and barn worth £60 were burned down at Killeglan, Taughmaconnell parish, in April 1837. The whole townland had been held collectively for many years but after the expiry of a lease the landlord had directed that the tenants should be granted individual leases. The victim of the arson attack, Bryan Dolan, was 'in comfortable circumstances' and had gained some of the best land, which was near his house. John Leaheny was assaulted at his home in Kilronan parish in July 1839 and sworn to surrender his 'choice division' of land to his partner. The demise of rundale usually accompanied attempts by landlords to improve or rationalize their estates, signifying changes in customary social and tenurial arrangements, and leading to conflict. When the townland of Erra, occupied by forty to fifty families, fell out of lease in September 1837, two men proposed to take a tenancy of the whole townland. Their proposal was followed by arson attacks on their turf and oats.[50]

In March 1836 a threatening notice was posted on Gregory Carroll's house in Bumlin parish, warning him:

> Take notice Gregory Carroll to have nothing to do with Hanleys land or if you do you may mark the consequence as you have a supply without it.

49 CSORP 18330/W46, Warburton to Gregory, 3 May 1830; CSORP 1834/25, Carr to Galbraith, 20 May 1834; OR 1835/22, Lowrie to Warburton, 1 Apr. 1835; OR 1835/30, Sparling to Warburton, 21 Sept. 1835; OR 1835/50, Curtis to Warburton, 20 Dec. 1835; OR 1837/48, Lowrie to Miller, 14 Apr. 1837; OR 1837/90, Lowrie to Miller, 19 July 1837; OR 1838/36, Sparling to Miller, 26 Mar. 1838.   **50** OR 1836/47, Blakeney to Galbraith, 12 Apr. 1836; OR 1836/107, Blakeney to Warburton, 17 Oct. 1836; OR 1839/4948, Alexander Henderson, constable, Boyle, to inspector general, 3 July 1839; OR 1837/121, Sparling to Miller, 1 Oct. 1837.

In November 1835 an armed party of men forced its way into six houses in Kilglass parish and swore the occupants not to bid for the lands of any man who was evicted. Implicit in this intimidatory action was a belief that a solidarity was required among the rural poor to dissuade landlords from evicting, or improving, as the landlord might have termed the action. Underpinning all attempts to regulate lands previously let in rundale was the belief that all members of the rural community had a right to a piece of land from which to gain subsistence.[51]

The maiming or killing of livestock continued to feature among the repertoire through which the customary code was enforced, including counter-theatrical and vengeful attacks on the landowner's own stock. Edward Hanly's sheep were houghed in June 1838 after he took land from which the previous tenant had been evicted. A week later Michael Daly's cow and his cabbage garden were destroyed after he took a few acres of land at Curramore, Kiltoom parish, which had previously been held by someone else. Disguise was still used during conflict over land, though considerably less frequently, as when a party of men with blackened faces attempted to storm Jacob Martin's house near Boyle in February 1836.[52]

These apparently archaic forms of action could, however, conceal a divergence between social classes. One example of an apparent neighbour dispute over land illustrates how such conflicts may be more usefully interpreted. At 2 a.m. on 18 December 1838, nine men assembled at John Hunt's house in Kiltullagh parish, scattering Hunt's oats, hay and a turf stack. Hunt recognized them as his nearest neighbours. All, including Hunt, were tenants of the marquis of Westmeath, then in the process of demanding rent increases. Chief Constable Carr reported that the tenants had combined against the marquis to fight the rent increases and evictions that were to follow any refusal to pay. Hunt, however, had complied with the rent demand. The apparently antiquated neighbour dispute, on investigation, proved to be an example of emergent associational organization, such as might be taken in an industrial context against a strike-breaker. The marquis being beyond the reach of the non-payers' associative capabilities, Hunt made a ready target. Indeed, while the marquis might have abandoned any sense of obligation, Hunt might still be expected to share the other tenants' conceptions of justice, a fair rent and the right to subsist. Further, while the collective activity was legitimized by a customary consciousness, it concealed possibilities of associational conflicts. As James Scott put it, 'the rights being defended represent the irreducible material basis of class interest'.[53]

---

51 OR 1836/38, enclosed with letter from Blakeney to Galbraith, 24 Mar. 1836; OR 1835/44, Galbraith to Warburton, 7 Nov. 1835. 52 OR 1838/73, Blakeney to Warburton, 21 June 1838; OR 1838/72, David Smyth, constable , Athlone, to Miller, 25 June 1838; OR 1836/18, Curtis to Crossley, 16 Feb. 1836. 53 OR 1838/114, Carr to Miller, 27 Dec. 1838;

Changing repertoires

The tactics described thus far in relation to land, wages, prices and law demonstrate the persistence of collective protests and actions that involved disciplining members of the community according to traditional, shared mores through
established tactics like the threatening letter, oath-swearing and incendiarism,
while the basis of such collective discipline was slowly being dissolved. Scott
has illuminated how similar mores functioned among the rural poor of south-
east Asia. Such comparisons locate Irish agrarian conflict in a wider context of
class relations in rural societies. Scott identified the characteristic themes of
agrarian protest as being that claims on their incomes are never legitimate
when they infringe on subsistence minima, and that everyone should be guar-
anteed a subsistence niche. He added that such 'safety-first' principles under-
lie the technical, social and moral arrangements of the non-capitalist agrarian
order. While the Irish agrarian economy was far from being a subsistence economy in this period, the poor undoubtedly enforced claims on the basis of the
need to subsist. Lewis anticipated Scott's observation, writing of the Irish
agrarian rebel, 'it is his wish to obtain some guarantee for his future subsistence
which drives him to Whiteboy outrage'. This need for the means of subsistence often meant an attachment to land. Joseph Tabuteau, a stipendiary magistrate in Co. Tipperary, told the Lords 1839 committee, 'the man who holds
the Tenement does not care under what Circumstances he is put out, whether
fairly or unfairly; … he thinks he ought not to be put out'. Scott's work has
described similar processes in places as far from Ireland as Burma and Vietnam.[54]

The response of the rural poor to developments like the ending of rundale
arrangements might be seen simply as a conservative reaction to the modernizing of landlords. However, an insistence on placing such conflicts in a
schematic framework is misplaced. While formally traditional methods may
have been used, these could have different contents. Smyth has suggested that
popular ideology in Ireland from the 1790s was a compound of custom and
the proselytizing of élites through newspapers, sermons and broadsheets.
This grafted Painite and 'half-digested French principles' on to customary
consciousness. Garvin has noted that 'secret societies … used agitation, intimidation and a primitive form of political mobilization to further their interests'. However, where nationalism may have been the political trajectory taken
by the Ribbon networks supported by publicans, shopkeepers and strong

J.C. Scott, 'Hegemony and the peasantry' (1977), 280.   54 Scott, *Moral economy of the peasant* (1975), 105; Beames, *Peasants and power*, 4; Lewis, *On local disturbances*, 253; SC 1839,
746, evidence of Joseph Tabuteau.

farmers, the evidence from the countryside suggests an embryonic repertoire of class, rather than national, affiliation. In July 1852 a bailiff and supporter of the Conservative candidate in a forthcoming election was presented with the ear of a horse and instructed to give the ear to the candidate, Pennefather Lloyd. Here a 'traditional' and symbolic tactic was deployed in an electoral context. Peter Burke has observed in relation to popular culture that the meaning of a ritual might change while the form remained more or less the same. It has also been noted that traditionalism could operate as a stimulus to revolt, rather than a restraint, as in the case of Pugachev's Cossack revolt in late eighteenth-century Russia. Thompson's observation that plebeian culture took conservative forms but that its meanings were not necessarily so, creating the apparent paradox of a rebellious traditional culture, is highly significant here. The sanctions deployed within plebeian cultures, such as intimidation and shame, may have been conservative in form, but particularly at transitional junctures they could prefigure associational forms, loyalties and solidarities that are usually considered modern (Luddism was an English case in point). In this significant sense, a historiography of modernization is an inadequate explanatory model for social conflict, which combined the traditional with the rebellious, the pre-modern with the modern and the parochial with the cosmopolitan.[55]

As a consequence of this eclecticism, tactics were adapted and transformed as direct conflict with landowners and representatives of the state became more common. The specific circumstances of illegality, severe penalties on conviction, and the early development of a professional police force to deal with agrarian disturbance, meant that many such actions could be no more than counter-theatrical demonstrations of class antipathy. For example, Edward Mills of Fairymount, the county's former high sheriff, who was encountered a number of times in the preceding chapter, died in 1829. The *Roscommon and Leitrim Gazette* reported bitterly that as his body was taken through Roscommon town on 20 February a 'rabble hooted and treated it disrespectfully'. This action is in contrast to the carefully observed rituals of respectful remembrance and affection reserved for those among the poor who met their end at places like Tyburn. However, counter-theatrical actions may also have been designed to have an intimidating effect, such as when stones were flung through the gatehouse windows at Castletenison, seat of a major landlord, early in 1836. In

55 Smyth, *Men of no property*, 3; T. Garvin, 'Defenders, Ribbonmen and others' (1987), 220; OR 1852/157, Kirwan to unnamed, Dublin Castle, 8 July 1852; P. Burke, *Popular culture*, 21; P. Longworth, 'The Pugachev revolt' (1974); Thompson, 'Introduction: custom and culture' (1993), 9; Thompson, *Making of the English working class*, 594.

April 1836 a former tenant of Alexander Lynch's near Athlone presumably gained some cathartic delight, though not reinstatement, when he burned down the unoccupied house he had been evicted from two months earlier. Chief Constable Alexander Lowrie observed of Lynch, 'this Gentleman, I am informed has used some severity with his tenants, by ejecting some, and raising the Rents of others.' Curtis reported a similar case shortly afterwards near Croghan. Dominick Breheny was suspected of burning down his house the night after his possessions were sold at auction under a court order for rent arrears, 'and nothing but the walls left him & he was orderd to quit & give them up to his Landlord'. Between 4 and 5 a.m. one November morning in 1836 forty-eight window panes were broken in Clarissa Masterson's house at Moss Hill in the half-parish of Clonaff, her son telling chief constable Carr that 'his mother had processed several of their immediate neighbours for conacre rent, who might have been induced through revenge to have committed the act'. Shots were fired into the glebe house of Kilgefin parish after the Revd W. Beech took land at Carroward in March 1842. Direct action was taken against Edward Kelly, a landlord who had evicted a tenant. Kelly's house at Curramore, Kiltoom parish, was set on fire. In January 1843 John Waldron was threatened directly over his conacre rent demands. Cattle sheds and stock worth £300 belonging to Archibald St George in Cam parish were burned in April 1847. In August the same year the thatch of Eleanor Egan's house in Creeve parish was set ablaze, suspicion surrounding two men who were engaged in a law suit with Egan over the house. The presence of the world of commerce in the lives of the rural poor was demonstrated when a gang of men visited Bridget Carty in Ardcarn parish, demanding money she had got at the agricultural bank. The visitors were wearing their coats turned inside out and had their faces blackened.[56]

Three roods of potatoes belonging to Bartholomew Moran were destroyed in July 1837 after he took lands in Ardcarn parish from which tenants had been evicted in May. Moran earned money through the distraint of goods, often livestock, on behalf of landlords. The letting of land to this man, in particular, would have compounded the wrong of evicting and re-letting. In November the same year Moran was again the object of attack, when a cow and a bull of his were poisoned. However, the whiteboys had still not finished with Moran

56 RLG, 28 Feb. 1829; OR 1836/17, Curtis to Galbraith, 14 Feb. 1836; OR 1836/52, Lowrie to Galbraith, 17 Apr. 1836; OR 1836/53, Curtis to Galbraith, 18 Apr. 1836; OR 1836/118, Carr to Miller, 3 Nov. 1836; OR 1842/5087, outrage report, 20 Mar. 1842; OR 1842/23727, outrage report, 17 Dec. 1842; OR 1843/1373, outrage report, 21 Jan. 1843; OR 1847/337, Gerard Barry, resident magistrate, Athlone to Redington 15 Apr. 1847; OR 1836/97, Carr to Miller, 24 Aug. 1836; OR 1836/103, Curtis to Miller, 5 Oct. 1836.

and they set fire to his house in May 1839, two years after he had been given the house and ten acres from which the former tenants had been evicted for non-payment of rent. In December 1839 oats belonging to Moran were scattered, Chief Constable Reed reporting that 'the only motive that can be assigned is, that Moran is a caretaker and driver to Mr Beggs, who has some property in that part of the country'.[57]

The memory of long-term occupation of land legitimized the continued or renewed possession of it among the rural poor, leading to conflict. Around a dozen men visited Bryan Lennon and Thomas Gallagher one evening in February 1839 and swore them to surrender the lands they had taken to Bryan Reilly and Mary Tully, by whom it was formerly held. A threatening notice was delivered to John Lavender in Cloonfinlough parish, warning him to have nothing to do with eviction proceedings planned by the Balfes, for 'to toss any person out of his Fathers Land where he was Bred and Born, you will rue the day'. Rent arrears were not seen as reasons for evicting someone. A notice sent via Carrick on Shannon post office (note here the contemporary means for conveying an apparently traditional form of rebuke) to a landlord near Keadue threatened:

> Will Loyd I hear what you have a mind to do, but look before you leap Loyd. Loid you say that you will dispossess a widow and six orphans of a piece of land they hold in Culbalkin and for which they are paying rent these twenty years ... if you have anything to do with this honest woman that you will not live to see next Christmas day ... Take notice of what I have said to you for by all the Tories in great Brittain and Ireland you will be made a riddle of ... I am no enemy to my queen or country.

The writer displayed the previously-noted rhetoric of loyalty, but at the same time an undisguised antipathy towards this particular landlord. Such a notice combines the formally traditional tactic of the threatening letter with an awareness of cosmopolitan politics and a memory of customary rights that had been enjoyed by the widow for twenty years. Its avowed loyalty may be rhetoric designed to legitimize it but it also suggests that the rural poor did not have a conception of such conflict being underpinned by any national struggle.[58]

57 OR 1837/94, Curtis to Warburton, 1 Aug. 1837; OR 1837/148, Curtis to Miller, 6 Nov. 1837; OR 1839/3257, Reed to inspector general, 4 May 1839; OR 1839/10542, Reed to inspector general, 20 Dec. 1839.   58 OR 1839/1433, Blakeney to Miller, 5 Mar. 1839; OR 1839/4075, Blakeney to inspector general, 8 June 1839; OR 1837/134, enclosed with letter from Curtis to Warburton, 23 Oct. 1836; OR 1839/1433, Blakeney to Miller, 5 Mar. 1839;

In the case of some landlords, it may not be too difficult to discern why this antipathy was felt. Seven men went to Patrick Byrne's house in Stoke Park, Kilmore parish, at 1 a.m. on 28 April 1838. The reporting chief constable said: 'It appears Mr Hogg the Land Lord wishes to dispossess said Byrne. In my opinion the said party was collected by Mr Hogg to dispossess said Byrne by force.' This was the same Hogg whose house had been attacked in September 1835 and who was to appear before the Devon Commission in Roscommon town, advocating recognition of tenant improvements. The *Roscommon and Leitrim Gazette* had described Mr Hogg, a member of a local Brunswick Club, as an 'indulgent' landlord.[59]

Other people facing eviction levelled their homes, rather than surrender them to the landlord, Constable James Sheron reporting such an instance at Kilbride, Kilmore parish, in March 1839.[60]

Protesters shot into a barn and left a threatening notice for a landlord named James Tumblety after his rent increases set a precedent. The notice warned Tumblety he would not receive the increase:

> you are the means of Riseing land in Taughmaconnell their was no land any higher than one pound an acre, until you put it thirty shillings.

The collective action of tenants against landlords was illustrated in May 1840 when two men serving eviction notices on forty tenants of two absentee ladies named Newcomen in Lisanuffy parish had to take refuge from a crowd of boys and women pelting them with stones. The men were chased into a house and the processes taken and torn up.[61]

Richard Crotty of Mount Plunket received three letters in July 1840 warning him against evicting tenants. One letter told Crotty:

> You tirant monster your death is decided on by the Dublin Society You are worse than an Orangeman You are without religion and no feeling for the poor, there are twenty five of us the lot fell on to do your job.

In the same month a notice was found posted on an uninhabited house at Slattaghmore in Kilglass parish, warning Patrick Balfe's bailiff not to continue sending people to jail at Mr Balfe's suit, he 'having ... assisted in the arrest

OR 1839/4075, Blakeney to inspector general, 8 June 1839; OR 1837/134, enclosed with letter from Curtis to Warburton, 23 Oct. 1836. 59 OR 1838/45, Johnston to Miller, 29 May 1838; Devon Commission, II, 348, evidence of Godfrey Hogg; RLG, 7 Mar. 1829. 60 OR 1839/1726, James Sheron, chief constable, Elphin, to inspector general of police, 21 Mar. 1839. 61 OR 1840/4111, Sheron to inspector general, 11 Mar. 1840; OR 1840/9933, Blakeney to inspector general, 26 May 1840.

of Persons Decreed, for Rent due ... and who had been committed to jail for non-payment'. Oats belonging to the same bailiff, Peter Derwin, were set alight the following month. He was also in conflict with tenants of Mr Balfe's on the townland of Knockhall, who had also been processed for rents due and witheld, the tenants claiming Mr Balfe was no longer the owner.[62]

The antipathy towards landlords reached such a level that agents like William Gorman petitioned for police protection in March 1841 to carry out evictions against his master's tenants in Kiltoom parish. The plea elicited an interesting response from the Castle: 'I am directed by His Excellency to inform you that the Constabulary cannot be allowed to go with you, but a party will be directed to go near the place, to be in readiness in case of a breach of the peace.'[63]

This response reveals the 'theatre' of the rulers. A guise of impartiality concerning the private business of landlord and tenant was adopted, but the police presence nearby would ensure that Gorman's work was done. The 1836 constabulary act had been formulated with this impartiality in mind. The police were not thenceforth to be used to 'levy tithe or to collect rent by distress', in accordance with Peel's vision of 'a stipendiary police acting ... under stipendiary magistrates'. Broeker has described this development as a 'tacit admission that government solely in the interests of the ascendancy was no longer feasible'. Gorman may have had good reason for requesting police assistance. Bryan Fallon was assaulted when he went to serve eviction processes in Kilbride parish that December. Denis Mahon wrote directly to the under-secretary, Edward Lucas, in March the following year, interceding for two bailiffs who wanted protection while they executed processes for non-payment of rent in the Strokestown area. Martin Mulligan, who was agent and bailiff to Mrs Anne Lyster of Athleague, was beaten after he distrained livestock in lieu of eighteen months' rent that was due from tenants at Fairymount in July 1842. The animals were taken from him. This was the same man who had been beaten for his services to the Lyster family in May 1839 after prosecuting people who removed timber from the Lysters' woods. At Stonepark, Kilronan parish, in December 1842, Edward Powell was threatened in order to prevent him serving eviction notices.[64]

62 OR 1840/12539, Blake to inspector general, 8 July 1840; OR 1840/13615, enclosed with letter from Blakeney to inspector general, 29 July 1840; OR 1840/15487, Blake to inspector general, 27 Aug. 1840.   63 OR 1841/3575, deposition of William Gorman, 20 Mar. 1841, and reply from Dublin Castle, signature illegible.   64 Broeker, *Rural disorder*, 222, 198, 234; OR 1842/1791, outrage report, 21 Dec. 1841; OR1842/3981, Denis Mahon to Edward Lucas, under-secretary, 4 Mar. 1842. Unfortunately there appears to be no record of the outcome of this request; Lucas, 4 Mar. 1842; OR 1842/17533, memorial of Martin Mulligan to lord chief justice, Dublin, 7 Sept. 1842; OR 1842/23309, outrage report, 17 Dec. 1842.

In the 1840s rents and availability of conacre gardens became a major issue to labourers. In 1839 the Lords had been told that tillage was being turned into pasture to send cattle to markets in Dublin and Liverpool. The growing need to feed cities was affecting the way agriculture was organized in Roscommon, leading to conflict over land. In October 1842 five people were sworn to pay no more than £2 10s. per acre for conacre at Tullyvarran, Lisanuffy parish, but the following month six persons were sworn not to pay more than £3 per acre on the same townland. However, at Rahara, a few miles to the south, persons paying more than £5 per acre were threatened, while in Cloonfinlough parish three oaths were administered to pay no more than £6 per acre. There were also continued threats against those who took land from which others had been evicted or persons who canted land. It is apparent that disciplining members of the same group remained a significant whiteboy tactic, despite threats to individual farmers about their prices, or general notices posted for the attention of landlords, farmers and agents.[65]

Actions against landlords who demanded, and tenants who paid, what were considered excessive prices for conacre, prompted a meeting of the county's magistrates on 7 February 1844. They noted that disturbance was prevalent in the central part of the county. The magistrates added that Mr Irwin (one of their number) had been fired at, a man named Brock had been murdered, Mr Malley's 91 sheep had been killed and he had been shot at, Mr Balfe and his horse had been shot, Mr Blakeney's horse driven off the field and his ploughman threatened with death and various other crimes. Government intervention was demanded. Resident magistrate David Duff wrote to Lucas explaining that 'the outcry is against the high rent demanded for conacre potatoe land which is let for from 5 to £9 per acre no manure with it ... Mr Balfe who was shot charged as high as £12 per acre'. Duff described the situation as 'the conflict between Landlord & Tenant & so far as I have seen the people are in the greatest poverty'. His judgement was confirmed by John Davis, a Co. Leitrim landlord, who swore to Duff he was afraid to visit his lands to demand rent after serving notices to quit on several tenants. Another landlord described the poor assembling to turn up pasture, shooting at a gentleman and maiming his cattle as they worked. In March 1845 Duff discovered that labourers were being charged £10 for unprepared conacre and a further £4 for preparation. Sixty labourers working for Arthur O'Connor near Castleplunket met the same

65 HL 1839, 1038, evidence of Tomkins Brew; OR 1842/20511, outrage report, 20 Oct. 1842; OR 1842/21427, outrage report, 7 Nov. 1842; OR 1842/23797, outrage report, 25 Dec. 1842; OR 1843/5729, outrage report, 10 Mar. 1843; For example, a notice posted at Carrownaskagh, reported at OR 1843/7059, 9 Apr. 1843, warned any 'persons ... who do not let land cheap'.

month and set conacre rates of £7 per acre. A labourer was reported as saying he would pay a reasonable price for conacre to ward off starvation. It is apparent that the practical need for land to grow subsistence potatoes was paramount, but that the rural poor generalized from such experiences, while taking specific actions over conacre rents.[66]

Michael Burke led a campaign over conacre in Cloonygormican parish and was imprisoned. He sent a striking memorial to the lord lieutenant appealing for clemency. Where most such memorials are the grovelling work of frightened men, Burke's was most unapologetic. He said he had only wanted 'potato ground at fair valuation', but then launched a general attack on landlordism:

> the poor of this county is in the State of death by the Cruelty of the Landlords – and Agents, Middlemen an stock masters … I mean the graziers who always make it appear to the Government contrary to the welfare of Ireland or the unhappy state of the poor who lies in oblivion – in hunger & threat, neighther Clothing or food or ahabitation to Shelter them from the inclemency of the weather – or – but poor huts with torrents of rain all through and they always … at the point of the swoord at time England was in need.

Duff reported that Burke had named himself Captain and had called meetings to dig up pasture, saying that he had the authority of the government. People believed he had been commissioned to let lands by the lord lieutenant, the queen and O'Connell. Burke had proclaimed that every labourer was entitled to five acres and more if he wanted. His proclamation said:

> A proclamation of distress as appears in the Townland of Bushfield and the adjoining Townlands. For the Hon[bl] James Nolan Esq.[r] occupier

> Sir, you are required to take your poor into consideration as to comply with their cry ov distress so far as to allow the Potatoe ground at fair valuation.

Burke then prescribed dates of payment and amounts to be paid, telling Nolan to accept what the labourers could pay,and concluding 'God save our sovereign Lady the Queen. Price by the acre 6£'.[67]

66 OR1844/3179, resolution of Co. Roscommon magistrates, 7 Feb. 1844; OR 1844/3549, Duff to Lucas, 22 Feb. 1844; OR 1844/4355, John Davis to Duff, undated (1844); OR 1845/3339, G. Lloyd, Croghan, to under-secretary, 18 Feb. 1845; OR 1845/5317, Duff to Lucas, 15 Mar. 1845; OR 1845/6963, information of Michael Dier, 27 Mar. 1845; OR 1845/10145, report of Roscommon petty sessions, 17 Mar. 1845.   67 OR 1845/11481, memorial of Michael Burke to lord lieutenant, 22 Mar. 1845; OR 1845/6055, Duff to

Despite the narrow geographic extent of Burke's campaign, the modest demands and the proclamations of loyalty, there are some striking features such as the openness of the meetings, which were attended by 300 people, as well as the degree of political generalization and the consciousness of conflict between landlords and tenants. The lingering expectation of paternalism is also note-worthy, James Nolan being expected to consider 'his' poor. Burke also employed a familiar oppositional discourse, of the labouring classes being expected to fight wars on behalf of their rulers and subsequently deserving reciprocity when they needed assistance. In the terms suggested by Antonio Gramsci, Burke may be seen as an 'organic intellectual' of the rural labourers. His story should not be dismissed as insignificant, for there were undoubtedly many more Burkes lead-ing local and regional struggles. The significance of these people was, as Scott put it, that 'the residue of local initiatives may form the potential nodes of class leadership and organization in later periods'. Burke was convicted at the sum-mer assizes in 1845 of delivering a threatening notice to Major Mahon's herds-man and was sentenced to seven years' transportation.[68]

Such campaigns could be effective. A Mr Hudson, who lived three miles from Roscommon town, could find no-one to work for him and all his conacre tenants gave up their lands after he took a farm which had been proposed for by others. Mr Hudson was a gentleman whose family had lived in the area for a hundred years.[69]

The assassination of Mahon was only the most celebrated example of the increased prevalence of direct conflict with landlords or their agents. The event afforded some satisfaction to those who warned James Fleming:

> Sir, This serves to give you notice that you are a marked man in the Coun-ty, and also to let you know that if you attempt to demand any rent from youre own tenant, or the Reverend Barre's tenants, you will meet with the fate of Major Mahon and have youre house burned over youre head.

Notices were served on Marcus McCausland and his wife. Mr McCausland was told:

> the cries of the Starved and Desolated have Reached the Heavens ... you will Share in the same Fate as y^r. Kindsman the Demon Major Mahon ... there is a fund at present formed in this Country for shoot-ing Opressors,

Lucas, 23 Mar. 1845.   **68** OR 1845/16805, Duff to Lucas, 6 Aug. 1845; Scott, *Moral econ-omy of the peasant*, 207; OR 1845/15015, H.B. Wray, resident magistrate, Castlerea, to Lucas, 13 July 1845.   **69** OR 1846/8863, Duff to Pennefather, 14 Apr. 1846.

while his wife was warned:

> unless Mr McCausland becomes a better landlord in this country he will
> share in the same fate as the Demon Major Mahon did There are Res-
> olutions in this Country to take down all the Tyranizeing Landlords.

McCausland had inherited a part of the Mahon estate some years earlier and
was a close relative of the Major. John Ross Mahon, of Dublin agents Guin-
ness and Mahon, was his agent.[70]

A Co. Kerry landlord reported his Co. Roscommon agent as saying that all
the tenants there had sworn not to pay a penny in rent. Furthermore, Dudley
Persse's Roscommon agent could not persuade tenants there to pay the rent,
even though the agent claimed they had ample means. Mr Persse had reduced
their rents from 23s. an Irish acre to 18s., and offered to cancel the arrears and
return the distrained cattle of those who surrendered possession of their holdings. However, none seemed inclined to do so. Mr Persse believed an armed conspiracy existed to protect defaulters, and that any evicting landlord would be
killed. Such demands should not necessarily be seen as evidence of a desire
among the poor to turn the world upside down, but suggest a decline in any
belief that it might be possible to return landlord and tenant relations to a former condition of reciprocity and the beginnings of organization to respond to
those changed circumstances. This decline accompanied the increasing incidence of direct threats to landlords and their agents. It should be acknowledged,
however, that attempts to return to an imagined or real equilibrium that pre-
dated the disturbance also continued to be a mechanism for legitimizing struggle and conflict.[71]

Among the first Molly Maguire notices was one posted in Castlerea in
March 1845. It coincided with a large and tumultuous daylight assembly at
Castleplunket to turn up pasture. Resident magistrate H.B. Wray reported: 'I
found a very violent & turbulent spirit among the people and several of them
using the most inflam'y language, particularly as regards the Police, and a
determination to dig up the ground regardless of all consequences.' Wray confronted the gathering and persuaded the people to disperse but they told him
that if Mr Macdonough would not consider their wants, they were determined
not to starve and might as well be shot. The whole crowd, numbering about
1,000, resolved to meet on St Patrick's day to show Macdonough what they
could do.[72]

70 OR 1847/736, threatening notice to James Fleming, 14 Nov. 1847; OR 1847/735, threatening notice to Mr McCausland and his wife, undated (1847); OR 1847/735, Marcus
McCausland to William Sommerville, 29 Nov. 1847.   71 OR 1845/22867, undated letter
from Kerry landlord, name illegible; OR 1847/688, statement of Dudley Persse, Co. Galway, regarding Co. Roscommon tenants, 31 Oct. 1847.   72 OR 1845/5001, Wray to Lucas,

The Revd John Lloyd of Smith Hill was shot dead on the way home from conducting a service in his parish church at Aughrim in November 1847. The assassination, two miles from Elphin, was attributed to Mr Lloyd's eviction of some tenants for rent arrears the previous month. Edmond Blake observed that 'there appears to be a regular organized system of Assassination got up against the Landlords of this County'. The previous year a deputation of Lloyd's workers had asked him for wages of 1s. a day, which he had refused. A magistrate named William Daniel survived an assassination attempt after he attempted to collect arrears he had bought with some land at Kilcorman. In January 1846 George Knox, the agent for crown lands in the area, received a notice ordering him to surrender the agency. The familiar demand for conacre land was also made. Some of Knox's own pasture land was turned up. An armed party approached two gentlemen riding in a gig near Frenchpark and handed a threatening notice to Arthur Irwin, who was walking with the gig party. Many people were watching and none assisted. The gentlemen gave chase and one of the armed men was drowned after he plunged into a river while trying to escape.[73]

Land was not Molly's only concern. Labourers engaged to work on a scheme to render the river Boyle navigable from Lough Key to the Shannon went on strike after two men said they could no longer pump water without assistance. Molly Maguirism was reported to be behind the dispute. Indeed, a printed notice was posted on a Catholic church in Carrick and circulated extensively. It attacked landlords, who cared less for Molly's children than for their dogs, and summoned Molly's family to action:

> it now lies with yourselves my dear children, not to starve in the midst of plenty.

The notice also prescribed rules allowing landlords 'fair value', no evictions unless two years in arrears, assistance to good landlords to collect rents, no night meetings or arms raids, no confrontations with the police, and 'no distinction to any man, on account of his Religion, his acts alone you are to look to … let bygones be bygones'. This notice is noteworthy for a number of reasons. First, the very fact that it was printed reveals a degree of organization. Thompson noted that in an agrarian context the anonymous letter remained

14 Mar. 1845. 73 OR 1847/760, Edmond Blake, resident magistrate, Elphin to Redington, 29 Nov. 1847; RLG, 16 May 1846; OR 1848/609, outrage report, 11 Nov. 1848; RLG, 24 Jan. 1846, 31 Jan. 1846. The story of Knox and the Crown estate at Ballykilcline is told by Robert Scally, *The end of hidden Ireland* (1995); OR 1846/12347, John Duckworth and Morgan Crofton, JPs, to under-secretary, 23 May 1846.

significant but that elsewhere in English plebeian culture the radical or Chartist printing press replaced it. By 1845 Irish agrarian protesters' texts had found their way into print. The existence of a printed Molly Maguire notice is a particularly significant example of the way in which class differentiation was developing on foundations of Irish tradition, and of the combined and uneven consciousness of the Irish rural poor. Second, Molly's notice prescribed general reforms to the conduct of landlord and tenant relations in the tenants' favour. These included radical but concrete reforms, which were neither millenarian nor revolutionary. Third, it was informed by an ideology of fraternity and disregard for religious affiliation that had been removed from opposition politics over the fifty years since 1798. It looked to a harmonious future, free from such distinctions. This suggests that an alternative conception of politics to confessional O'Connellite nationalism was forming out of the customary practices of Irish popular culture, as those traditions increasingly became identified with the rural poor alone (although under economic pressure, lesser tenant farmers could resort to similar tactics, particularly as there were now many more direct lettings from landlords to occupiers of land). Thompson noted the emergence of 'a plebeian Painite underground culture' by 1800 in England. The story of agrarian rebellion in Co. Roscommon was of the development of an underground culture of class antagonism, in the early nineteenth century appropriating Jacobin and Painite emblems and later influenced first by radicalism and then by trade unions and Chartism, all grafted on to Irish traditions. It would be difficult to ignore the social dimension of late Chartism, since informal links were made official between the English Chartists and the Irish Confederates in the spring of 1848.[74]

The Molly Maguire disturbances may be seen as the maturation of this phase of agrarian conflict, when overt conflicts between self-conscious classes became more or less open. Landlords who were the owners of estates were the victims, as were the substantial farmers they let their lands to. It has already been observed that the number of intermediate layers in the social pyramid of rural Ireland was not so significant as the relations between immediate landlord and tenant. As this frequently became a direct relationship between owner and occupier as the first half of the nineteenth century progressed, prominent persons like Mahon increasingly became targets.

Patterns of conflict in the Roscommon countryside evolved as the nineteenth century proceeded. In addition, while the language of custom may have

---

74 RLG, 21 June 1845, 5 July 1845; E.P. Thompson, 'The crime of anonymity' (1975), 295; J.C. Belchem, 'English working class radicalism and the Irish' (1985); the tension between Chartist and nationalist politics in Ireland is considered in M. Huggins, 'Democracy or nationalism?' (2005).

been the legitimizing discourse behind agrarian and other disturbances, there is also much evidence that this language, (and the forms through which conflicts were articulated), was being strained by the other changes affecting social, economic and political relations. Political is used here not in the sense of the high politics practised by such as the O'Conor Don and Viscount Lorton, but the popular politics of the rural poor. That is not to say different discourses could not co-exist, and mutate. The motifs of Paine and France, expressed along with chiliastic aspirations, were incrementally being transformed into expressions of class antagonism and developing associational forms. Gibbons acknowledges only that 'abstract political ideas' were present in threatening notices but suggests that they played a minor role. The pervasiveness of the modernization approach has led to an underestimating of the extent of political and class-consciousness among the rural poor. Historians have not found evidence of embryonic political and class awareness because they have not expected to. However, by the mid-1840s it seems that the demands of agrarian combinations were often practical and reformist.[75]

The distinction between confessional nationalism and the politicization of the rural poor may be discerned in a notice posted just outside Roscommon in 1830. The writer had not moved from general statements of the need for change, which had their roots in chiliastic dreams and which had no clear organizational vehicle or programme for achieving such change. However, the fact that such general statements were being made at all demonstrates that the consciousness of the rural poor was not limited by parochial, family or confessional identities. The notice proclaimed:

> General Notice to the people of Ireland to be firmly united together without any distinction whatsoever in either church or creed but true and Loyal to each other oppressing Land Lords and Clergy tythes and taxes all overbearing men of Ireland be ready when called on and throw off the yoke which we are long under God Save the King.

Despite the syntax and punctuation, the writer's meaning was plain. The sentiments echoed French notions of universal fraternity, not unlike those of 1798. What makes these expressions so interesting, however, is that this notice was posted a time when the 'common name of Irishman' espoused by the United Irishmen was being abandoned for confessional identity. It suggests a popular politics that did not follow the lead of élite confessional discourses of identity, whether derived from O'Connell on one hand or Musgrave on the other.[76]

75 Gibbons, 'Rockites and Whitefeet', 210.   76 CSORP 1830/W103, copy of notice post-

However, it has usually been assumed that the 'political movements of the 1820s and 1830s ... successfully enshrined Catholic nationalism as the primary loyalty in Irish rural society'. Smyth has suggested (albeit for a slightly earlier date than covered in this study) that the 'most meaningful' class demarcation divided a 'broad popular category' from the landed gentry and aristocracy. This model would bury the conflicts that racked Ireland in the half century before the famine (which have become apparent here in the case of one county) in a discourse of national oppression and resistance. Such views are inconsistent with the findings from Co. Roscommon. Before the famine there existed a powerful alternative discourse of lower class antagonism to employers, retailers, clergymen, landlords (of whatever status and whether head landlords or strong farmers) and to the state. This antagonism had organic roots among the rural poor, which was nourished by an ideological interchange with cosmopolitan oppositional discourses. This also involved direct and no less intense class conflict with Catholic landlords and agents, and conflict with the Catholic clergy, where they opposed the perceived interests of the rural poor. In March 1846 a farmer named Kean at Annagh, near Strokestown, was sworn to surrender a tenancy he had held for seventeen years. The *Roscommon and Leitrim Gazette* observed, 'so much for the stability of mob-popularity. There could not have been a more violent Repealer at the time of the monster meetings than Mr Kean'.

Like many members of social élites, John Bromell of the *Gazette* could not understand the antagonism of the crowd to the Catholic farmer, cutting as it did across monolithic confessional identity and solidarity. He relied instead on the well-worn image of the fickle mob. It has taken social historians many years to disengage from the élite characterization of the crowd as a mob. Unfortunately, in the case of Irish agrarian protesters, because of the durability of popular nationalist conceptions of social identity in the nineteenth century, and modernization theories of social conflict, that process has not been satisfactorily completed.[77]

A qualitatively similar, although more violent, incident was recounted to the Lords committee of 1839 by the crown solicitor in Co. Tipperary. Charles O'Keefe, a Catholic, O'Connell supporter and land agent was murdered for evicting someone for rent arrears and for taking land from which a man had been evicted. However, the divisions within the Catholic population revealed by these events were consistent with the view of agrarian organization taken by the leader of nationalist Ireland. O'Connell stayed over night at Boyle in October 1845. On his way there from Carrick he had stopped his carriage and

ed at Mohill market place, Co. Leitrim, enclosed with letter from Warburton to Gregory, 14 Nov. 1830.   77 J. O'Neill, 'Popular culture and peasant rebellion', 375–6; Smyth, *Men of no property*, 7; RLG, 14 Mar. 1846.

made an impromptu speech, emphasizing that Repeal would be granted if Molly Maguirism and Ribbonism were abandoned. The success of the monster meetings as an organizational tactic has become a tablet of stone in nationalist historiography and has been considered of international significance but, as Cronin and others have suggested, its hegemony was limited. Indeed, there was an independent political impulse among the rural poor that could, at times, co-exist with O'Connellism and at other times displace it among the rural poor. Just as the Catholic Committee had not controlled the Defenders in the 1790s, O'Connell's opposition to agrarian organization did not lead to its being abandoned. This awareness of class antagonism did not come in a neatly labelled package, complete with a political theory, programme and party, but that does not mean that it was not there. An independent political impulse was also present in the Captain Swing agitation in southern England in the autumn of 1830, when the labourers claimed to have been misled by Radicals into believing place men, taxes and an unreformed parliament were the root of their problems, when in fact their problems were rather more concrete.[78]

The trades political unions were an interesting attempt to appropriate the vigour of plebeian protest for the national movement. Warburton submitted a paper entitled the 'Objects of the Carrigallen Trades Political Union', from Co. Leitrim. This paper espoused support for the king in accomplishing parliamentary reform against 'a faction'. This was 1832. At exactly the same time in England the reform campaign had generated agricultural Political Unions which sought to combine political demands with economic muscle. The notice aimed to unite rich and poor well-wishers, although only the 'manufacturing, commercial and agricultural classes' had a right to join, to seek repeal of the union and 'promote the interest and better the condition of the industrious and working classes'. The O'Connellite movement was making some serious attempt at providing an associational framework that would retard the development of separate associational forms for the pursuit of lower class ends in the Irish countryside.[79]

Another example from around the same time had a more specifically plebeian inflection, purporting to be a resolution from 'Terry and his mother'. It provides evidence of a process whereby 'traditional beliefs might, instead of becoming abandoned, be transformed and adapted to meet new needs'. It outlined detailed frameworks for the setting up of parish committees plus delegate meetings for

78 SC 1839, 829, evidence of John Cahill; RLG, 18 Oct. 1845; Smyth, *Men of no property*, 76; E.J. Hobsbawm and G. Rudé, *Captain Swing* (London, 1985 ed.), 43.   79 R. Wells, 'Social protest' (1990); CSORP 1832/1247, enclosed with letter from Warburton to Gosset, 23 July 1832.

every twelve parishes. The document solemnly proclaimed that 'private picques and anomosities shall not in future disgrace the systim' which would prevent 'persons coming clandestinely by their neighbours place'. The delegates should have patriotic principles and the main object was to struggle for the reduction of conacre and rack rents (it should be remembered that 'patriotic' could have a number of inflections, including a discourse claiming that the labouring poor were the true patriots). No notice would be served unless there was absolute conviction of the justice of the case or without a superior's clearance. Minimum wages (and maximum conacre rents) were set with an instruction to quit the job if the member couldn't get that amount. The resolution concluded, 'we can no longer Exist under the yoke of our Landlords and Employers'. The sanctions for breaking this resolution were that the person would 'fall into the hands of our noble sharp shooters'. The resolution clearly referred to family and private disputes, but distinguished them from the legitimate collective struggle it aimed to pursue. The comprehensive prescriptions for rents and wages are evidence of a consciousness that was able to make general conclusions about the need for working people to pursue collectively held interests, and it identified the enemies of those working people concretely as the landlord and employers. That such sentiments were generally current is suggested by a report from the county in 1843 that reported an overheard conversation in which 'it was observed that it would be good – to rid the County of Tyrant Landlords'. They were also sentiments that were shared across a wide geographic area. In March the same year fires were lit across the county and in neighbouring counties Mayo and Sligo to celebrate the acquittal of persons charged with whiteboy offences in Co. Roscommon. This suggests at least a regional dimension to these organizational efforts. It has been suggested that the period between the end of the wars and the famine saw a change in the quality of conflict: 'Participation of some members of the peasantry in such supra-local agitation suggests the beginning of a qualitative change in the nature of peasant protest and the level of political mobilization.'[80]

Similar sentiments to those advocated by 'Terry and his mother' appeared in a Molly Maguire notice that accompanied the mass assembly to turn up Macdonough's grazing land in Baslick parish. The resident magistrate found a 'turbulent spirit' among the crowd of 1,000, especially in antagonism to the police. The confrontation was also notable because it was in daylight, undisguised. It specifically referred to the encroachment of commercial economic pressures:

80 Rudé, *The crowd in history*, 234; CSORP 1832/1479, 'resolution' of Terry and his mother dated (erroneously?) 29 July 1831. Located in Co. Roscommon correspondence but possibly Co. Leitrim or Co. Galway; OR 1843/1995, anonymous information, 31 Jan. 1843; J. O'Neill, 'Popular culture and peasant rebellion', 333.

see before your eyes all the fine lands of that parish – to see the produce sent off every year without ... getting a mouthful of these in any form or even a days work ye are asleep but I will waken ye ... when they will give ye no Conacre, I'll let them know that might is not always right – if ye fail ye deserve to starve or worse if such could be ...

_____ your Countrys regenerator

Molly Maguire.

Molly generalized about relations between landlords and tenants from the specific experiences of the enormous pressure on conacre. There is also a hint of political rhetoric and vanguardism in the notice. That ability to generalize the experience of the labourers was evident from the size of the crowd that turned up a few days after the assembly of 1,000 people on Macdonough's land near Castlerea. This time around 3,000 people assembled at Ballintober, about five miles distant, with the intention of turning pasture into conacre. No land was dug up after the crowd agreed to give the landlords, a man named Dignan and Lord Hartland, a chance to respond to their demands. Such an incident appears like the negotiation of contested rights between different classes that is usually associated with organizations like trade unions. Similarly, around 3,000 people had gathered at Crossna in September 1837 to send a deputation to Tobias Peyton, claiming that tithe collection was causing rebellion. Thompson suggested that rural custom and ritual, because of its oral transmission, was unrelated to trade union oaths and ceremonies. He believed that Luddism drew on Irish tradition but that unions drew on masonic and craft traditions. However, the notices of Terry and his mother and Molly Maguire suggest protean trade combinations, albeit from an Irish rural tradition. While archaic forms persisted, new layers of meaning and new ways of articulating meaning (often borrowed) were heaped on top of old traditions, not supplanting them but adding supplementary languages to the repertoires of agrarian rebels. It is doubtful whether these notices can be called threatening notices at all in the common, pre-modern understanding of the term. The conacre assemblies of the 1840s in Co. Roscommon were similar to other cases a few years earlier when on one occasion 3,000 people assembled at Ballaghadereen and appointed deputies (on the advice of magistrates) from each townland to approach the landlords with their concerns. Similarly, a crowd of between ten and fourteen thousand had assembled a few miles away at Ballina, Co. Mayo, and the magistrates had parleyed with representatives of the crowd over their demands. The size of these assemblies, from the 1830s onwards, is particularly striking, although nobody has ever labelled them 'monster meetings'.[81]

81 OR 1845/5001, copy of notice enclosed with letter from Wray to Lucas, 11 Mar. 1845;

It should be noted that part of the development of a collective identity among the rural poor was the insistence of élites in defining them as separate. Representatives of the state, too, did not possess a 'pure' consciousness. Blakeney's anxiety about the removal of Roscommon market is an example of an élite perspective that was not necessarily singularly antipathetic to the peasantry or to custom, and there were a number of instances when resident magistrates and police officers expressed anxiety about poverty and the insensitivity of landlords. The correspondence of magistrates like Duff is in contrast with the more commonly encountered attitudes of colleagues like Thomas Conry. Conry, it may be recalled, was Mahon's agent. In his capacity as a magistrate he ordered police protection for bailiffs working on the Strokestown estate and expressed the now-prevailing élite view of the correct relations between the landowners and the mechanisms of the state: 'If life and property is not to be protected by the police what use are they or what more necessary duty can they perform.'[82]

An agent named Bentley, of Ballinastruve House near Strokestown, wrote, 'it is in contemplation amongst those barbarians in the event of my going thither [a planned journey to Roscommon town] during the sitting of the Grand Jury, which was my intention, to have me and my sub agent stopt on the road, and either threatened into a total forbearance of all further proceedings, or perhaps our lives sacrificed on the spot'. Bentley's dislike of the rural poor can not simply be attributed to obsessive suspicion. Thomas Jordan of Strokestown wrote in 1843 to the lord lieutenant that 'Sistim business is got to such a hight in this Nabourhood the hold nightly meetings and assemblies'. Jordan's spelling and grammar suggest he was an uneducated man and not a member of a local élite. He was therefore likely to know the extent of whiteboy organization and his evidence is less likely to be tainted by imagined conspiracy theories, although he may have had other unknown agendas. Anthony McDonnell of Co. Mayo described how the Rockite disturbances of 1831 were being repeated in 1844 under the leadership of Captain Smart. His brother, an agent in Co. Roscommon, had been ordered not to collect rents, his herdsmen and labourers had been sworn not to work for him and he observed that 'the persecution is now revived under the mandate of ruler Smart'. McDonnell's son was a farmer near Castlerea and a mob came to his home one night when he was not in. They beat his herdsman 'on the rage of disappointment at missing him'. While the conclusions drawn by the county

OR 1845/6017, Wray to Lucas, 25 Mar. 1845; RLG, 23 Sept. 1837; E.P. Thompson, 'Rough music' (1993), 525; Thompson, *Making of the English working class*, 557–8; D. McCabe, 'Social order', 104.   82 OR 1846/11349, T. Conry, land agent, to Pennefather, 8 May 1846; OR 1844/4263.

grand jury: 'We are satisfied that a most wide spread conspiracy exists … arms & money collected by the disaffected, committees of assassination are regularly organized and supplied with fitting instruments to carry out their orders', may appear overstated, there is enough evidence to suggest that their fears were well founded. Co. Roscommon had reached a heightened pitch of conflict on the eve of the famine.[83]

Writing of the inhabitants of early nineteenth century Irish townlands in his study of the crown lands at Ballykilcline in Co. Roscommon, Robert Scally has suggested that they were 'insulated to a startling degree for Europeans from up-to-date knowledge of the outside world'. Contrarily, the world of the Irish rural poor was, certainly from the late eighteenth century onwards, not so parochial and enclosed as supposed by Scally. While it has been acknowledged that the English countryside during this period was not isolated, it remains widely believed that the Irish countryside was insulated within a shell of confessional, cultural and national antipathy towards the Ascendancy. The élite world of Brunswick Clubs organized by Lorton and electoral politics contested by people like Lorton and nationalists was transmitted from London and Dublin to places like Co. Roscommon along clear lines of communication which have become historians' sources – police reports, newspapers, parliamentary enquiries. Although the transmission of non-élite culture is obscured by illiteracy, a lack of written texts and on occasions a language barrier, it should not be assumed that it remained a consciousness that was dependent on élite patronage and leadership. It may also be that in Ireland the hedge school masters, or other intermediaries like the itinerants considered previously, performed the role of the semi-literate conduits of written texts from élite culture to the townlands' inhabitants that Peter Burke has identified across Europe. Roger Wells has identified a 'radicalised, rural plebeian culture' emerging from English beer shops in the mid-1830s, accompanied by a radical press and presenting a contrast with Ireland, where the radical press was in the hands of nationalists (such as Tully of the *Roscommon Journal*).[84]

It has been necessary to uncover Irish rural plebeian radicalism in the fragmentary evidence provided by threatening notices and a careful examination of élite sources. While the emblems of Paine and France formed part of the libertarian imagery deployed in agrarian collective action in the early part of the

83 G. Bentley, Strokestown, to unnamed, Dublin Castle, 19 Feb. 1844; OR 1843/277, Thomas Jordan, Strokestown, to Earl De Grey, lord lieutenant, 11 Jan. 1843; OR 1844/4557, memorial of Anthony McDonnell, Palmfield, Co. Mayo, undated, (1844); OR 1845/15147, resolution of Co. Roscommon grand jury, undated, July 1845.   84 Scally, *End of hidden Ireland*, 7; Wells, 'Social protest', 127; See RLG, 4 Oct. 1828, for a report of the foundation of a Brunswick Club in Boyle; Burke, *Popular culture*, 63; Wells, 'Social protest', 191.

century, they were displaced as time went on by a diction appropriated from other cosmopolitan developments, like Reform and Chartism. A paper entitled 'Obligations of the Fraternal Society' was read to the 1839 Lords committee, swearing allegiance to the king. Such papers demonstrate how different traditions might be synthesized in a combined and uneven plebeian consciousness. The presence of radicalism in Boyle has already been noted, and there are further clues about the fusion of agrarian conflict and popular plebeian politics. The *Roscommon Journal* reported extensively the Captain Swing movement in south–east England during the autumn of 1830. Headlines from October to December spoke of the 'Disturbed State of England' and, significantly, 'Captain Rock in England'. However, historians have generally failed to make such a connection, whether determined to find in Ireland pure oppressed Gaels or parochial peasants who saw no further than their neighbours' coveted acres. The *Journal* also reported extensively the trials of the Chartists in Birmingham in August 1839. The subscribers to these newspapers may have been predominantly members of local élites, but it is unsustainable that the whiteboys were unaware of Swing or Chartism, just as they were evidently aware of the reform battle in 1832.[85]

Indeed, it is possible to go further than this, for Chartism enjoyed an organized efflorescence in Ireland during 1841, with branches of the Irish Universal Suffrage Association opening in Dublin, Belfast, Cork, Sligo, Newry, Cashel, Chapelizod, Donabate, Lucan, Ballyraggett, Drogheda, Loughrea, Kells, Navan and Waterford. Chartist organization was first mentioned in early June, when an informer reported that there were three meetings a week in Dublin, and that the number of members was growing rapidly, having now reached fifty-three. A visitor from Manchester told a Dublin meeting that the members should prepare themselves for 'the Charter would never be obtained but by the sword and the Pike'. The secretary, Peter Brophy, read a letter from an Irish man living in Bradford 'recommending Physical Force for the Charter, and denouncing Mr O'Connell and his Humbug Repeal Association'.[86]

Proselytizing by Irish men returning from England appears to have provided the impetus for the Irish movement, as an undercover policeman reported from Drogheda in August that he had been taken to a house 'where Peter Hoey the Chartist delegate from England stops'. Hoey had been there for eleven weeks, paid for by English Chartist funds. Hoey has been identified by Dorothy

85 SC 1839, 172, 161, evidence of H.W. Rowan; SC 1839, 198–9, evidence of William Fausset, magistrate, Co. Sligo; See RJ, 30 Oct. 1830, 13 Nov. 1830, 4 Dec. 1830, 18 Dec. 1830; For example, RJ, 10 Aug. 1839.   86 PRO, CO 904/8, 'PM' to James O'Connor, police inspector, 9 June 1841.

Thompson as an Irish man residing in Barnsley, returning home periodically to advocate the charter. He was staying on this occasion with a local Chartist named Pat Murphy, who had formerly resided in England. There were at that time more than 300 'real teetotal Chartists' in Drogheda. That an Irish inflection has been grafted on to the English associational and political form is evident in the references to pikes and abstinence from alcohol. However, these words are more frequently associated with nationalism and cleric-backed abstinence campaigns. Their presence in this context demonstrates that consciousness was neither pure nor monolithically nationalist and Catholic. Dorothy Thompson has, along with others, overlooked the significance of the radical alternative to O'Connellite hegemony in Irish popular politics, suggesting that any such significant alternative was located 'particularly outside Ireland', as 'the Chartist movement had little support' in Ireland. The numbers game alone does not bear out this conclusion during the growth spurt of the autumn of 1841. The Irish Chartists sustained two newspapers between 1848 and 1850 and were a constant presence in the Dublin political scene for ten years.[87]

Even though the numbers of active Chartists may be many fewer than the numbers that had been formally affiliated to the emancipation campaign through the Catholic Rent, or attended O'Connell's monster Repeal meetings, it has been established that the figures for Catholic Rent collection must be treated with great caution. It should also be remembered that much of the historiography of O'Connell's movements has been dependent on partial and hagiographic works. Some light has recently been shed on O'Connell's technique for creating the sense of solidarity at monster meetings. This involved a preliminary procession deploying banners with a familiar symbolism, the liberal use of stock phrases from the Irish language, and, in O'Connell's speech, addressing the concrete concerns of many in the audience but offering only ill-defined and general solutions. Maura Cronin has concluded that O'Connell's 'speeches were tailored to meet popular material expectations'. One resident magistrate observed that 'the people dispersed under the firm conviction that each man would shortly be in the possession of a farm of twenty acres of land which they were told would be given to them at low rent and with long leases'. Cronin suspects that the issue of repeal had little independent existence for the crowds who gathered at monster meetings. Indeed she suggests that the peacefulness of the meetings may signify some apathy in the cause of repeal. Writ-

87 PRO, CO 904/8, John O'Ferrall, police commissioner, Dublin, to under-secretary, 14 Aug. 1841; PRO, CO 904/8, O'Ferrall to under-secretary, 14 Aug. 1841; See, for example, T. Koseki, 'Patrick O'Higgins and Irish Chartism' (1990); P. Pickering, ' "Repeal and the suffrage": Feargus O'Connor's Irish mission' (1999); D. Thompson, 'Ireland and the Irish in English radicalism' (1982); M. Huggins, 'Democracy or nationalism?'.

ing of O'Connell's Repeal campaign in the 1830s and 1840s, and addressing directly the tension between O'Connellism and whiteboyism, Cronin has gone so far as to suggest:

> the frequency of more spontaneous types of crowd activity throughout the two decades under review show the consensus of O'Connellite meetings to have been largely illusory or temporary.

The poor were perhaps unlikely to join the charter campaign formally, although it is apparent that the general political aspirations of this movement had penetrated the language of threatening notices. At this point there was a visible synthesis of cosmopolitan lower-class political ideas and Irish traditions.[88]

It may be objected that the Irish Chartists were an anglophone urban minority, based upon trades rather than agrarian organization. However, there is significant evidence of the dissemination of Jacobin, Reform and later Chartist ideas in the Irish countryside during the first half of the nineteenth century. It should not be assumed that a language and literacy barrier prevented agrarian rebels from hearing and appropriating the popular politics of England for use in an Irish agrarian context. Indeed, Marianne Elliott and Kevin Whelan have both noted that there were clear lines of communication along which such ideas might be transmitted. Elliott notes that the remote parts of Ireland learned of Paine and the French revolution via local anglophone reform groups and 'that the language of the more radical reformers, and the claim to natural human rights – which the American and French revolutionaries had put forward against the threat of despotism – had been absorbed into the threats and oaths of Irish popular protest'. Whelan has found these lines of communication not only in the way the *Northern Star* was distributed and read collectively during the 1790s, but also in the proliferation of ballads, chapbooks, prophecies and other genres which permeated the language and literacy barriers in the countryside. A magistrate near Strabane, Co. Tyrone, noted of one chapbook that 'the ignorant country people will take many meanings out of it that suit their present way of thinking, as there is a levelling principle in it'. This demonstrates the way in which the rural poor might appropriate cosmopolitan discourses and adapt them for their own purposes, insofar as they had a 'levelling' content.[89]

88 M. Cronin, ' "Of one mind"?' (2000), 147; OR 1843 17/15487, quoted in Cronin, ' "Of one mind"?', at 148; idem, 167.   89 M. Elliott, *Partners in revolution* (1982), 16; Whelan, 'The republic in the village' (1996), 66; idem, 74, letter accompanying *Christ in triumph coming to judgement* (Strabane, 1795), copy in National Archives of Ireland, Rebellion Papers 620/22/63.

The loyal Catholic parish priest from Roscommon town, the Revd Madden, among others, noted that seasonal migrants brought weapons back from British cities with them, as well as an ideology that connected with Irish traditions of collective conflict. Such interfaces with the cosmopolitan world encouraged the growth of organic leadership of the rural poor like Michael Burke's in Cloony-gormican (a more substantial comparable instance would be Zapata in Mexico). In Ireland this leadership never became more significant than local leaders like Burke, although these matters inevitably prompt speculation on what might have happened if the great famine and mass emigration had not intervened. A correspondent from Carrick on Shannon wrote to the Castle in April 1845 to warn that the peasants would obtain more weapons in England during the harvest and that the 'better class of persons' would be at their mercy. Madden wrote to the Castle in 1839 that three men from Roscommon town had returned from England and organized the rural poor 'under the Chartist system', as well as returning with the hardware of collective violence. Many had been sworn in at pubs and their local leader, James Hanly, was in contact with co-conspirators in Birmingham. He also possessed the papers, rules and regulations of the system. The *Roscommon Journal* proprietor, Charles Tully, warned readers in January 1843 that the Chartists were trying to entrap Irish peasants into 'their wicked associations' through opposition to the poor rates. It is questionable whether the labourers and cottiers were otherwise so innocent of levelling instincts as Tully claimed to believe. His opposition to lower class associational forms resonates with a familiar fear of the labouring poor organizing for themselves. It has long been acknowledged that Irish traditions had been exported to the manufacturing districts of England with migrants. In Manchester, for example, Luddism had been added to a Painite radical group 'with an ebullient Irish fringe'. Historians of nineteenth-century England have written of the influence of Irish traditions on English lower class organization. The close relations between Irish conspiracy and Chartism in England have been explored, but only in the nationalist dimension, connected with confederacy and ribbonism. No account has been available of the impact of Chartism on Irish agrarian combinations. The 1831 select committee was told that Irish rural labourers who had been to England for seasonal work had returned with trade union ideas, having seen the way English labourers were fed and clothed. They said English labourers' practice 'was to swear to be true to each other, and join to keep the people upon their ground'. No doubt, symbiotic exchanges such as these occurred between Irish and English workers, suggesting the manufacturing cities of England had becomes a crucible where traditions of agrarian rebellion, working class organization and politics were blended, producing a highly combustible mixture. These exchanges led in Ireland to a rich fusion of egalitarian notions, a nascent class-consciousness and an assertion of a need for general political change. National policies, rather than the failures of individuals to obey the moral economy, were increasingly a focus for organization. A witness from Ballinasloe, on the border of Co. Roscommon and Co. Galway, articulated the muddled nature of these political thoughts when he told the Lords 'the poor People fancy they should be much better off if there was a Change of Measures in some Way'. He had previously seen assemblies carrying banners proclaiming: 'Half Rent, no Tithes, no Taxes, and certain Rates of Wages'.[90]

The idea of an Irish agrarian combination meeting during daylight and carrying banners proclaiming such demands should no longer be surprising. The notion that Irish agrarian rebellion remained definitively secret, nocturnal, parochial and pre-modern must be abandoned.

90 G. Huizer and R. Stavenhagen, 'Peasant movements and land reform in Latin America' (1974), 383; OR 1845/8705, C. McArthur, Carrick-on-Shannon, to unnamed, Dublin Castle, 13 Apr. 1845; OR 1839/7398, information of Revd J. Madden, undated, (Aug. 1839); RJ, 18 Jan. 1843; HL 1839, 292, evidence of John Wright, former chief constable; Thompson, *Making of the English working class*, 651; see, for example, Belchem, 'English working class radicalism and the Irish'; Lewis, *On local disturbances*, 90, quoting evidence of Revd Nicholas O'Connor to select committee; early nineteenth-century food riots in Manchester, England, had taken a similar direction, see Bohstedt, *Riots and community politics politics*, 92; SC 1839, 728, 727, evidence of Captain Bartholomew Warburton.

6

The moral economy of the Irish crowd

Reviewing revisionist assaults on the nationalist historiography of the eighteenth century, Sean Connolly has suggested that agrarian movements like the Whiteboys and Rightboys 'could be fitted without difficulty into the frameworks' suggested by the work of Rudé, Hobsbawm and Edward Thompson; but there have as yet been no studies which make such a task central to their aims. Donnelly has noted that, although the outbreaks of agrarian conflict in Ireland were as intense as the Captain Swing conflict and happened every decade between 1760 and 1840, no account like Hobsbawm's and Rudé's has ever been forthcoming for Ireland. Bartlett, Whelan and others have used Thompson's concept of a moral economy. It has been peripheral to their main concerns, although one historian has noted the presence of 'an acute awareness as to who had rights to what, and to a concept of landholding defined by tradition and customary right' and another that whiteboyism was motivated by 'conservative assumptions not unlike those of the English poor'. The remainder of this book will consider more thoroughly what is meant by moral economy, and how it may relate to the evidence of social conflict in pre-famine Co. Roscommon. It will also be useful to consider peasant societies more generally, and theories about the capacity of peasants for collective action, in the context of Samuel Clark's model for class differentiation in the nineteenth century Irish countryside. It will conclude with a survey of critiques of the idea of a moral economy, and their relevance to the case of Co. Roscommon.[1]

Anonymous threats, counter-theatre and direct action

On an initial reading, the stories of whiteboys in pre-famine Ireland are similar to the romantic legends which surrounded the early years of trade unionism in England, described by E.P. Thompson as meeting 'on dark nights on the peaks, moors, and wastes', bound together by 'awe-inspiring oaths'. Just as the Pentridge rising of 1817 in Derbyshire was 'accompanied by signal lights on the hills', an anonymous letter to Dublin Castle on 1 April 1816 from Stroke-

1 Connolly, 'Eighteenth century Ireland', 22; Donnelly, 'Rightboy movement', 121; see Bartlett, 'Militia disturbances'; Whelan, 'An underground gentry'?; M. Elliott, 'The Defenders in Ulster' (1993); McCabe, 'Social order', 93.

stown, Co. Roscommon, warned that 'last night the hills around were lit with fires as signals from the rebels of this county to their friends'.[2]

These similarities between the early years of trade unionism in England and whiteboyism in Ireland can be elaborated further, when considering the moral pressure of the brick through the window, the vandalizing of machinery, assassination, and other tactics pursued by groups such as the Wiltshire shearmen, the Luddites and the Rebecca rioters. Such groups were asserting the primacy of their moral economy over political economy, much as it has been suggested that the redresser movements in Ireland did. What does 'moral economy' mean and is it viable as a conceptual tool for the study of pre-famine Irish agrarian conflict?[3]

Thompson first deployed the concept in a 1971 essay on food riots in eighteenth-century England to challenge the view that such actions were the blind, compulsive reactions of a 'mob' to dearth. He asked how the behaviour of the hungry was modified by custom, culture and reason, and suggested that in every eighteenth-century crowd action there was a legitimizing notion grounded in a perception among the participants of the proper economic functions of the parties to the riot; disturbances were not compulsive, blind, unselfconscious reactions to economic stimuli but that a consciousness underpinned them. Hobsbawm and Rudé described this consciousness as 'the usual baggage of the pre-political poor, the belief in the rights of poor men by custom, natural justice and indeed law which must not be infringed by the rich'.[4]

Thompson saw the Black Act of 1723 as being a defining moment in England. This signified the end of the pre-eminence of crime between people – breaches of fealty or deference – and the beginning of the primacy of crime against property. Judicial and bureaucratic responses to Irish agrarian conflicts also reflected the Whig world-view, a product of a society where the moral economy was being abandoned by those able to accumulate capital and defended tenaciously by those resisting such change. Thompson said that 'recourse to the Act was most likely in a context of agrarian disturbance, especially when this was combined with class insubordination – as, for example, when resistance to enclosure took the form of firing into windows, threatening letters or the houghing (malicious wounding) of cattle'. These were as much the symptoms of whiteboyism in rural Ireland as of social conflict in southern England during the eighteenth century.[5]

2 E.P. Thompson, *The making of the English working class*, 556, 732; SOCP1 1767/36, anonymous letter from 'A Protestant', Strokestown, to Sir Edward Littlehales, 1 Apr. 1816. 3 Whelan, 'An underground gentry?', 26. 4 E.P. Thompson, 'The moral economy of the English crowd', 187; E.J. Hobsbawm and G. Rudé, *Captain Swing*, 43. 5 E.P. Thompson,

How, then, did notions of custom and duty affect English social protest, and do these have anything to reveal about the Irish situation? Thompson identified three characteristics of popular action: anonymous threats, counter-theatre and direct action. The first of these was identified with 'a society of total clientage and dependency', where overt challenges to the established order might result in retaliation and loss of job and home. It was the other side of the forelock-touching deference which might have characterized the daylight hours, a deference that was often without the least illusion. These actions included the posting of anonymous letters or notices, setting fire to stacks or outhouses, houghing of cattle, shooting or hurling a brick through a window, taking a gate off its hinges, chopping down an orchard and opening a fish-pond sluice at night. This sort of action was characteristic of Irish as well as English conflicts and was found especially in rural societies where there were no overt or institutional forms of resistance available; it characterized social relations in which labour was not free and able to organize itself. The central concept of feudal custom had not been that of property rights but of reciprocal obligations. As Thompson put it, the mutuality of the manor had not yet been completely replaced by the 'reification of usages into properties which could be rented, sold or willed'. English wreckers of the eighteenth century believed they had a 'perfect right' to their plunder, seeing nothing incompatible in rescuing and plundering. They refused to recognize the coastguard's authority. Likewise, smugglers didn't believe their activities were criminal, but the assertion of a right. Their activities have been described as 'partly a defence of local economies against the development of commercial capitalism'.[6]

The rural poor in early nineteenth-century Ireland frequently took such actions. Nocturnal visits, attacks on property and intimidation were a constant feature of the period, referred to with weary regularity by Dublin Castle's correspondents. Threatening notices were common, too. Part 2 of this book considered a number of such notices. A typical example posted on a chapel door threatened vengeance against 'any person daring to drive cattle for rent', swearing to 'burn the houses, haugh the cattle and murder the families of any landholder who should on any account pay more for his holding than he did sixteen years ago'. This notice is also striking for the way it illustrates how a demanded norm – the rent paid sixteen years previously – is a recent assertion added to the expectations of the person who posted the notice. It is an example of how the paternalist model of customary dealing was reconstructed selectively

Whigs and hunters, 207, 246.   6 E.P. Thompson, 'Patricians and the plebs', 66; E.P. Thompson, 'Eighteenth century English society' (1978), 157; see also P. Linebaugh, 'The Tyburn riot'; E.P. Thompson, 'Custom, law and common right', 127, 135; J.G. Rule, 'Wrecking and coastal plunder' (1975), 176; C. Winslow, 'Sussex smugglers' (1975), 150.

by the poor. It also reflects the sense in which the 'primitive' form of protest (the threatening letter or arson attack) could remain in use for a time in a new economic situation where social arrangements were changing quickly.[7]

Actions such as incendiarism reached their height in England in the last decade of the eighteenth century, when rural class relations were changing rapidly. Many 'threatening letters and the burning of buildings and stacks' were provoked by attempts to restrict commoners' rights in forests. So, similar tactical manoeuvres were employed by Irish and English agrarian protesters during the same period, even though the economic contexts of the English and Irish countrysides were different. While in England a moral economy could operate in the context of the repeal of specific paternalist legislation, in Ireland it might function in a more 'ambient' consciousness of custom, that is to say in which custom informed attitudes as much as it was reflected in specific statutes. Thompson did allow such an extension of the concept, as long as it was firmly anchored to a specific set of social relations.[8]

A splendid example of the ambient nature of agrarian custom is provided by an incident which took place on 2 July 1816, in the parish of Dysart, a few miles from Athlone. A tenant voluntarily surrendered a lease, owing eighteen months' rent; the night before an 'improving' tenant was due to move in, the house was burned down. This action, taken despite the voluntary surrender of the house by the previous tenant, implies a belief that people had an inalienable right to land in order to sustain life, irrespective of economics. The arsonist was expressing a generalized value system conflicting with the rights of property which in England had been reinforced through legislation like the Black Act. The former tenant clearly did not have a modern sense of contract law, and the fact that he surrendered the tenancy did not persuade him that he had no right to nurse a grievance. He felt that there was a moral economy which had greater validity than political economy. In 1839 three witnesses to a Lords enquiry spoke of the sense of customary rights to land which prevailed among the poor in Ireland. John Barnes, a Co. Longford stipendiary magistrate, described how Lord Lorton had evicted between 30 and 40 Catholic families from his Longford estates and replaced them with Protestants; he added that 'the People in Ireland, no Matter what the law is, look to the Possession as giving them a Right'. The earl of Donoughmore, a Co. Tipperary landlord, described how Catholic landlords agreed with his views but that 'the Principle of the Peasantry of Tipperary is,

7 SOCP1 1776/97, quoted in letter from yeomanry Brigade Major S. South, to Lt. Col. Murray, 25 Oct. 1816, enclosed with letter from Mahon to Peel, 2 Nov. 1816; R. Wells, 'The development of the English rural proletariat' (1990).   8 Wells, 'Social protest', 158; Thompson, 'Custom, law and common right', 102; Thompson, 'The moral economy reviewed', 340.

that when once in the Possession of Land they have a Right to continue on it', and that there was a general combination among the peasantry to prevent land-lords from exercising their just property rights. Co. Tipperary stipendiary magistrate Joseph Tabuteau attested:

> I think the man who holds the Tenement does not care under what Circumstances he is put out, whether fairly or unfairly; that he thinks he ought not to be put out.[9]

E.P. Thompson described a number of forms of action as 'counter-theatre' – the wearing of ribbons, toasts and seditious (often Jacobite) oaths. Similar forms are to be found in the evidence from Co. Roscommon. Thompson also cited the instance of the Tyburn mob trying to stop surgeons from snatching the deceased's body as a symbolic instance of solidarity with the person who suffered the extreme outcome of a law they knew to be predisposed against them. These were responses to the theatre of the rulers, which was most apparent to the rural poor in the law courts, where the major actors even wore costumes. It is just such a sensibility that informed the agrarian rebels of early nineteenth-century Ireland. On 4 April 1812 two captured Threshers, one wearing women's clothes, were paraded through the streets of Roscommon in an example of self-conscious élite theatre. Edward Mills, reported:

> I brought the wounded prisoners in as solemn a manner as I could thro the town of Roscommon (this being a very crowded market day) and left them in view of a ... multitude for some time for their contemplation.

The functions of law were constructed in such a way as to obscure any partiality or injustice that might be inherent in defending the rights of property. The use of legalistic forms by agrarian rebels was the assertion of a contrary consciousness, based on endangered customs which were increasingly abandoned by the gentry. Many Irish threatening notices suggest this alternative jurisprudence, which was applied to anyone interfering with custom.[10]

Examples of counter-theatre abounded in the forests of southern England. Thompson's discovery of a Hampshire Black leader called King John is reminiscent of the titles claimed by Irish agrarian rebels years later. The title of 'King John' also suggests an alternative allegiance and authority, and a code of customary usages that was parallel to the official laws. As we have seen, agrar-

9 SC 1839, 930, 955, 746.   10 Thompson, 'Patricians and plebs', 85; SOCP1 1408/40, Edward Mills, Fairy Mount, to Sir Charles Saxton, under-secretary, 4 Apr. 1812; Gibbons, *Captain Rock*, 22.

ian rebels in early nineteenth-century Ireland also chose fanciful titles and ranks. For example, a number of threatening notices were recovered in March 1812 in Co. Roscommon and sent to Dublin Castle. They were signed by a Captain James Farrell. At almost the same time another notice attached to a church door near Ballaghadereen was signed by Mr Fair Play. Other titles adopted at various periods in pre-famine Co. Roscommon (and in many other Irish counties) included Captain Moonlight, Captain Rock and Captain Right. Interestingly, Captain Farrell's notices began 'God save the king'. Such declarations of loyalty might have been 'rhetorical stratagems' (perhaps similar in nature to the deferential tugging of the forelock during daylight hours).[11]

Hobsbawm and Rudé also noted English rebels asking 'how could justice be against the king and Government?' If anything, Irish agrarian rebels stressed their loyalty rather more often than English ones. They shared the same predilection for whistling subversive airs, swearing people to seditious oaths and wearing ribbons, but they were less likely to have access to radical newspapers, those vehicles for political opposition which were said (with alarm) to have led to an increased availability of information among the English peasantry (although it has become apparent that they attained a basic associational status). The obvious Irish parallel to the development of a radical press would be the penetration of the *Northern Star* into the depths of the countryside in the early 1790s, despite the fact that this revolution was a revolution of literate, anglophone Ireland. The Enlightenment-inspired pre-suppression United Irishmen were rather less republican than reformist, and some of their ideas were drawn from the same stock of motifs as the custom-inspired agrarian rebels – Paine, France and the tree of liberty. It has become apparent that there was a much greater symbiosis between the popular custom-inspired politics of Irish agrarian combinations and radical politics in England than has generally been supposed. Interestingly, the language of threatening notices was English. The relationship with a hedge-school master or other intermediary would be one way in which the poor became familiar with cosmopolitan politics. As Marianne Elliott has observed of Ireland in the 1790s, 'an inability to read was not necessarily a barrier to knowledge of contemporary events'. Hugh Dorian's recollection of the significance of newspaper readings at late-night meetings should also be recalled. Similar scenes occur in William Carleton's work. It appears that radical ideas could have been disseminated by itinerants and translated aloud in public by sympathetic residents, much as the *Northern Star* was distributed in the 1790s, a process which had at that time led to 'the jacobinising of the secret societies'.[12]

11 Thompson, 'Patricians and plebs', 92–3.   12 Hobsbawm and Rudé, *Captain Swing*, 63; Wells, 'Social protest', 191; M. Elliott, *Partners in revolution*, 16; for example, W. Carleton,

It has become apparent that the range of grievances nursed by Irish agrarian rebels was wide, and often underpinned by a conception of a fair price, much like instances of food riot in England. Grievances included the dues levied by Catholic priests for performing various rites; tithes payable to the established church; the prices of commodities like potatoes and spirits; the conversion of tillage to pasture and land being let at higher rents than prescribed by the protesters. It has also been seen that Irish protests over prices were often similar in form to price-fixing actions like the characteristic marketplace English food riot.[13]

Direct actions by Irish protesters were sometimes violent. They tended to be visited upon the same kind of people as themselves, for example, people who had taken land at higher rents than prescribed by the protesters. In England, similarly, violence was used against blacklegs rather than employers in protests against job-threatening technological advances. The Irish countryside being heavily militarized, it may have been much easier to exert discipline on members of the rural community than on the landlords, protected as they were by magistrates and soldiers. The poorest in rural society were asserting the demands of custom against people who were relatively easy to influence. This might also be suggested by a relative lack of recourse to legal remedies. There seem to have been more frequent attempts by English protesters to use the law than by the Irish.[14]

Paternalism and deference

Histories written from a nationalist view might suggest that the lack of recourse to law was because two opposing nationalities did not share the same concept of duties and rights. If the notion of a moral economy involves a previously-shared sense of customary mutual obligation, does not the replacing of the 'natural' layer of Irish aristocrats with British landowners through much of the island during the seventeenth century invalidate an attempt to use the concept in Ireland? In this case it would be necessary to set aside Thompson's model and once more consider conflicts between landlords and tenants in eighteenth- and nineteenth-century Ireland as symptoms of a proto-national struggle. However, as Barnard has argued, landlord-tenant relations in eighteenth-century Ireland were often characterized by laxity and not the vigorous oppression suggested by

Traits and stories of the Irish peasantry (1843), vol. i, 9; K. Whelan, 'The republic in the village', 73, 75.   13 SOCP1 1120/47, C. Seymour, Ballaghadereen, 15 July 1807, to unnamed, Dublin Castle; SOCP1 1408/27, Lt. Gen. Thomas Meyrick, Athlone, to unnamed, Dublin Castle, 7 Jan. 1812; SOCP1 1401/15, Meyrick to W. Wellesley Pole, chief secretary, Dublin Castle, 1 Jan. 1812.   14 Randall, 'The shearmen and the Wiltshire outrages'.

nationalist historiography. Vertical ties between landlord and tenant were
stronger than has been suggested. Even if the freeholder of a piece of property was English and remote from Irish customs, conflict was most often not
between such people and their Irish tenants but between Irish sub-strata. The
Co. Roscommon evidence challenges the notion of inherent national discord.

Modernization explanations of pre-famine agrarian conflict echo the explanations of primitive rebellions suggested by Hobsbawm and Rudé in their
work on Captain Swing. In pre-modern social arrangements, where vertical ties
between master and labourer or landlord and tenant persisted, social conflict
might result in the kinds of communal or personal action proposed by Fitzpatrick in his work on Cloone (although Fitzpatrick, Hobsbawm and Rudé
have all tended to dismiss the capacities of the poor for 'horizontal' solidarities
rather more readily than Thompson).

These 'pre-class' social relations could only exist in conditions of dependence, when élites controlled the entire lives of labourers and before non-mon-
etary relations were translated into payments. These social relations were
characterized by a 'paternalism–deference equilibrium'. However, for Thompson, equilibrium did not necessarily mean consensus. Plebeian culture was not
wholly deferential, especially as the eighteenth century wore on and the gentry
increasingly abandoned its paternalism under the imperative of capital accumulation. The gestures of paternalism tended, in any case, to be a 'studied
technique of rule' and, besides, total paternalist control over life was being
eroded by the extension of trade and industry. This may have created a space
in which new horizontal ties might begin to be formed, without necessarily
meaning that all deferential notions were discarded. An overall hegemony of
the gentry might well co-exist with a non-deferential sense of custom. A key
component of this can be seen in the tendency of 'rights' and customs to be
relatively new assertions on the part of the plebeians and that if there was any
consistent model of custom adopted by participants in collective action it was,
at most, 'a selective reconstruction of the paternalist one'.[15]

Paternalism might also be theatrical as much as substantive, and deference
was never unconditional. Thompson qualified significantly the idea of an equilibrium, suggesting that such arrangements were invariably the site of contes-
tation. The gentry's paternalism was not accepted on its own terms and
deference was habitually not accompanied by illusions:

15 Thompson, 'Eighteenth century English society', 150; idem, 'Patricians and plebs', 37,
41, 64; E.P. Thompson, 'Introduction: custom and culture' (1993), 2; Thompson, 'Moral
economy of the English crowd', 212.   16 Thompson, 'Patricians and plebs', 37, 38, 64, 85,

> It is necessary also to go beyond the view that labouring people, at this
> time, were confined within ... the fraternal loyalties and 'vertical' con-
> sciousness of particular trades; and that this inhibited wider solidari-
> ties and 'horizontal' consciousness of class.

Thus, while a 'vertical' equilibrium may have persisted through much of the
eighteenth century, this was not static and unchanging. When élites attempted
to renege on their responsibilities, they were challenged. Sean Connolly has
found an analogy between this conditional deference and popular attitudes to
the Catholic clergy in pre-famine Ireland, attitudes 'of genuine submissiveness
and of equally genuine resentment'. Another historian has considered the Irish
tenant's attitude to be one of 'feigned humility'. However, it needs to be established that any challenge to a paternalism–deference equation in Ireland did
not have a national dimension.[16]

First, it is no longer considered axiomatic that ethnic conflict characterized landlord and tenant relations in post-confiscation Ireland. As noted in
chapter two, Whelan and Barnard have agreed on that much. A recent historiographic survey by Sean Connolly has made a similar assertion. The disengagement by the gentry from a shared sense of obligations and rights
during the last quarter of the eighteenth century, and their espousal of new
concepts of property rights, led to conflict legitimized through the assertion
of customary rights by the rural poor. James O'Neill devoted a chapter of
his thesis to the 'estrangement of the upper classes from popular culture',
once shared. This was due to the emergence of a new upper class culture,
less indulgent and more market-orientate (it is the same process described
fictionally by Edgeworth). James Scott described similar processes in south-
east Asia, when peasants complained that landlords' 'sons and grandsons no
longer follow their old patriarchal customs; they exercise their rights and
neglect their duties'.[17]

However, James O'Neill surrendered to the notion that the gap between
popular and élite culture which arose in Ireland was due to the overwhelming
prospect facing the Irish peasantry of a foreign, arbitrary legal system which
could be capriciously altered according to the whims of the dominant (and foreign) classes. O'Neill granted too prominent a place to national cultural characteristics and concepts of property rights understood by tenants (Irish) and
landlords (English), 'one popular and Irish, the other elitist and foreign'. Similarly, Robert Scally has suggested that the 'predominantly Protestant landed

57; Connolly, *Priests and people*, 270, Clarke, *Christopher Dillon Bellew*, 26.   17 J. O'Neill,
'Popular culture and peasant rebellion', 136, 236; Connolly, 'Eighteenth-century Ireland';
Scott, *The moral economy of the peasant*, 88.

gentry ... lay like a crust over the native culture'. It is not inevitable that the problem should be put in this way in Irish historiography. The conflicts arising from increased class differentiation in the Irish countryside are misrepresented when they are characterized as between colonists and natives. Stanley Palmer's assertion that in Ireland there was no deference or paternalism is misplaced – even Lord Hartland, of Strokestown Park, Co. Roscommon, was 'under some constraint from the long tradition of paternalism'.[18]

Barnard claims that shared recreational culture was 'regardless of confession or ethnicity'; it depended much more on status:

> The reciprocity between landlord and tenant, patron and client or master and servant, was well understood by upstart as willingly as by veteran.

His objection to Whelan's 'underground gentry' is thus not on the basis of increasing divisions between land-owners and occupiers; in fact, he sees no great difference between 'upstart' and 'veteran' owners, that is between those who had become freeholders as a result of plantation or confiscation and the native aristocrats. Scally has suggested (surprisingly, given his description of the Protestant gentry 'crust') that rich and poor enjoyed a 'fraternal slovenliness', whatever their confessional allegiance.[19]

Whelan also argues, however, that conflict could arise from disappointed expectations of reciprocity between native Irish élites and land occupiers as well as between the 'upstarts' and land occupiers. He has pointed out that Irish middlemen themselves abandoned any sense of a Gaelic moral economy just before the period of greatest pre-famine agrarian conflict. Beneath the landlord stratum there were intermediate strata which could potentially be influenced by demands that appealed to custom and duty. The head landlord class was rarely, as has been observed, in direct contact with the cottiers, labourers and small farmers living on the land; the layer of tenant farmers and middlemen with substantial holdings directly from the head landlord was much more likely to be in regular contact (and dispute) with the rural poor, to whom they rented cabins and conacre gardens and whom they employed on their leasehold farms. A layer of Catholic middlemen had emerged who, as the eighteenth century progressed, increasingly abandoned the sense of vertical interdependence clung to by the rural poor. New social attitudes emerged (including family val-

18 O'Neill, 'Popular culture and peasant rebellion', 212, 219; R. Scally, *The end of hidden Ireland*, 13; S.H. Palmer, *Police and protest in England and Ireland*, 52; Scally, *The end of hidden Ireland*, 38.   19 Barnard, 'The gentrification of eighteenth century Ireland', 144; Scally, *The end of hidden Ireland*, 42.

ues) as the Catholic strong farming and middle classes distanced themselves from calendar custom, hurling, cock-fighting, horse-racing, patterns, wakes, bardic poetry and public drinking (the change was also reflected in the adoption of the English language). A Catholic Irish tenant was indeed quite likely to be the landlord of a Catholic labourer or cottier, once agricultural rationalization led to increasing stratification among the peasantry. Moreover, the stronger cottiers were able to rent directly from head landlords, who increasingly employed agents and other professionals, rather than middlemen. The emergence of this agent group, which Whelan contends was directly descended from the dispossessed Gaelic aristocracy, was recognized by James O'Neill:

> Expressions of popular unrest were embarrassing to the emerging Catholic middle classes as well as to the hierarchy of the church.

This might appropriately be described as the adoption by the emerging Catholic farming and middle class of values based upon a political rather than on a moral economy. A similar process has been noted in England when, as coal-mining encroached upon Cannock Chase in Staffordshire, the 'tangled skein of alliances in small communities' tended to be broken.[20]

Peasants and conflict

Similarities between Nedd Ludd and the Wiltshire shearmen in England and Captain Moonlight in Ireland need further qualification. There were indeed descriptive and tactical similarities, but we need to consider the social nature of peasant production, and how this might modify the forms collective action could take. Hobsbawm and Rudé identified the issue when they declared that peasants predominated in Ireland but that by the time of Captain Swing they were already unimportant minorities in England. Can conceptual models developed to consider rapidly industrializing Britain be applied to Ireland? To pursue this we need to consider some examinations of the nature of peasant production, and evaluate the usefulness of Beames's and Clark's reflections on economic strata and their status as sources of conflict in rural Ireland.[21]

First, let us consider the extent to which the term 'peasant' confers social, economic and cultural homogeneity on a certain group of people, and examine

20 Whelan, 'An underground gentry?', 26; J. O'Neill, 'Popular culture and peasant rebellion' 46, 286; D. Hay, 'Poaching and the game laws' (1975), 200.   21 Hobsbawm and Rudé, *Captain Swing*, 3; Beames, *Peasants and power*, and Clark, 'The importance of agrarian classes', pay much attention to the potential for conflict between social groups differentiated economically in sub-landlord Irish rural society during this period.

the complex relations that obtained among the rural population in Ireland, in the light of Samuel Clark's delicately stratified model of Irish rural society in the nineteenth century.

Rodolfo Stavenhagen, writing of Latin America, noted:

> nothing is further from the truth than the once widely held idea of an undifferentiated peasant mass, a homogeneous and unchangeable rural substratum.

The same point has been made in regard to the Irish rural population – that it was not simply a homogeneous mass groaning under the oppressive English yoke. It should be kept in mind that the landlords were wholesalers, rather than retailers, of land, and that beneath them were further sub-strata – middlemen and agents, farmers, plus further sub-lessees like cottiers, and farm labourers whose land consisted of nothing more than a potato patch to feed the family. Indeed, O'Connell told the 1825 Lords investigation into Irish disturbances that there were as many as six or seven layers of landlords between the owner and the occupier. The potential for conflict between and among these sub-landlord strata has been pointed out in Clark's revision of nationalist ortho-doxy, as well as in theoretical terms by historical sociologists.[22]

A helpful starting point is Michael Beames's description of peasant pro-duction being one where farms worked by family labour constitute the basic unit of production. This kind of definition allows almost everyone who worked in the countryside to be described as a peasant, but it may not be so useful for understanding their relation to the land they worked, to their immediate land-lord or, for that matter, to their tenants. It may suggest a homogeneity among the rural population beneath the élite that held title to the land, and may par-tially account for Beames's attention being focused on attacks on such élites and less on the conflicts among the population beneath this numerically tiny layer.[23]

Similar examinations of the defining characteristics of peasant producers have been developed for English society during the period in question, using Lenin's description of Russian peasant producers as a starting point. He iden-tified four kinds of peasant producers. They were, first, rural proletarians engaged in small-scale agricultural production for wage labour (the pre-famine Irish farm labourer might be aligned with this category, albeit on a consider-ably lower income). Second, the household producer who neither sold nor

---

22 R. Stavenhagen, *Social classes in agrarian societies* (1975), 64; Ó Gráda, *Ireland: a new eco-nomic history*, 30; SC 1825, 51, evidence of Daniel O'Connell.   23 Beames, *Peasants and power*, 1. See also Beames, 'Rural conflict in pre-famine Ireland'.

bought labour (certain small-scale Irish agricultural land holders, such as cottiers, might fit into this category). The third category is middling producers
who make a meagre surplus that might be converted into capital, for example
through the hiring of seasonal labour. Fourth are richer peasants – effectively
capitalist entrepreneurs in the countryside, connected to the peasantry only
through shared traditions and through continuing to work on the land. This
means that someone who rents a family farm may be both a peasant and a capitalist if, for example, he is subletting or employing labour.[24]

There are some similarities between Lenin's description and the models
adopted by Stinchcombe, who distinguished between hacienda farming, family tenancies, family smallholdings, plantation agriculture and capital-inten-
sive ranching. However, they would all need to be modified to some extent to
fit the Irish context. Their relation to Samuel Clark's stratified class model for
the Irish case is also evident. Whatever variant is accepted (there are numerous potential regional and national variations), and whatever criticisms of particular models may be made, what seems not to be at issue is that there were
sharp antagonisms within rural populations which confirm that the non-élite
rural population was anything but homogeneous. There was a space for antagonisms in the Irish countryside between people who were all peasants in so far
as the family farm was the basic unit of production. This could lead to polar-
ities within the same kin, communal, ethnic or religious group which would
militate against senses of reciprocity and mutuality derived from ideas of
nation, kin or community, and tend towards horizontal, rather than vertical
loyalties. It also means that using a general term like 'peasant' is of limited
value when considering social relations among the sub-élite Irish rural population in the late eighteenth and early nineteenth centuries, or indeed when
considering pre-famine agrarian conflicts. The complex pyramid of landlord-
tenant relations confirms Stavenhagen's view and suggests that it is necessary
to discard the term 'peasant' when talking about the people engaged in agrarian conflict.[25]

It is also important to consider whether these apparently primitive conflicts
were expressions of other kinds of divisions among the peasantry. Referring to
Irish agrarian conflicts in the first half of the nineteenth century David Fitzpatrick has suggested that 'the primary change in the pattern of unrest was not
class but family structure'. If he meant that changing family structures affected rural disorder, it is notable that the middling Catholic orders were increasingly adopting the notion of impartible inheritance, where one child inherited
the family farm and other children were dispersed among the professions and

24 M. Reed, 'Class and conflict in rural England' (1990).   25 A. Stinchcombe, 'Agricultural enterprise and rural class relations' (1961–2).

the Church. Such practices would lead to family conflict when first adopted in preference to the former practice of sub-division. The possibilities of settling scores and the difficulty of distinguishing between private and public issues has been acknowledged in an English context around the Captain Swing conflict, and the same difficulty does arise in an Irish context.[26]

As has been seen in relation to Co. Roscommon, there are occasional references among the manuscript sources to collective action being used as a cover for the settling of private grievances in Ireland. For example, a Dublin Castle enquiry into disturbances near Ballaghadereen in August 1808 concluded that cattle had been houghed due to the 'jealousy of one faction to another for taking a farm'. There are doubtless others. But the private/public distinction may be of limited analytical value. It could be argued that all grievances were individual and thus private; public grievances, or ones which were expressed by groups, undoubtedly expressed individual discontents. It has already been noted that factions were commonly associated with the interests or leadership of a family that had long-established authority in an area. Additionally, abductions and attempts to compel marriage were most often perpetrated by the sons of stronger farmers, anxious to secure a viable future. These private issues spilling into the area of public crime can be seen as a result of the adoption of commercial economic practices by a particular stratum in Irish rural society. Increasingly, individuals resolved their subsistence problems through loose associations which responded to the structural and economic changes taking place, changes that made these combinations the most viable way of opposing the reordering of rural social relations. This is not to collapse pre-famine social conflicts into a modernization model in which repertoires of dissent can only reflect a particular stage of development of economic forces. I have rejected notions that Co. Roscommon agrarian conflicts could only be 'pre-modern'. However, that does not mean that such conflicts can only be understood in terms of a fully-developed class-consciousness or conflict. Thompson's moral economy model demonstrates the ways in which custom and tradition could be deployed in changed circumstances, expressing consensual views about the proper conduct of social and economic relationships.[27]

Undoubtedly breakdowns in family relations and disputes among kin over land could persuade people to settle private scores through the collective medium of the agrarian combination, but the scale and widespread distribution of agrarian conflict shows that conflict reflected the very substantial economic changes taking place, as well as the reorientation of the middling Catholic family towards commercial farming.

---

26 Fitzpatrick, 'Class, family and rural unrest', 39; Wells, 'Social protest', 164.   27 SOCP1 1192/7, Stephen Brannick, Ballaghadereen, to unnamed, Dublin Castle, 7 Aug. 1808.

Marx suggested that the cultural nodes through which economic distinctions are transmitted are individualistic and aspirational, rather than collective, and that these are significant limitations on the capacity of peasants for collective action. It is in this sense that it is perhaps most useful to talk of peasants as a broad category. However, disunity has been noted far beyond Ireland during agrarian protests. During the revolution of 1873 in Spain, for example, Spanish socialists complained of the difficulty of organizing and forging unity among a stratified peasantry that included day labourers, tenant farmers and small landowners. When considering peasants in Ireland, it is apparent that collective actions did indeed take place, rather than rural protest being merely the fissiparous activity of individuals. Marx's potatoes model needs some qualification. Payment of rent to someone, or working for someone who might well also be paying rent and working the land, complicates the picture.[28]

Further, collective appeals to a moral economy could continue to mediate collective actions in circumstances which were changing. What seems certain from examining these models is that, while the term 'peasant' may describe a broad range of a rural population, it can also conceal a number of important divisions. The word is perhaps best used to refer generally to the sub-élite rural population that worked in agriculture, or when referring to sources that use the term loosely. Co. Roscommon whiteboys usually belonged to what may broadly be termed the 'rural poor', that is, they were cottiers and labourers. In times of crisis tenant farmers might be drawn into conflict on the same side as the rural poor, although more often they were the objects of whiteboy agitation.

It would be wrong, then, to say that the numerical predominance of agricultural labourers or small-scale farmers who accumulate no capital confers a social homogeneity or cohesion upon the peasantry which is reflected in the forms taken by rural conflict. While continuing to be peasants, tenant farmers who sub-let have a different relation to land than their sub-lessees – and this may produce conflict within the peasantry. Lenin's theory involving four categories of peasant was not necessarily definitive, but such a scheme at least showed how there can potentially be conflicts in the countryside within the peasantry; it is not unlike the models outlined by Clark and Stinchcombe. It seems reasonable to suppose that if a farmer employs only one or two labourers regularly, the potential for farmer and employee to perceive an identity of interests is greater than where a large-scale farmer employs many labourers, from whom he is distanced by the scale of the enterprise as well as by income. The defining characteristic of agrarian conflict might therefore be seen as rela-

28 K. Marx, 'The eighteenth Brumaire of Louis Bonaparte' (1968 ed.), 170; M. Molnár and J. Pekmez, 'Rural anarchism in Spain' (1974).

tion to the land – with the sources of conflict being more easily blurred in the small-scale enterprise where the farmer is less separated from the labourer, culturally, socially and economically. In those circumstances, bonds of interdependence are lived out daily. It was also in such situations that conflicts within and between families might be most apparent, in the manoeuvres of families over inheritance, marriage and the security of family farms. In the Irish situation (where such bonds had been cemented by kinship or community) the vertical reciprocity between tenant and sub-tenant may have been increasingly undermined, as farming became commercially orientated. While the ability to accumulate capital may be a critical economic distinction between different kinds of peasant producers, it may coexist with cultural expectations which pre-date the reorientation of relations on the land towards commerce. Vertical ties of paternalism, deference and customary practice based on the mutuality of the peasant community break down in the process of economic change, but conflict could still be legitimized through a backward-looking consciousness. It could take some time for the cultural and social milieux which could legitimize collective action to adapt to new circumstances. A social hierarchy that produced social cohesion at one time might be increasingly strained by the breakdown of a sense of customary duty and reciprocity. By incremental mutations and under the impact of structural change, rural social relations in Ireland were thus transformed. Yet the question of how various groups in the Irish rural population legitimized the collective actions they took has not previously been fully addressed.

In this consideration of peasant production, economic categories which suggest potential for conflict have been explored, revealing layers in the rural population, but these categories do not reveal the conscious loyalties or identities articulated by rural populations (or parts of them) engaged in collective action. It should also be noted that, while Clark was correct to point to the strata within the peasantry, potential conflicts cannot simply be read off from the economic relations between these strata. How they formed new collectives – of class or nation, for example – in the context of economic change, would be intimately related to the forms and cultural expressions of conflict.

Despite appeals to custom, economic imperatives were straining the moral economy. A structural change in class relations seems to have been under way by the late eighteenth century, as improving head landlords emerged and middlemen, agents and strong tenants began to abandon notions of customary reciprocity. Such men now began to look towards using land as capital in a commercial economy, not as a resource for modest private gain or for sustaining the life of the community. Where these men were Catholics, they began to look to an extension of political rights in the form of Emancipation and Repeal as a way to assert their growing economic strength. One observer, writing in the second decade of the nineteenth century, characterized middlemen as 'low farmers, a set of harpies who spread misery and oppression on the unhappy creatures who are compelled to live under them'. Rural social structures became increasingly differentiated in the pre-famine years.[29]

Thus by the early nineteenth century in Ireland the rural poor were alone in attempting to assert the primacy of custom. If the passage of the Black Act in 1723 was a defining moment in the shift from a moral economy to political economy in England, then the same kind of process occurred in Ireland, certainly in the last quarter of the eighteenth century, when agents, middlemen and the Catholic tenant farming class increasingly adopted a commercial ethic.[30]

The explanation of agrarian revolt as a response to economic modernization found its clearest expression in *Captain Swing*, where Hobsbawm and Rudé's found that:

> a rural society which was in some senses traditional, hierarchical, paternalist, and in many respects resistant to the full logic of the market, was transformed under the impetus of the extraordinary agricultural boom ... into one in which the cash nexus prevailed, at least between farmer and labourer. The worker was simultaneously proletarianised – by the loss of land, by the transformation of his contract ... and deprived of those modest customary rights as a man (though a subordinate one) to which he felt himself to have a claim.

This sense of placing conflicts in a broader process of modernization was also clearly identified by Charles Tilly in his studies of collective violence. Stanley Palmer has suggested that 'Ireland's agrarian criminals, like England's food rioters, were preindustrial or reactionary'.[31]

As noted, Charles Tilly has rejected his earlier view of grand narratives which describe the evolution from unfree to free labour, from pre-capitalist productive forces to capitalism. Tradition and culture imposed their own contingencies on the forces of modernization. It may be that the Irish agrarian conflicts contained elements of different types of collective violence, but if the forms were conservative, the meanings were not necessarily so. Despite taking the forms of appeals to custom and being against practices which can loosely be described as modernizing, they contained elements which give them a greater interest than if they were merely spontaneous, primitive acts of rebellion.

29 W. Eastwood, 'An account of the parish of Tacumshane' in W. Shaw Mason, *A statistical account or parochial survey of Ireland*, 3 vols (Dublin, 1814–19), iii, 426, quoted in Whelan, 'An underground gentry?' at 53; K. O'Neill, *Family and farm*, 106.   30 Whelan, 'An underground gentry?', 18.   31 Hobsbawm and Rudé, *Captain Swing*, xxi–xxii; Palmer, *Police and protest*, 48.

This is not to go so far as to say that these kinds of action were fully associ-ational – there are few suggestions in the Co. Roscommon evidence of the asso-ciational forms usually connected with class-consciousness. Perhaps historians need to reconsider what constitutes evidence of such a consciousness.

The repertoires of popular protest that emerged in the first half of the nine-teenth century in Co. Roscommon were quite separate from those of the emerging Catholic nationalist class, led from the 1820s by O'Connell. A com-parison of the peaks of disturbance and the peaks of O'Connell's campaigns reveals no congruence. It may well be that the monster rallies attended, pre-sumably, by many agrarian activists, were a reflection of the downturns and defeats of agrarian struggles as well as the political ascendancy of the upward-ly mobile Catholic middle class. The actions of oath-bound combinations in Ireland indicate that Marx's sack of potatoes had unusual properties. Thomp-son said that class should become possible within cognition before finding insti-tutional form, and this is evident in the wide range of motifs used by Irish agrarian protesters in the half century before the famine. While dissenting repertoires that, formally, looked backward were deployed to cope with the challenges created in the processes of structural change, such challenges could also adopt languages from outwith their spatial and cultural matrix.[32]

Thus the intriguing notice posted in Co. Tipperary in 1819 refers to the 'murdered patriots of Manchester'. If such a phrase had been used fifty years later it might be expected to refer to the Manchester Martyrs. In 1819, it was an expression of solidarity with the poor of England. It is a suggestion of a consciousness operating in a quite different way to that of nationalism, a con-sciousness that was silenced by subsequent Irish historiography.[33]

32 Gibbons, 'Rockites and Whitefeet', 204; Thompson, 'Eighteenth century English soci-ety', 157.   33 Gibbons, 'Rockites and Whitefeet', 204.

7

The secret Ireland

Acknowledging that Irish traditions and circumstances affected the way repertoires of rebellion were constituted and played out, it is nevertheless apparent that Irish agrarian conflict resonates with similar legitimizing customary attitudes as English price-fixing riots. However, this account of collective conflict in Co. Roscommon also suggests that Irish agrarian unrest can not simply be placed on a linear continuum of modernization. This is in distinction to some 'history from below', which has missed an opportunity to gain a better understanding of the pre-industrial crowd by dismissing it as composed of primitive rebels.

In conclusion, first, it is apparent that the notion of a moral economy might be extended to explain acts of collective protest, resistance and rebellion in Co. Roscommon during the first half of the nineteenth century. The rural poor in Ireland demonstrated a combination of custom and culture that legitimized resistance to social and economic disruption and change. Bartlett maintains the view that the focus of violence in Ireland was on land, but acknowledges that 'the legitimization of that violence was common to both countries'. The relevance of the moral economy has been shown through this examination of conflict in Roscommon, dispelling the notion that price-fixing and other forms of collective action used to regulate prices, wages, terms of employment and rents were unknown in Ireland. The price of provisions, wage rates, clerical duties, tithe impositions and poor rates, for example, have been considered, as well as the more familiar grievances of rents and access to land.[1]

Second, the term moral economy does not necessarily imply one-sided deference and acceptance of the terms and conditions of élite dominance. Thompson was careful to assert that although customary outlooks were formally backward looking, they contained within them the embryos of mutated collectives, as 'discrete and fragmented elements of older patterns of thought become integrated by class'. This was the basis of what may be termed a paradoxical consciousness. It was apparent in the mid-eighteenth century Whiteboy and Rightboy movements. Rightboys marched under banners to join Protestant churches, their bands playing the White Cockade to show *loyalty*. The Whiteboys were capable of proclaiming loyalty to both Queen Sive, symbolizing Ireland, and to George III. While these specific paradoxes demonstrate the absence

1 Bartlett, 'An end to moral economy', 194.

of a monolithically nationalist consciousness, others demonstrate a consciousness that upsets the linearity of explanations of agrarian violence as pre-modern. It has been suggested that Irish agrarian collectives relied on 'outmoded
appeals to the moral economy which both the rulers and ruled had shared'.
However, a number of features of agrarian conflict which suggest a combined
and uneven consciousness can be discerned, much like the one which could proclaim loyalty to both Ireland and to the crown. Maurice Bric has suggested that
the Rightboys could not be characterized merely as a pre-industrial crowd,
clinging stubbornly to a past of protectionist legislation as their rulers abandoned it. Just as E.P. Thompson discovered the inadequacy of notions of economic progress and backwardness in considering English upland weaving
communities in the early nineteenth century, so this study of Co. Roscommon
suggests the need to re-evaluate Irish agrarian collectives.[2]

Thompson saw movements like Luddism as transitional forms. On the one
hand, Luddism looked backward to old customs and paternalist legislation
which could never be revived; on the other hand, it tried to revive ancient rights
in order to establish new precedents. The agrarian conflicts of pre-famine Ireland might be profitably reinterpreted in a similar way. This examination of
conflict over fifty years in Co. Roscommon has provided evidence that such an
approach is valuable.[3]

Hobsbawm and Rudé claimed that the organization of the Captain Swing
disturbances was entirely traditional but Tilly has noted that while the Swing
events might look 'like a fragment of another world', because of their justifica-
tion by reference to time-honoured rights, there were evident connections to
national politics. By incremental mutations, customary forms like the shaming
rituals of rough music merged into disciplined demonstrations. Thompson
noted that the English working class between 1790 and 1840 was not simply
'made' by the industrial revolution but brought with it legacies and traditions
from Paine, Methodism and the legend of the free-born Englishman. Indeed,

> The factory hand or stockinger was also the inheritor of Bunyan, of
> remembered village rights.

In the context of Roscommon it has become apparent that cosmopolitan discourses (Painite, French, Reform and Chartist, for example) were imported
and grafted on to indigenous traditional ingredients, thus modifying the repertoires of rebellion. Peter Burke has noted that 'the political education of the

2 Thompson, 'Eighteenth century English society', 156; Donnelly, 'The Rightboy movement'; Donnelly, 'The Whiteboy movement; J. O'Neill, 'Popular culture and peasant rebellion', 393; M.J. Bric, 'Priests, parsons and politics' (1987); Thompson, *Making of the English
working class*, 322.   3 Thompson, *Making of the English working class*, 603.

common man' took place when political consciousness among European peasants 'was suddenly transformed following the French Revolution'. In the Irish
context, it might be argued that the agrarian protesters of the first half of the
nineteenth century were inheritors of vertical reciprocities that pre-dated the
changes of political dispensation and landownership in the late seventeenth
century. Yet, by the late eighteenth century they were adapting language and
actions that located them within pan-European traditions of protest. As has
been demonstrated, there were striking similarities between some of the repertoires of action and dissent in Ireland and repertoires from across Europe and,
indeed, beyond.[4]

The incremental changes in repertoires of collective action are highly significant in demonstrating responses to structural changes. James O'Neill has
suggested that after 1815 the concerns of the rural poor ceased to be exclusively agrarian, and agitations became 'supra-local', suggesting a qualitative
change in the nature of rural protest and the level of political mobilization.
Captain Rock operated from Cork to Larne, according to the *Roscommon and
Leitrim Gazette*. Other agrarian movements evidently spread across regions,
rather than being merely local. Where the movements were unrelated, as many
were, there can be little doubt that the similarities in manifestations of conflict
suggest a broader significance. Writing of England, Tilly suggested changes in
repertoires occurred as a result of structural changes involving a great concen-
tration of capital, a substantial augmentation and alteration of the national
state's power, and struggles in response to those changes. Ritual humiliation
and violence declined as public meetings and associations prevailed. In relation
to Ireland, demographic and economic change, especially integration into the
UK's internal market, had powerful effects on relations between landowners
and occupiers, on land use and on emigration. Imported repertoires increasingly supplemented traditional ones. It has been noted that in 1821 Rockites in
Co. Kilkenny carried banners demanding 'no taxes, no tithes, 60 per cent
reduction in rents', while ten years later 'Ribandmen' in Co. Cavan carried banners demanding 'Half Rents, no Tithes, no Taxes and certain Rates of Wages'.
The demands themselves are significant, but so are the forms in which they
were expressed. Banners, placards and mobilizing slogans are habitually considered part of the modern associational repertoire, yet they were appearing in
rural Ireland when such activities were supposedly unknown outside the élite
Catholic politics of O'Connell. Nocturnal meetings, disguise and threatening
notices had not been completely displaced, but other tactics were supplement-

4 Hobsbawm and Rudé, *Captain Swing*, 253; Tilly, *Popular contention*, 315–16, 332–3;
Thompson, *Making of the English working class*, 212–13; Thompson, 'Rough music', 525;
Coleman, *Riotous Roscommon*, 15; Burke, *Popular culture*, 269, 266.

ing them. Nor do these demands merely look back for the restoration of a pre-vious equilibrium. By the mid-nineteenth century the Roscommon rural poor were viewing the matrix of economic and social relations in which they lived in terms of horizontal social solidarities, without having created durable insti-tutional forms for the expression of class-consciousness.[5]

These changes also demonstrate the ways in which ideas of community norms were gradually being replaced by horizontal consociations, as landown-ers and farmers attempted to respond to change through 'private gain at the expense of the community', and as improvement displaced laxity as the pre-dominant ethos of landlordism. It might be observed that:

> The old and newer modes of production each supported distinct kinds of community and characteristic ways of life. Alternative conventions and notions of human satisfaction were in conflict with each other.

The additions to the repertoires of collective conflict signify a redefinition by the whiteboy of the people 'whose motives and interests he understands ... with whom interaction and understandings are possible on the basis of com-mon premises'. It has also been suggested that in the processes of widespread structural change, the legitimacy of landlords as a class may have been ques-tioned, by means of a formally backward-looking focus on their non-compli-ance with their obligations.[6]

However, where Thompson's approach was once widely recognized as sig-nificant, it has been under attack in recent years. One source of attack has been the historians of what has been known as the 'linguistic turn' in English social history. This has involved the suggestion that Thompson's conception of social and economic relations in late eighteenth- and early nineteenth-century Eng-land reduced the linguistic, cultural and discursive complexities of popular protest to a grand narrative of the development of productive forces, which created new forms of social identity, that is, the emergence of a working class.

The charge of economic determinism laid at Thompson's door is closely related to the way in which historians writing from materialist perspectives have been associated with the construction of grand narratives. The most obviously relevant metanarrative to this study would be one of economic modernization, in which the actions, forms of association and languages of

5 J. O'Neill, 'Popular culture and peasant rebellion', 333; RLG, 3 May 1823, 10 May 1823; Reed, 'Class and conflict in rural England'; Tilly, *Popular Contention*, 16, 7–8; McCartney, *Dawning of democracy*, 93; SC 1839, 727, evidence of Bartholomew Warburton; Thomp-son, *Making of the English working class*, 157.   6 J. O'Neill, 'Popular culture and peasant rebellion', 222; Thompson, *Making of the English working class*, 485; E. Wolf, *Peasants* (1996), 47; Scott, *Moral economy of the peasant*, 51.

the rural poor would be determined by macro-economic change. The charge against Thompson has been made most vociferously by the post-modern epigones of Foucault, among whom a favourite example of metanarrative has been 'Marx's drama of the forward march of human productive capacities'. This is not the place to discuss whether human productive capacities have over a very long period 'marched forward', despite long periods of stagnation, nor whether such an assertion is based upon a caricature of classical Marxism. What is hard to doubt is that there is no necessary, immediate and direct link between social being (your place in the world) and social consciousness (your beliefs about your place in the world). The links in the chain of historical change are inherited traditions and cultures. Thus any viable 'historical materialism' requires agency as well as social and economic structures, in which historical outcomes are not simply determined by economic positions and relations of production. Thompson's moral economy makes room for just such an account of agency, an introduction of contingency to the historical process.[7]

The activity of Roscommon agrarian combinations displayed the significance of agency. Any social formation may, in the totality of its production relations, have a number of different modes of production. While factory production was, in the period under study here, beginning to predominate in certain regions of England, the productive relations in which the rural poor of Roscommon participated were generally of a different sort. Roger Wells has speculated about how far rural evidence may be useful in extending Thompson's view of class formation. In so far as Thompson's key criterion of consciousness of an identity of interests against employers and rulers is satisfied, it is surely useful.[8]

What is most interesting is how the cultural and rebellious traditions frequently associated with one set of production relations (so-called pre-modern, pre-capitalist, pre-industrial) could be cross-fertilized with another (Painite, radical, Chartist, for example), as has become apparent, resulting in transformed languages and repertoires of dissent and rebellion. Thus, for example, not only did Irish agrarian rebels appropriate languages of formal judicial authority in threatening notices, but also they used associational forms. Not only did they post notices and assemble at night in disguise, they also marched openly by day, bearing placards proclaiming political demands.

This is at odds with a number of accounts of protests and collective action by the rural poor. They have therefore been inclined to interpret agrarian protest and collective action in ways that have been limited by expectations of

7 K. Jenkins, 'Introduction: on being open about our closures' (1997), 7.   8 Wells, 'Social protest'.

the kind of forms protest might take in particular modern or pre-modern circumstances. As previously noted, Tilly made this view explicit in a 1969 essay:

> Reactionary disturbances ... center on rights once enjoyed but now
> threatened, while modern disturbances center on rights not yet enjoyed
> but now within reach.

Tilly suggested in a 1978 work that collective action in Europe tended to move
from the local to the national, from the reactive to the active and from the
communal to the associational. James O'Neill views the increasing separation
of élite and popular culture in Ireland as a symptom of this process:

> As the gentry adopted values and pastimes more characteristic of the
> modern world, and as they came to view their estates more rationally
> and instrumentally, the familiar sort of relationship which had existed
> between them and the peasantry under the old order deteriorated.

The enemies of Hobsbawm's primitive rebels were those outsiders, foreigners,
lawyers, dealers and money-lenders who upset 'traditional' peasant life.[9]

Huizer and Stavenhagen's study of Mexico and Bolivia suggested that political consciousness only developed among the peasantry as a result of exposure
to modernizing influences. Chirot and Ragin's study of rebellion in Românía
suggested that, under the impact of modernization, there is an 'optimal' period
for peasant rebellion, before peasant traditions and solidarities are destroyed for
ever. In a study that attempts to reconcile signs that peasants were not limited
to local, primitive rebellion to the idea of modernization, Hildermeier suggested that primitive rebels could make a leap to being modern revolutionaries. The
modernization theory was implied in Stavenhagen's assertion that all over the
world 'new mechanisms of social integration' displaced 'integrative mechanisms
based on kinship, locality and primary relations'. Wolf considered that the trans-
formation of agriculture into an economic enterprise aimed at maximum output rather than subsistence was critical in this process. However, he did note
that caution should be exercised in drawing up an evolutionary scale in these
matters, saying the pre-modern and modern could co-exist. As has already been
suggested, Hobsbawm and Rudé's study of Captain Swing also uses a linear
model for the development not only of economic forces but also of the kind of
struggles that could be precipitated by such developments. For Rudé, new
notions of natural wages and prices replaced old notions of just prices and

9 Tilly, 'Collective violence in European perspective', 34; Tilly, *From mobilization to revolution*; J. O'Neill, 'Popular culture and peasant rebellion', 266; Hobsbawm, *Primitive rebels*, 22.

wages that had been sanctioned by custom. Yet, analyzing mediaeval Europe, Rodney Hilton showed that peasants were not an 'undisciplined or easily dispersed mob'. Scott has acknowledged some relationship between modern and pre-modern collective action in the formative potential of local collective actions. He has also asserted that 'peasant social structure, values and organization … are not nearly so atomistic and amorphous as Marx assumes'. However, none of these views entirely escapes from a linearity which precludes the co-existence of modern and pre-modern forms of culture and popular politics.[10]

Thompson suggested that class relations were processes, not static relationships to particular configurations of the forces of production. There is no contradiction between this and the materialist assertion that, in any specific case, the relations of production are critical to an understanding of class. New assertions based on changing production relations may be perceived within a rebellious traditional culture as no more than the assertion of customary rights.[11]

This is not to say that there was no directionality in the development of productive forces in early nineteenth century Britain and Ireland, only that there was no inevitable outcome of class–consciousness among lower class protesters like Irish agrarian rebels. However, economic circumstances profoundly affect the capacities of human agency, and these must be acknowledged when considering the capacity for collective action of the rural poor in Co. Roscommon. Thompson maintained that 'class relations have rôles intrinsic to the system and cannot transcend it'. As Tilly suggests:

> Over the longer run … transformations of the economy shaped not only the grievances on which ordinary people were prepared to act but also their capacity to act collectively.[12]

These relations of production do appear critical. Although Scott and Hilton have noted a greater capacity for peasant collective action than has sometimes been acknowledged, the desired outcomes of these actions should not be inferred as the same as those of working class associations. Co. Roscommon whiteboys were able to appropriate some of the languages and associational forms of urban workers and cosmopolitan political movements, but the demands of their organic intellectuals like Michael Burke were ultimately

10 Huizer and Stavenhagen, 'Peasant movements and land reform'; D. Chirot and P. Ragin, 'The market, tradition and peasant rebellion' (1975), 442; Hildermeier, 'Agrarian social protest'; Stavenhagen, *Social classes in agrarian societies*, 65; Wolf, *Peasants*, 36, 54; Rudé, *The crowd in history*, 226; R. Hilton, 'Peasant society, peasant movements and feudalism in medieval Europe' (1974); Scott, *Moral economy of the peasant*, 207; Scott, 'Hegemony and the peasantry', 270.   11 Thompson, 'Eighteenth century English society', 133–65.   12 Thompson, 'Eighteenth century English society', 161; Tilly, *Popular contention*, 204.

structured by the life conditions of the basic unit of production in the mid nineteenth-century Irish countryside, the family farm or conacre plot. These included a piece of land to provide economic security, or the regulation of rents, prices and wages. In this sense they created qualitatively and politically the kind of associational forms that Lewis described as a 'vast trades union of the rural poor', but little more. Thompson's writing on 'class society without class' is of utmost importance here. Writing of 'the mob' in eighteenth-century England, Thompson suggested that 'the mob may not have been noted for an impeccable consciousness of class, but the rulers of England were in no doubt at all that it was a horizontal sort of beast'. The 'horizontal' consciousness of the rural poor in Co. Roscommon has become apparent.[13]

However, this nascent self-consciousness of Roscommon agrarian rebels should not be tested against class indicators that might be used to measure the existence of an industrial proletariat like, for example, degrees of workplace trade union organization. The proceedings of the select committee investigating disturbances in counties Monaghan, Armagh and Louth in 1852 are an appropriate place to conclude the chronology of this investigation. The committee discussed demands by stronger farmers for peasant proprietorship. It should be remembered that the famine and mass emigration were having a rapidly homogenizing effect on rural social structures in which the numbers and proportions of cottiers and labourers (and thus whiteboys) to farmers were falling rapidly. Edward Golding, a magistrate in Armagh, said that conacre had been 'done away with completely'. Nevertheless, the demands for proprietorship indicate the general trajectory of peasant movements.[14]

Peasant proprietorship, rather than the primitive class politics of the Roscommon rural poor, is much more easily reconciled with Marx's well-known characterization of the peasantry as profoundly atomistic, 'much as potatoes in a sack form a sack of potatoes'. For classical Marxists, the political guidance of another class was deemed necessary to overcome the tendency to individualism inherent in peasant proprietorship.[15]

Clark and Donnelly suggested that while it is not clear that external leadership was required for Irish peasant movements, their political aspirations were limited by O'Connellism. However, given the calamity of the great famine and the absence thereafter of organized labourer and cottier movements, the question was never tested further in Ireland. It would be projecting later conceptions of class antagonisms back on to agrarian class distinctions to claim that

13 Lewis, *On local disturbances*, 80; Thompson, 'The patricians and the plebs', 64.   14 SC 1852, 68–9, evidence of Captain George Fitzmaurice; SC 1852, 77, evidence of Edward Golding.   15 Marx, 'The eighteenth Brumaire of Louis Bonaparte', 170; T. Shanin, 'Peasantry as a political factor' (1971).

the 'territorial imperative jostled confusedly with class criteria of community, anticipating in microcosm the relationship of nationalism and socialism in later generations'. Hildermeier suggested that the integrative processes of econom- ic change removed some of the parochial limitations on peasant organization- al capacities, enabling the emergence of an 'agrarian populism' that contests the validity of Marx's approach and 'displays a typical mix of backward-look- ing and progressive forces'.[16]

This is both to overstate the case and to reduce it to a reflex of economic development, a tendency among accounts constructed in a modernization par- adigm, which make direct connections between the development of economic forces and available repertoires of collective action. Agency and consciousness, informed as they were by cosmopolitan developments, stretched the limits of the structural capacities of Irish peasants in the pre-famine decades in ways pre- viously largely unexplored by historians. But they alone never threatened wide- spread social and political upheaval. Scott and Hildermeier's views of the capacity of peasant movements to generate organically an independent politics that is capable of challenging for state power do not seem borne out by twenti- eth century events in, for example, Cuba and China, where exogenous social groups like intelligentsia provided political generalization and leadership for peasant populations.

Furthermore, Thompson's critics have raised important questions about his- torical narrative itself, in a departure that is of great significance for the study of whiteboyism because this approach may be used to reduce the history of Irish agrarian conflict to a conflict of national identities, consistent with nationalist explanations. Given that this study has taken care to demonstrate the inade- quacies of nationalist narratives of whiteboyism, it requires some attention.

The starting point for this approach is the unremarkable recognition that knowledge of the past can only be through textual representations of that past. Applied rigorously to the issue at stake here, the formation of social identity, it means that

> Class is therefore increasingly, and rightly, seen less as objective reality than as a social construct, created differently by different historical actors. The seemingly simple recognition that the category of 'experi- ence' (out of which historians such as E.P. Thompson argue comes class consciousness) is in fact not prior to and constitutive of language but is actively constituted by language, has increasingly been recognised as having far-reaching implications.[17]

16 Clark and Donnelly, 'General introduction'; Lee, 'Patterns of rural unrest in nineteenth century Ireland' (1980), 228; Hildermeier, 'Agrarian social protest', 330, 331.   17 P. Joyce,

Thus one determinism has been swiftly substituted for another. The focus on the category of class is intended to demonstrate that ideas like class are registered in language, constituted by and therefore not pre-existing the language in which they are narrated. What is especially misleading about the reduction of class (as the favoured example of historians pursuing the linguistic approach) to narrative is the tendency to treat it as a hermetic category. Some years ago Eric Hobsbawm noted the congruence between the national and the social in late nineteenth-century political movements. Hobsbawm noted that 'the class appeal of the socialists, the confessional appeal of religious denominations and the appeal of nationality were not mutually exclusive'. National movements articulated lower class demands, often accompanied by vague promises of social and economic change, as we have seen in the case of Daniel O'Connell. These abstractions connected with the specific economic and social concerns of the lower class audience. Nationalists utilized homogenizing rituals and emblems that were at once familiar and thus helped in the discursive creation of the nation. By this means all members of a particular language or other group on the claimed national territory might be persuaded to support nationalists. Hobsbawm made a most significant point in relation to the appeal of the national and the social – that for many, much of the time, the two overlapped without any sense of inconsistency. For a great number of people in later nineteenth-century Europe there was neither the exclusively national nor the incorruptibly social. Indeed, such convenient categories of social identity as 'national' and 'social' have been created after the event. While Hobsbawm's study concerns an earlier period, his remarks remain helpful.[18]

For it is doubtless the case that individual subjects speak 'different, overlapping and often competing "discourses",' rather than possessing a monolithic consciousness. Thus a Moldavian farm labourer participating in the rebellion alluded to earlier may have said the Jewish leaseholder was his oppressor because the leaseholder was Jewish, a leaseholder or both of these. A Roscommon cottier may have said the Protestant middleman was his oppressor because the middleman was a Protestant, a middleman or both. That competing discourses are born in the plurality of social relations is not surprising, but the determinist impulse among historians is sometimes overpowering. As it has been put recently, 'the view that meanings are unitary and fixed is as far from a genuinely historical view as is the view that meanings are infinitely plural and unstable'.[19]

Visions of the people (1991), 9.   18 E.J. Hobsbawm, *Nations and nationalism since 1780* (1990 ed.), 123.   19 Joyce, *Visions of the people*, 8; Chirot and Ragin, 'The market, tradition and peasant rebellion'. In Moldavia during the rebellion of 1907 most peasants owned land but had nevertheless also to labour on farms leased out by major landowners. Forty per cent of such lessees were Jewish; P. Mandler, 'The problem with cultural history' (2004), 109.

The meanings of language can also be contested. For example, Patrick Joyce suggested that class was not evident in the looser terms he discovered in use among English working people, a language of contrasts between the rich and the poor. He made this claim on the basis that the rich/poor distinction was moral, not economic. This mechanical separation of the discursive practice through which the distinction between rich and poor was made by working people and the 'economic' distinction being described, was constructed by Joyce (emplotting hermetic discourses of the moral and the economic, and on the basis of the kind of reductive definition of class supposed to have been disposed of), not the people whose practices he was considering. For the rural poor in pre-famine Ireland, there was no language available to them to articulate a difference between the moral and the economic. When the discursive practices of English working people appear unquestionably to be languages of class, they have been dismissed as the 'spurious facticity' of 'popular common sense'. To allow plurality would be to allow a dialogic view of language in which language does not create class, nationality or whatever discourse you will, but forms and narrates the material past.[20]

It appears that, for the historians of the linguistic turn, there is no external reality beyond language and discourse, because 'the events, structures and processes of the past are indistinguishable from the forms of documentary representation, the conceptual and political appropriations, and the historical discourses that construct them'.[21]

Such assertions lead to major epistemic questions, which should be acknowledged briefly here because of their direct relevance to the construction of nationalist narratives. The emphasis on language recreates historical practice as a self-referential activity with no greater claim to discovering the past than the novel. This is a reasonable claim only if language does constitute, rather than mediate, the relationship between human agency and structures. Thus, in a pugnacious engagement with postmodernism, Richard Price notes:

> The postmodernist approach to history rests upon a conception of history that reduces it to another form of literary fiction.

While the representation of something may be the starting point for an enquiry into it, it can not precede or originate that something. The question is how to characterize the relationship between language and that past. While the presence of class (or other) structures is not dependent on their registration in language, the study of language may be one element in a wider framework 'which embraces agency and structure, saying and doing, the conscious and the

---

20 Joyce, *Visions of the people*, 247; Joyce, 'The end of social history?' (1995), 85; R. Price, 'Postmodernism as theory and history' (1997), 28.   21 N. Kirk, 'History, language, ideas and postmodernism' (1994); Joyce, 'History and postmodernism' (1991), 208.

unconscious, and the willed and unintentional consequences of individual and social action and thought'.[22]

The connection between consciousness and action was made by Gramsci, when he described 'the co-existence of two conceptions of the world, one affirmed in words and the other displayed in effective action'. People may have consciousnesses that are submissive and subordinate, but in their relations to structures they enter into groups which act according to a praxis of shared interests. Gramsci went on to describe these conceptions as two theoretical consciousnesses, or one contradictory consciousness. One is implicit in activity and the other made explicit verbally. The verbal consciousness may even directly contradict the practical consciousness, as it is often absorbed as a result of subordination to another group. This can be seen in the appropriation by Roscommon rebels of languages and symbols of authority, not only in attempts to order their understanding of the circumstances they lived in, but also when trying to re-order that world. Such a model is surely of more utility in considering the multi-layered actions, emblems and words of agrarian rebels than any modernizing or linguistic determinism.[23]

There may be many different conceptions of the world affirmed in language by the same subject, for example when, as noted earlier, confession and class intersect. It is these discourses that can be equated with the paradoxical consciousness of the Roscommon agrarian rebel. Peter Burke has enumerated five discourses of response to perceived wrongs in the popular culture of early modern Europe. They are fatalist, modernist, traditionalist, radical and millenarian. Burke suggests that these attitudes are points on a continuum. The moral economy may correspond most closely to the traditionalist response, but it has been established that tradition could frequently be put to radical uses, legitimizing new demands. In the context of significant structural change at the end of Burke's period of study of early modern Europe, the interaction of Gramsci's two 'theoretical consciousnesses' shifted incrementally, with new repertoires of action and new collectives being established. In his study of English collective action, Tilly has identified that conflict itself, that is human agency, affected how those struggles eventuated. This is far removed from the structural determination that has been identified with Thompson's historical materialism. This is not to say that there is no element of determination within materialist conceptions of social processes, merely that it also accounts for the capacity of human agency to affect outcomes and structures.[24]

22 Price, 'Postmodernism as theory and history', 34; P. Zagorin, 'Historiography and postmodernism: reconsiderations' (1990), 269; Kirk, 'History, language, ideas and postmodernism', 238, 239.   23 A. Gramsci, *Selections from the prison notebooks* (1991 ed.), 326–7, 333.
24 Burke, *Popular culture*, 174; See for example, Tilly, *Popular contention*, 42, 37.

Without an account of structure, it is difficult adequately to account for historical change. So proponents of the linguistic turn seem not to attempt to get by without such an account. In relation to nineteenth century England, Joyce acknowledged that 'quite simply factory production had irrevocably strengthened its hold on older forms of production and many of the views and practices associated with the older forms no longer made sense to workers'. Put another way, structural change affected the consciousness and discourses constructed by working people. Another advocate of the linguistic turn, Gareth Stedman Jones, has described how, at the end of the Napoleonic wars, 'radicalism found itself forced to stretch its vocabulary to encompass new sources of distress and discontent within its terms'. A few years further on, the old radical image of placemen, sinecurists and fundholders had been displaced by 'something more sinister and dynamic – a powerful and malevolent machine of repression, at the behest of capitalists and factory lords'. Joyce would concede only that there are 'instances ... that have social contexts essential to their meaning, but no underlying structure they are expressing'. Here, an Althusser-derived caricature of historical materialism is deployed to ignore the critical factor of human agency in affecting outcome. In this caricature, human activity could only be an expression of determining structures, rather than itself affecting the eventuation of structures.[25]

A second critique of Thompson's approach to popular contention was developed by Mark Harrison, who sought to integrate analysis of all crowds into a single conceptual framework. Harrison complained that historians like Rudé and Thompson had conflated 'crowd' and 'riot', and that most crowds were consensual. This criticism would be acceptable if it could be demonstrated conclusively that a single conceptual framework is desirable or possible. Harrison suggested, quite reasonably, that 'riots must be regarded as such multi-layered manifestations at the local level of national concerns that they cannot be crammed into the existing methodological straightjacket of "pre-industrial" and "industrial" collective activity'. He also sought to depart from the examination of contentious assemblies to consider consensual displays, often called into existence by élites. A recent attempt to extend Harrison's approach to the consideration of Irish crowds goes so far as to suggest that 'the normative crowd was one sanctioned and even brought into being by urban élites'. This suggestion is made possible by entirely excluding whiteboyism from the discussion. Adopting Harrison's taxonomy of a crowd as 'a large group of people assembled outdoors in sufficient proximity to be able to influence each other's behaviour and to be identifiable as an assembly by contemporaries', Peter Jupp and Eoin Magennis main-

25 Joyce, *Visions of the people*, 102; G. Stedman Jones, *Languages of class* (1983), 103, 173; Joyce, 'History and postmodernism', 208.

tain that secret night meetings do not fall within this definition. The members of an assembly might not be identified because of the darkness, but it was very much identified as a crowd by contemporaries.[26]

The assembling of a crowd involves a collective act of self-identification, of inclusion and of exclusion. Harrison was aware of this in respect of the con- sensual Bristol crowd's identification of the people present as Bristolians, and thus with a common identity and interests. However, because Jupp and Magennis have excluded one particular important kind of Irish contentious crowd from their analysis, they decline to consider the senses of social identi- ty demonstrated by those kinds of crowd. Instead they concentrate on the ways in which the O'Connellite crowd aimed to 'subvert the development of the much les controllable physical force pressure groups' and achieve the political integration of lower class Catholics under the nationalist umbrella. Unfortu- nately this has precisely the effect of shoehorning Irish contentious gatherings into the kind of 'convenient demarcations' Harrison has objected to, in which 'élite sanctioning increased and spontaneous crowd activity declined'. This would, of course, lead unsurprisingly to the apparent hegemony of O'Connel- lite nationalism. As has been shown, so-called 'spontaneous' crowd activity (shown in this study to have been rather more than spontaneous) continued until the famine, the effects of which may have been much more closely con- nected to the decline of this type of activity than the success of O'Connell. If consensual and contentious gatherings were considered evenly, it would be apparent that collective assemblies in Ireland characteristically displayed com- plex, combined and uneven elements of consciousness, evading categoric def- inition as consensual or contentious. Much more compelling is Maura Cronin's exploration of the tensions within the O'Connellite crowd, reflecting Sean Connolly's observation that 'the vision of emancipation that moved the mass of the catholic population was in many cases radically different from that held by the small-town notables and strong farmers'.[27]

In Ireland, according to Jim Smyth, at the same time as the English work- ing class was being made, 'lower class solidarity and collective awareness found expression through opposition to the ascendancy, religion and an as yet inchoate nationalism'. It is clear from this study of Co. Roscommon that the hegemony of nationalism was anything but as complete and uncontested as Smyth appears to suggest. It remains to note the ways in which the assump- tions of Thompson's critics help breathe new life into the nationalist account of a homogenous Gaelic peasantry oppressed by Saxon landlordism.[28]

26 P. Jupp and E. Magennis, 'Introduction: crowds in Ireland' (2000), 4–5, 25; M. Harri- son, *Crowds and history* (1988), 198, 37.   27 Jupp and Magennis, 'Introduction: crowds in Ireland', 25, 29; Connolly, 'Mass politics and sectarian conflict' (1989), 92–3.   28 Smyth,

It is evident that if, as the proponents of the linguistic turn suggest, there is no past independent of the discourses which construct it, any narrative of the past may be as valid as another. This accords the same significance to constructions of the past by historians and novelists and allows the kind of narratives of Irish history practised by writers like Sullivan, O'Brien and O'Hegarty, or the teaching proffered by the Christian Brothers, as much importance as historical enquiry. The relativism and absence of external referents in the postmodern approach are especially prone to the mythologies of the nation, because they allow the construction of such imagined communities as much significance as evidence derived from a close inspection of sources. In this way the linguistic turn coincides with conservative accounts of nationality and ethnicity as self-evident, fundamental categories, as totalizing, unitary conceptions of identity that disallow alternative discourses. The approach adopted by Harrison in the investigation of consensual crowds is similarly susceptible. His focus on the 'perceptions and interpretations of contemporary participants and observers' makes close interrogation of sources irrelevant. Neither approach can explain the apparent paradoxes of loyalty to Queen Sive and George III, or the singing of the *White Cockade* to demonstrate loyalty, nor antagonism to Catholic clergy, farmers and landlords. A continuous interrogation of the sources and close attention to the language in which they were constructed has revealed another account of whiteboyism. The close examination of agrarian conflict in Co. Roscommon undertaken in these pages reveals enormous cracks in the gloss of national oppression discourses. The suggestion made by Hobsbawm, that social identities often seen by historians as hermetically discrete were not necessarily experienced as such by the historical subjects themselves, ought to be borne in mind. In addition, Irish historiography is still engaged in a long process of dragging itself out from beneath the weighty corpus of nationalist narratives of the nineteenth century. Reviewing the creation of nationalist 'stories of Ireland', Roy Foster has suggested that 'there are other models, tales within tales, which might allow more room for alternative truths and uncomfortable speculations'.[29]

Accounts of peasant collective action in colonial settings also reveal the widespread difficulties in 'national liberation' accounts of agrarian unrest. French officials in Vietnam reported that communal lands had fallen into the hands of local notables and mandarins, 'abuses which belong in the category of those committed by the natives against their own compatriots'. This study has demonstrated many instances of conflict in Co. Roscommon between 'natives'

Men of no property, 8.   **29** A. Callinicos, *Theories and narratives* (1995), 71; idem, *Making history* (1987), 208; Price, 'Postmodernism as theory and history', 13; R.F. Foster, 'Storylines: narratives and nationality' (1998), 52.

and 'compatriots', but the potency of national myth-making has led to the historiographic submergence of such conflicts.[30]

The question of a continued loyalty to the descendants of dispossessed
landowners has also been noted in colonial settings (leaving aside the much-
debated question of whether Ireland was strictly a colony). In Vietnam, 'dynas-
tic pretenders' provided ready leadership in Nghe Tin province. Similarly, on
his travels in Ireland de Tocqueville discerned the memory of dispossession 'as
a vague instinct of hatred against the conquerors'. Despite the deference and
paternalism that appears to have characterized relations between the dispossessed Gaelic aristocracy and the descendants of their peasant kinsmen and
tenants, (which, Barnard has shown, was also characteristic of the relations
between land occupiers and their new lords after the Treaty of Limerick), it
should not be assumed that such vertical ties persisted or were still widespread
until the time of de Tocqueville's journey in the mid-1830s. The perpetuation
of the memory of estate forfeiture was by people such as the farmers who were
said, in evidence to the 1824 select committee, to entertain hopes of recovering
those estates their ancestors had lost. Russell's catechism had involved 'divid-
ing the ancient estates among the descendants of those ancient Irish families,
who were pillaged by English invaders'. It seems that de Tocqueville and others gained their impressions from members of a new Catholic élite that was re-
emerging, according to Whelan's argument, from among the descendants of
those who had been dispossessed in the seventeenth century. Whelan suggested that 'almost invariably' such families assumed political rôles which could be
traced after the confiscations through Jacobite, Catholic Committee, United
Irish, O'Connellite and Confederate phases. However, the critical point here is
to recall Whelan's description of the disengagement of such people from popular culture in the last quarter of the eighteenth century, so that the ties with
popular culture snapped, leading to a more formal relationship.[31]

This disengagement may be seen now as the opening of a window through
which Jacobin, Painite, Radical and Chartist notions blew in to Ireland during
the half century before the famine. Sectarian and nationalist manifestations
(such as the Ribbon oath to wade three leagues in Orange blood) of secret society activity in Co. Roscommon were much more frequently associated with
people such as publicans, shopkeepers, artisans, minor leaseholders and other
aspiring non-élite Catholics than with whiteboys. Beames suggested that
whiteboyism did not share their religious nationalism.[32]

---

30 Scott, *Moral economy of the peasant*, 129, 132.   31 Scott, 'Hegemony and the peasantry';
SC 1824, evidence of George Bennett; Smyth, *Men of no property*, 168; Whelan, 'An underground gentry?', 18, 24.   32 Beames, *Peasants and power*, 26.   33 Bartlett, 'An end to

I have demonstrated in detail that whiteboyism in Roscommon cut straight across the familiar confessional component of nationalism. Bartlett reports on a 1794 discussion of this problem:

> The peasants no longer confide in their clergy, they suspect them and they are also of the opinion that their gentry have abandoned them; thus a great mass of uninformed men are for the first time thrown to depend on themselves ... the peasants are binding themselves on oath to protect each other.[33]

It seems that, as O'Farrell has suggested:

> popular rebellious elements ... were too remote from their nominal religion ... and too opposed by its ministers to entertain any notion of setting their protests in a religious context.[34]

James O'Neill's remark that historians should not insist on a display of class-consciousness and modernity before recognising plebeian movements for what they were is most apposite. O'Neill also acknowledged that Irish peasants demonstrated an ability to organize independently on 'quite a large scale'. Unfortunately, O'Neill's assessment of pre-famine whiteboyism collapsed into a familiar nationalist discourse. He identified the authority of the village priest as a critical factor in the emergence of Catholicism as a solidarity mechanism at the base of nationalism, which was 'enshrined' in the 1820s and 1830s as the 'primary loyalty' in Irish rural society. This does not accord with the evidence adduced in this study. O'Connell admitted that disturbances would not disappear with the granting of emancipation because of the 'double oppression' suffered by the rural poor. De Tocqueville asked Edward Nolan, bishop of Kildare and Leighlin, about whiteboyism and was told of the outlook of a Whitefeet leader, a Michael Burke of Co. Kilkenny. On being reprimanded by a priest for his activities, Burke had replied:

> The law does nothing for us, we must save ourselves. We are in possession of a little bit of land which is necessary to our and our families' survival. They chase us from it, to whom do you wish we should address ourselves? We ask for work at 8d. a day, we are refused – to whom do you want us to address ourselves? Emancipation has done nothing for us. Mr O'Connell and the rich Catholics go to Parliament. We are starving to death just the same.

moral economy', 216, quoting John Keogh to Nepean, 15 Apr. 1794, PRO, HO 100/46/154–7.   34 P. O'Farrell, 'Millennialism, messianism and utopianism', 47.

It is important to retain a sense of how unknown and contingent future social and political developments in rural Ireland must have been in the half century before the famine, and how contested the hegemony of confessional nationalism was. I have traced how agrarian rebels contested that hegemony, justifying collective defiance by tradition and custom, freely importing and adapting class discourses and actions. The Irish agrarian rebel who described the 'murdered patriots of Manchester' may have been talking of the United Kingdom or of a parallel patriotism in Ireland. The available text does not reveal which was meant. What it reveals (which is as significant as whether Ireland was conceived of as a separate nation) is the same understanding of patriotism as among the nascent English working class, embodied in a self-consciousness that expressed horizontal solidarities. Those solidarities were considerably more complex and sophisticated than might be expected of pre-modern agrarian rebels.[35]

Through an examination of texts about collective conflict I have suggested new ways in which historians might profitably re-examine Irish agrarian conflict, ways which must be located outside the monolithic identities of confession and ethnicity which have dominated the historiography. I have suggested that, in particular concrete circumstances identities were not given by the texts of O'Connell or Davis, but increasingly by a challenge mounted through the legitimizing power of tradition and the simultaneous stirrings of a different social identity.

Robert Scally's work on the townland of Ballykilcline, in Co. Roscommon, demonstrates the ways in which the legacy of nationalist historiography lingers. In *The end of hidden Ireland*, Scally writes about the destruction of Corkery's Ireland by the twin evils of eviction and emigration, words that have been hallmarks of a nationalist historiography of Ireland. The result is to return to Corkery's *The hidden Ireland* of a shared Gaelic past, the unity of rich and poor native and the writing of historical discourse for the purpose of nation–building. I have examined a secret Ireland, which has been obscured from view by the legends of the hidden Ireland.

35 J. O'Neill, 'Popular culture and peasant rebellion', 393, 375, 376; SC 1825, 127, evidence of Daniel O'Connell; Larkin, *De Tocqueville's journey*, 41.

Bibliography

MANUSCRIPT SOURCES

National Archives of Ireland
State of the country papers, series 1
State of the country papers, series 2
Outrage reports
Chief secretary's office registered papers
Religious survey of the diocese of Elphin (1749), MS 2466

National Library of Ireland
Clancarty manuscript, MS 31761
   Historical Manuscripts Commission reports: Fortescue MSS, viii, (1912), 463–8. Letter
   of Marquis of Buckingham to Lord Grenville and reply on Captain Thresher's campaign
   against tithes, 11 Dec 1806
Lorton papers, MS 3104
Lorton papers, MS 3105
King papers, MS 4120
Pakenham-Mahon papers, MS 2597
Pakenham-Mahon papers, MS 9471

National Archives of England and Wales
Records of the Colonial Office, CO904

Public Record Office of Northern Ireland
King-Harman papers, D4168

Royal Irish Academy
Ordnance Survey memoirs, Box 50, Co. Roscommon
Extracts ... relating to the topography and antiquities of Co. Roscommon, collected by the
   Ordnance Survey, MS 14 F.6–7
Letters containing information relative to the antiquities of the county of Roscommon, col-
   lected during the progress of the Ordnance Survey in 1837, MS 14 F.8–9

John Rylands University Library of Manchester
Collectanea de rebus Hibernicis, inc. Revd J. Keogh's statistical account of Roscommon for
   Sir W. Petty (1683), MS 498 (a copy of the original in Trinity College, Dublin)

NEWSPAPERS

Roscommon and Leitrim Gazette
Roscommon Journal and Western Impartial Reporter
Roscommon Journal and Western Reporter
United Irishman

PARLIAMENTARY PAPERS

Census of population of Ireland, 1831. 1833 (23) xxxix.3

Census of population of Ireland, 1841. 1843 (354) li.321

Census of population of Ireland, 1851. 1852–3 (1555) xcii.515

A statement of the nature and extent of the disturbances which have recently prevailed in Ireland, and the measures which have been adopted by the government of that country, in consequence thereof, by the lord lieutenant of Ireland, Lord Whitworth, to Viscount Sidmouth, 5 June 1816 (479) IX.569

Select committee to inquire into disturbances in Ireland. *Report, appendix* 1824 (372) viii.1 and *Minutes of evidence,* indices 1825 (20) vii.1

Select committee to inquire into the state of Ireland with reference to disturbances. *Reports, minutes of evidence,* index 1825 (129) viii.1

Select committee of the House of Lords to inquire into the state of Ireland with reference to disturbances. *Minutes of evidence* 1825 (181) ix.1; *Minutes of evidence, appendix, index* 1825 (521) ix.249; *Report* (1825) 1826 (40) v.659

Select committee of the House of Lords on the nature and extent of disturbances in Ireland. *Minutes of evidence* (1824) 1825 (200) vii.501

Select committee on the disturbed state of Ireland. *Report, minutes of evidence, appendix, index* 1831–2 (677) xvi.1

Select committee of the House of Lords on the state of Ireland. *Report, minutes of evidence, appendix, index* 1839 (486) xi.1, xii.1

Memorial presented to the Boyle board of guardians on 26 May 1843. 1843 (443) L.403

Royal commission of inquiry into the state of the law and practice in respect to the occupation of land in Ireland. *Report, minutes of evidence, Part I 1845* (605)(606) xix.1,57; *Minutes of evidence, Parts II and III* 1845 (616)(657) xx.1, xxi.1

Select committee on outrages (Ireland). *Report with proceedings of the committee, Minutes of evidence, appendix and index.* 1852 (438) xiv.1

BOOKS AND ARTICLES

Alexandrov, Y.V., 'The peasant movements of developing countries in Asia and North Africa after the second world war' in H.A. Landsberger (ed.), *Rural protest: peasant movements and social change* (London, 1974), 351–77

Barnard, T.C., 'The gentrification of eighteenth century Ireland' in *Eighteenth-Century Ireland* 12 (1997) 137–55

Bartlett, T., 'An end to moral economy: the Irish militia disturbances of 1793' in Philpin (ed.), *Nationalism and popular protest in Ireland* (1987), 191–218

Beames, M.R., *Peasants and power* (Brighton, 1983)

——, 'The Ribbon societies: lower class nationalism in pre-famine Ireland' in C.H.E. Philpin (ed.), *Nationalism and popular protest in Ireland* (Cambridge, 1987), 245–62

——, 'Rural conflict in pre-famine Ireland: peasant assassinations in Tipperary 1837–1847' in *Past and Present* 81 (1978) 75–91

Belchem, J.C., 'English working class radicalism and the Irish, 1815–1850' in S. Gilley and R. Swift (eds), *The Irish in the Victorian city* (London, 1985), 78–93

Bohstedt, J., *Riots and community politics in England and Wales, 1790–1810* (London, 1983)

Booth, A., 'Food riots in the north-west of England 1790–801' in *Past and Present* 77 (1977) 84–107

Brady, J., and P.J. Corish, 'The church under the penal code' in idem, *A history of Irish Catholicism,* iv (Dublin, 1971), 1–88

Bric, M.J., 'Priests, parsons and politics: the Rightboy protest in County Cork, 1785–1788' in Philpin (ed.), *Nationalism and popular protest in Ireland* (1987), 163–90

Broeker, G., *Rural disorder and police reform in Ireland, 1812–1836* (London, 1970)

Burke, P., *Popular culture in early modern Europe* (Aldershot, 1994 ed.)
Callinicos, A., *Making history* (Cambridge, 1987)
——, *Theories and narratives* (Cambridge, 1995)
Carleton, W., *Traits and stores of the Irish peasantry*, 2 vols (Dublin, 1843)
Cawley, M., 'Aspects of continuity and change in nineteenth century rural settlement patterns: findings from County Roscommon' in *Studia Hibernica* 22–3 (1982–3) 106–17
Clark, S., 'The importance of agrarian classes: agrarian class structure and collective action in nineteenth century Ireland' in P.J. Drudy (ed.), *Ireland: land, politics and people* (Cambridge, 1982), 11–36
Clark, S., and J.S. Donnelly (eds), *Irish peasants: violence and political unrest, 1780–1914* (Manchester, 1983)
——, 'General introduction' in Clark and Donnelly (eds), *Irish peasants* (1983), 3–21
——, 'The tradition of violence: introduction' in Clark and Donnelly (eds), *Irish peasants* (1983), 25–35
Clarke, J., *Christopher Dillon Bellew and his Galway estates, 1763–1826* (Dublin, 2003)
Chirot, D., and C. Ragin, 'The market, tradition and peasant rebellion: the case of România in 1907' in *American Sociological Review* 40 (1975) 428–44
Coldrey, B.M., *Faith and fatherland* (Dublin, 1988)
Coleman, A., *Riotous Roscommon* (Dublin, 1999)
Connolly, S.J., 'Mass politics and sectarian conflict, 1832–1830' in W.E. Vaughan (ed.), *A new history of Ireland* v (Oxford, 1989), 74–107
——, 'The Houghers: agrarian protest in early eighteenth-century Connacht' in Philpin (ed.), *Nationalism and popular protest in Ireland*, (Cambridge, 1987), 139–62
——, 'Eighteenth century Ireland, colony or ançien régime?' in D.G. Boyce and A. O'Day (eds), *The making of modern Irish history* (London, 1996), 15–33
——, ' "Ag Déanamh *Commanding*": élite responses to popular culture, 1660–1850' in J.S. Donnelly and K. Miller (eds), *Irish popular culture, 1650–1850* (Dublin, 1998), 1–29
——, *Priests and people in pre-famine Ireland, 1780–1845* (Dublin, 1982)
Corkery, D., *The hidden Ireland* (Dublin, 1967 ed.)
Cronin, M., ' "Of one mind"?: O'Connellite crowds in the 1830s and 1840s' in Jupp and Magennis (eds), *Crowds in Ireland c.1720–1920* (2000), 139–72
Cullen, L.M., 'Catholics under the penal laws' in *Eighteenth-Century Ireland* 1 (1986) 23–36
——, 'The hidden Ireland: reassessment of a concept' in *Studia Hibernica* 9 (1969), 7–47
Dickson, D., 'Middlemen' in T. Bartlett and D.W. Hayton (eds), *Penal era and golden age* (Belfast, 1979), 163–85
Donnelly, J.S., 'The social composition of agrarian rebellions in early nineteenth-century Ireland: the case of the Carders and Caravats, 1813–1816' in P.J. Corish (ed.), *Historical Studies* 15 (1983): *Radicals, rebels and establishments*, 151–69
——, *Landlord and tenant in nineteenth-century Ireland* (Dublin, 1973)
——, 'Factions in prefamine Ireland' in A.S. Eyler and R.F. Garratt (eds), *The uses of the past: essays on Irish culture* (London, 1988), 113–30
——, 'The Rightboy movement, 1785–1788' in *Studia Hibernica* 17–18 (1977–78) 120–202
——, 'The Whiteboy movement, 1761–1765' in *Irish Historical Studies* 21:81 (March 1978) 20–54
Dorian, H., *The outer edge of Ulster: a memoir of social life in nineteenth-century Donegal*, ed. D. Dickson and B. Mac Suibhne (Dublin, 2001 ed.)
Drudy, P.J. (ed.), *Ireland: land, politics and people* (Cambridge, 1982)
Edgeworth, M., *Castle Rackrent* (Oxford, 1995 ed.)
——, *The absentee* (Oxford, 1995 ed.)
Eley, G., and K. Neild, 'Starting over: the present, the post-modern and the moment of social history' in *Social History* 20 (1995) 355–64
Elliott, M., 'The Defenders in Ulster' in D. Dickson, D. Keogh and K. Whelan (eds), *The United Irishmen* (Dublin, 1993), 222–33
——, *Partners in revolution* (New Haven and London, 1982)

Fitzpatrick, D., 'Class, family and rural unrest in nineteenth century Ireland' in Drudy (ed.), *Ireland: land, politics and people* (1982), 37–75

Foster, R.F., 'Storylines: narratives and nationality in nineteenth-century Ireland' in G. Cubitt (ed.), *Imagining nations* (Manchester, 1998) 38–56

Freeman, T.W., *Pre-famine Ireland: a study in historical geography* (Manchester, 1957)

Gacquin, W., *Roscommon before the famine* (Dublin, 1996)

Garvin, T., 'Defenders, Ribbonmen and others: underground political networks in pre-famine Ireland' in Philpin (ed.), *Nationalism and popular protest in Ireland* (Cambridge, 1987), 219–44

Gibbon, S., *The recollections of Skeffington Gibbon from 1796 to the present year, 1829* (Dublin, 1829)

Gibbons, S.R., *Captain Rock, night errant* (Dublin, 2004)

——, 'Rockites and Whitefeet, Irish peasant secret societies', unpublished PhD thesis (University of Southampton, 1983)

Gramsci, A., *Selections from the prison notebooks*, ed. and trans. Q. Hoare and G. Nowell-Smith (London, 1971 ed.)

Harrison, M., *Crowds and history* (Cambridge, 1988)

Hay, D., 'Property, authority and the criminal law' in Hay et al. (eds), *Albion's fatal tree* (1975), 17–63

——, 'Poaching and the game laws on Cannock Chase' in Hay et al. (eds), *Albion's fatal tree* (1975), 191–255

Hay, D., et al. (eds), *Albion's fatal tree* (New York, 1975)

Hildermeier, M., 'Agrarian social protest, populism and economic development: some problems and results from recent surveys' in *Social History* 4 (1979) 319–32

Hilton, R., 'Peasant society, peasant movements and feudalism in medieval Europe' in H. Landsberger (ed.), *Rural protest: peasant movements and social change* (London, 1974), 67–94

Hobsbawm, E.J., 'Social banditry' in H. Landsberger (ed.), *Rural protest* (London, 1974), 142–57

——, *Nations and nationalism since 1780* (2nd ed., Cambridge, 1990)

——, *Primitive rebels* (London, 1969 ed.)

Hobsbawm, E.J., and G. Rudé, *Captain Swing* (London, 1985 ed.)

Huggins, M., 'Democracy or nationalism?: the problems of the Chartist press in Ireland' in O. Ashton and J. Allen (eds), *Papers for the people: a study of the Chartist press* (London, 2005), 129–45

Huizer, G., and R. Stavenhagen, 'Peasant movements and land reform in Latin America: Mexico and Bolivia' in H. Landsberger (ed.), *Rural protest* (1974), 378–409

Hutton, A.W. (ed.), *Arthur Young's tour in Ireland (1776–1779)* (London, 1892)

Jenkins, K., ed. 'Introduction: on being open about our closures' in idem (ed.), *The postmodern history reader* (London, 1997), 1–30

Jordan, D., *Land and popular politics in Ireland* (Cambridge, 1994)

Joyce, P., 'History and postmodernism' in *Past and Present* 133 (1991) 204–9

——, 'The end of social history?' in *Social History* 20 (1995) 73–91

——, *Visions of the people* (Cambridge, 1991)

Jupp, P., and E. Magennis, 'Introduction: crowds in Ireland, c.1720–1920' in Jupp and Magennis (eds), *Crowds in Ireland, c.1720–1920* (2000), 1–42

Jupp, P., and E. Magennis (eds), *Crowds in Ireland, c.1720–1920* (Basingstoke, 2000)

King-Harman, A.L., *The Kings of King House* (Bedford, 1996)

Kirk, N., 'History, language, ideas and postmodernism: a materialist view' in *Social History* 19 (1994) 221–240

Knott, J.W., 'Land, kinship and identity: the cultural roots of agrarian agitation in eighteenth century Ireland' in *Journal of Peasant Studies* 12 (1984) 93–108

Koseki, T., 'Patrick O'Higgins and Irish Chartism', *Hosei University Ireland Japan papers* 20 (Tokyo, 1990)

Larkin, E. (trans. and ed.), *Alexis de Tocqueville's Journey in Ireland* (Dublin, 1990)

——, 'The devotional revolution in Ireland, 1850–75' in *American Historical Review* 77 (1972) 625–52

Landsberger, H.A., 'Peasant unrest: themes and variations' in idem (ed.), *Rural protest* (1974), 1–64

——, (ed.), *Rural protest: peasant movements and social change*, (London, 1974)

Lee, J., 'The Ribbonmen' in T.D. Williams (ed.), *Secret societies in Ireland* (Dublin, 1973), 26–35

——, 'Patterns of rural unrest in nineteenth century Ireland: a preliminary survey' in L.M. Cullen and F. Furet (eds), *Irlande et France XVIIe–XXe siècles: pour une histoire rurale comparée: actes du premier Colloque franco-irlandais d'histoire économique et sociale* (Paris, 1980), 223–37

Lewis, G.C., *On local disturbances in Ireland*, (London, 1836; Cork, 1977)

Linebaugh, P., 'The Tyburn riot against the surgeons' in Hay et al. (eds), *Albion's fatal tree* (1975), 65–117

Longworth, P., 'The Pugachev revolt: the last great Cossack-peasant rising' in Landsberger (ed.), *Rural protest* (1974), 195–256

Lyotard, J.F., 'The postmodern condition' in K. Jenkins (ed.), *The postmodern history reader* (London, 1997), 36–8

McCabe, D, 'Social order and the ghost of moral economy in pre-famine Mayo' in R. Gillespie and G. Moran (eds), *A various country: essays in Mayo history, 1500–1900* (Westport, 1987), 91–112

McCartney, D., *The dawning of democracy* (Dublin, 1987)

Macken, W., *The silent people* (London, 1965 ed.)

MacRaild, D., *Irish migrants in modern Britain, 1750–1922* (New York, 1999)

Magennis, E., 'In search of the "moral economy": food scarcity in 1756–7 and the crowd' in Jupp and Magennis (eds), *Crowds in Ireland, c.1720–1920* (2000), 189–211

Mandler, P., 'The problem with cultural history' in *Cultural and Social History* 1 (2004) 94–117

Marx, K., 'The eighteenth Brumaire of Louis Bonaparte' in K. Marx and F. Engels, *Selected works* (London and Moscow, 1968 ed.), 94–179

Mattimoe, C., *North Roscommon: its people and past* (Boyle, 1992)

Mitchel, J., *Jail journal* (London, 1983 ed.)

——, *The last conquest of Ireland (perhaps)* (Glasgow, 1861)

Molnar, M., and J. Pekmez, 'Rural anarchism in Spain and the 1873 cantonalist revolution' in Landsberger (ed.), *Rural protest* (1974), 158–193

Moody, T.W. (ed.), *Irish historiography, 1936–70* (Dublin, 1971)

O'Brien, R.B., *A hundred years of Irish history* (London, 1911)

O'Farrell, P., 'Millennialism, messianism and utopianism in Irish history' in *Anglo-Irish Studies* 2 (1976) 45–68

O'Ferrall, F., *Catholic emancipation, Daniel O'Connell and the birth of Irish democracy 1820–1830* (Dublin, 1985)

——, *Daniel O'Connell* (Dublin, 1981)

Ó Gráda, C., *Ireland: a new economic history, 1780–1939* (Oxford, 1994)

O'Hegarty, P.S., *A history of Ireland under the Union* (Dublin, 1952 ed.)

O'Neill, K., *Family and farm in pre-famine Ireland* (Madison, 1984)

O'Neill, J.W., 'Popular culture and peasant rebellion in pre-famine Ireland', unpublished PhD thesis (University of Minnesota, 1984)

Orser, C.E., 'Archaeology and nineteenth century rural life in Co. Roscommon' in *Archaeology Ireland* 39 (1997) 14–17

——, 'In praise of early nineteenth-century course earthenware' in *Archaeology Ireland* 54 (2000) 8–11

Palmer, S.H., *Police and protest in England and Ireland, 1780–1850* (Cambridge, 1988)

Philpin C.H.E. (ed.), *Nationalism and popular protest in Ireland* (Cambridge, 1987)

Pickering, P., ' "Repeal and the suffrage": Fergus O'Connor's Irish mission, 1849–50' in O. Ashton, R. Fyson and S. Roberts (eds), *The Chartist legacy* (Woodbridge, 1999)

Price, R., 'Postmodernism as theory and history' in J. Belchem and N. Kirk (eds), *Languages of labour* (Aldershot, 1997), 11–44

Randall, A.J., 'The shearmen and the Wiltshire outrages of 1802: trade unionism and industrial violence' in *Social History* 7 (1982) 283–304

Reed, M., 'Class and conflict in rural England: some reflections on a debate' in Reed and Wells
(eds), *Class, conflict and protest in the English countryside, 1700–1880* (1990) 1–28

Reed, M., and R. Wells (eds), *Class, conflict and protest in the English countryside, 1700–1880* (London, 1990)

Roberts, P.E.W., 'Caravats and Shanavests: whiteboyism and faction fighting in east Munster,
1802–1811' in Clark and Donnelly (eds), *Irish peasants* (1983), 64–101

Rudé, G., *The crowd in history, 1730–1848* (London, 1964)

Rule, G., 'Wrecking and coastal plunder' in Hay et al. (eds), *Albion's fatal tree* (1975), 167–88

Scally, R., *The end of hidden Ireland* (Oxford, 1995)

Scirocco, A., 'Fenomeni di persistenza del ribellismo contadino: il brigantaggio in Calabria prima
dell'unità' in *Archivio storico per le province napoletane* 3rd series, 20 (1981), 245–79

Scott, J.C., *The moral economy of the peasant: rebellion and subsistence in southeast Asia* (New Haven
and London, 1976)

—, 'Hegemony and the peasantry' in *Politics and Society* 7 (1977) 267–96

Smyth, J., *The men of no property: Irish radicals and popular politics in the late eighteenth century*
(London, 1992)

Shanin, T., 'Peasantry as a political factor' in idem (ed.), *Peasants and peasant societies* (London,
1971), 238–63

Stavenhagen, R., *Social classes in agrarian societies* (New York, 1975)

Stedman Jones, G., *Languages of class: studies in English working class history, 1832–1982* (Cambridge, 1983)

Smith, A.W., 'Irish rebels and English radicals, 1798–1820' in *Past and Present* 7 (1955) 78–85

Stinchcombe, A., 'Agricultural enterprise and rural class relations' in *American Journal of Soci-
ology* 67 (1961–2), 165–176

Sullivan, A.M., *New Ireland* (London, 1877)

Thompson, D., *The Chartists* (New York, 1984)

—, 'Ireland and the Irish in English radicalism before 1850' in D. Thompson and J. Epstein
(eds), *The Chartist experience* (London, 1982), 120–151

Thompson, E.P., 'The crime of anonymity' in Hay et al. (eds), *Albion's fatal tree* (1975), 255–308

—, 'Custom, law and common right' in idem, *Customs in common* (London, 1993 ed.), 97–184

—, *Customs in common* (London, 1993 ed.)

—, 'Eighteenth century English society: class struggle without class?' in *Social History* 3 (1978)
133–65

—, 'Introduction: custom and culture' in idem, *Customs in common* (1993 ed.), 1–15

—, *The making of the English working class* (London, 1980 ed.)

—, 'The moral economy of the English crowd in the eighteenth century' in idem, *Customs in
common* (1993 ed.), 185–258

—, 'The moral economy reviewed' in idem, *Customs in common* (1993 ed.), 259–351

—, 'The patricians and the plebs' in idem, *Customs in common* (1993 ed.), 16–96

—, 'Rough music' in idem, *Customs in common* (1993 ed.), 467–538

—, *Whigs and hunters* (London, 1990 ed.)

Tilly, C., 'Collective violence in European perspective' in H.D. Graham and T. Gurr (eds), *Violence in America: historical and comparative perspectives* (New York, 1969), 4–42

—, *Popular contention in Great Britain, 1758–1834* (London, 1995)

—, *From mobilization to revolution* (Reading, MA, 1978)

Wall, M., 'The whiteboys' in T. Desmond Williams (ed.), *Secret societies in Ireland* (Dublin, 1973)

Walton, J.K., *Chartism* (London, 1999)

Weld, I., *A statistical survey of County Roscommon* (Dublin, 1832)

Wells, R., 'The development of the English rural proletariat and social protest, 1700–1850' in
Reed and Wells (eds), *Class, conflict and protest in the English countryside, 1700–1880* (1990),
29–53

——, 'Social protest, class, conflict and consciousness in the English countryside, 1700–1880' in Reed and Wells (eds), *Class, conflict and protest in the English countryside, 1700–1880* (1990), 121–214

——, 'The Irish famine of 1799–1801: market culture, moral economies and social protest' in A. Randall and A. Charlesworth (eds), *Markets, market culture and popular protest in eighteenth-century Britain and Ireland* (Liverpool, 1996)

Whelan, K., *The tree of liberty* (Cork, 1996)

——, 'An underground gentry? Catholic middlemen in eighteenth century Ireland' in idem, *The tree of liberty* (Cork, 1996)

——, 'The republic in the village: the United Irishmen, the Enlightenment and popular culture' in idem, *The tree of liberty* (Cork, 1996)

Williams, T.D. (ed.), *Secret societies in Ireland* (Dublin, 1973)

Winslow, C., 'Sussex smugglers' in Hay et al. (eds), *Albion's fatal tree* (1975), 119–66

Wolf, E., *Peasants* (Saddle River, NJ, 1966)

Zagorin, P., 'Historiography and postmodernism: reconsiderations' in *History and Theory* 29 (1990) 263–74

Index

Abbeytown, 56
abductions, 67, 117, 121–2, 182
absenteeism, 23, 52, 65–6
Henry Addington, Viscount Sidmouth,
   home secretary (1812–22), 20, 28, 95, 96
agrarian conflict (*see also* whiteboyism)
   and arms raids, 20, 27, 37, 98, 125, 142
   and arson, 26, 98, 102, 142, 145, 147, 172
   and custom, 14, 40, 47, 49, 51, 62, 71, 86,
      100, 101, 104, 108, 111, 125–6, 128,
      132, 179, 184, 185, 187, 204
   and land (including evictions and rents),
      62, 63, 103, 104, 107, 111, 113, 142,
      143, 144, 147–55, 156, 158, 162, 168,
      175, 187, 191,
   and law, 109–10, 111, 115–16, 125, 127,
      129–30, 132, 173
   and modernization, 23, 28
   and nationalism, 18, 19, 23, 30, 34
   and pasture/grazing, 28, 51, 52, 89, 100,
      116, 123, 129, 151, 154, 160, 161, 175
   and Roman Catholic church, 36, 42, 74
   legitimation, 13, 49, 51, 84, 108, 128,
      129, 170, 187, 204
America (including United States) 77, 142,
   166
Annagh, townland (Kilronan), 63
Annagh, townland, (Kilmore),158
archaeology, 54
Ardcarn, parish, 119, 126, 137, 138, 147
Ardgower, townland, 56
Ardkina, townland, 56–7, 62, 133
Ardmore, townland (Dunamon), 101
Ardmore, townland (Boyle), 122
Arigna iron works, 118, 126–7
Armagh, Co., 194
ascendancy, Protestant, 25, 61, 163
Asia, south-east, 55, 145
Athleague, 150
Athlone, 53, 58, 65, 71, 76, 85, 100, 101, 102,
   103, 107, 123, 134, 135, 141, 147, 172
Atkinson, Robert, chief constable, 125
Aughamore, Ballaghadereen, 120
Aughrim, parish, 71, 126, 155

Balfe, Patrick, landlord, 149, 151
Balkans, 39
Ballagh, townland (Kilgefin), 43, 83
Ballaghadereen, 58, 104, 109, 120, 161, 174,
   182
Ballina, Co. Mayo, 161
Ballinafad, townland, 119
Ballinamene, 119, 131, 135
Ballinamuck, 63
Ballinasloe, Co. Galway, 101, 168
Ballinastruve, house, Strokestown, 162
Ballintober, parish, 57, 110, 161
Ballyfarnon, 127, 137, 139
Ballyforan, townland, 107
Ballyglass, townland (Dysart), 102
Ballykilcline, townland, 121, 163
Ballymartin, townland (Kilglass), 141
Ballymote, 53
Ballyraggett, Co. Kilkenny, 164
Banagher, Co. Offaly, 140
bandits, 39
Barnard, Toby, historian, 47, 48, 93, 177,
   178, 202
Barnes, John, stipendiary magistrate, 172
Barnsley, England, 164
Barrington, Matthew, crown solicitor, 20, 23
Bartlett, Thomas, historian, 48, 169, 203
Baslick, parish, 57, 60
Bath, 48
Battlefield, Boyle, 71
Beames, Michael, historian, 42, 43, 50, 70,
   71, 73, 82, 115, 179, 180
Becher, W., 80
Beech, Revd. W., 147
Belfast, 164
Bellanagare, 136
Bellew estate, Co. Galway, 64
Bennett, George, crown prosecutor, 21
Bentley, George, agent, 162
Betheridge family, 122
Birmingham, England, 167
'Black Acts', 106, 170, 172, 173, 185
Blackburne, Francis, barrister, 20, 23, 72, 85
Blake, John, magistrate, 121